teach
yourself

DISCARD spanish

teach
yourself

spanish
juan kattán-ibarra

For over 60 years, more than 40 million people have learnt over 750 subjects the **teach yourself** way, with impressive results.

be where you want to be
with **teach yourself**

For UK order enquiries: please contact Bookpoint Ltd, 130 Milton Park, Abingdon, Oxon OX14 4SB. Telephone: +44 (0) 1235 827720. Fax: +44 (0) 1235 400454. Lines are open 09.00–17.00, Monday to Saturday, with a 24-hour message answering service. Details about our titles and how to order are available at www.teachyourself.co.uk

For USA order enquiries: please contact McGraw-Hill Customer Services, PO Box 545, Blacklick, OH 43004-0545, USA. Telephone: 1-800-722-4726. Fax: 1-614-755-5645.

For Canada order enquiries: please contact McGraw-Hill Ryerson Ltd, 300 Water St, Whitby, Ontario L1N 9B6, Canada. Telephone: 905 430 5000. Fax: 905 430 5020.

Long renowned as the authoritative source for self-guided learning – with more than 40 million copies sold worldwide – the **teach yourself** series includes over 300 titles in the fields of languages, crafts, hobbies, business, computing and education.

British Library Cataloguing in Publication Data: a catalogue record for this title is available from the British Library.

Library of Congress Catalog Card Number: on file.

First published in UK 1998 by Hodder Education, 338 Euston Road, London, NW1 3BH.

First published in US 1998 by The McGraw-Hill Companies, Inc.

This edition published 2003.

The **teach yourself** name is a registered trade mark of Hodder Headline.

Copyright © 1998, 2003 Juan Kattán-Ibarra

Typeset by Transet Limited, Coventry, England.
Printed in Great Britain for Hodder Education, a division of Hodder Headline, 338 Euston Road, London, NW1 3BH, by Cox & Wyman Ltd, Reading, Berkshire.

Hodder Headline's policy is to use papers that are natural, renewable and recyclable products and made from wood grown in sustainable forests. The logging and manufacturing processes are expected to conform to the environmental regulations of the country of origin.

Impression number   20 19 18 17 16 15 14 13
Year   2008 2007 2006

The author wishes to thank Juan Luzzi for his assistance at all stages of production of the manuscript. Thanks are also due to the following people for their help with recordings: Carlos Fernández, Marisa Julián, Eliud Porras, Mariluz Rodrigo, Sarah Sherborne.

The author and publisher would like to thank the following for permission to use material in this volume: Revista de difusión científica *Quo*, Restaurante Aeropuerto El Prat (Barcelona).

Every effort has been made to obtain permission for all material used. In the absence of any response to enquiries, the author and publisher would like to acknowledge the following for use of their material: Revistas *Tiempo*, *Mía*, *Guía del Ocio*, *Buena Salud*, *Tú*; Diarios *ABC*, *El Periódico de Catalunya*, *La Nación*, *La Tercera*, *El Mercurio*; Oficina de Información y Turismo de Fuengirola, Renfe, Consorcio de Transportes de Madrid, Conserjería de Salud y Servicios Sociales (Junta de Andalucía), Julía Tours, *Guía Turística de San Telmo*, Halcón Viajes, Cosmo Service, Hotel Condes, Hotel Excelsior.

acknowledgements

About the author

Juan Kattán-Ibarra was born in Chile, and lived in Spain for a number of years. He has degrees in foreign language teaching from the University of Chile, Michigan State University, Manchester University and the Institute of Education, London University. He taught Spanish at Ealing College and Shell International, and was an examiner in Spanish for the London Chamber of Commerce and Industry and the University of London School Examinations Board. He is now a full-time author.

He is the sole author of *Teach Yourself Spanish Extra!*, *Teach Yourself Spanish Grammar*, *Teach Yourself Latin American Spanish*, *Conversational Spanish*, *Conversando*, *Panorama de la prensa*, *Perspectivas culturales de España*, *Perspectivas culturales de Hispanoamérica*, and co-author of *Working with Spanish*, *Talking Business Spanish*, *Se escribe así*, *España nuevo siglo*, *Sueños – World Spanish 2*, *Modern Spanish Grammar* and *Modern Spanish Grammar Workbook*.

contents

introduction

Welcome to *Teach Yourself Spanish!*

Is this the right course for you? If you are an adult learner with no previous knowledge of Spanish and studying on your own, then this is the course for you. Perhaps you are taking up Spanish again after a break from it, or you are intending to learn with the support of a class? Again, you will find this course very well suited to your purposes.

Developing your skills

The language introduced in this course is centred around realistic everyday situations. The emphasis is first and foremost on *using* Spanish, but we also aim to give you an idea of how the language works, so that you can create sentences of your own.

The course covers all four of the basic skills – listening and speaking, reading and writing. If you are working on your own, the audio recordings will be all the more important, as they will provide you with the essential opportunity to listen to Spanish and to speak it within a controlled framework. You should therefore try to obtain a copy of the audio recordings if you haven't already got one.

Use it or lose it!

Language learning is a bit like jogging – you need to do it regularly for it to do any good! Ideally, you should find a 'study buddy' to work through the course with you. This way you will have someone to try out your Spanish on. And when the going gets tough, you will have someone to chivvy you on until you reach your target.

Where can I find real Spanish?

Don't expect to be able to understand everything you hear or read straight away. If you watch Spanish-speaking programmes on TV or buy Spanish magazines you should not get discouraged when you realize how quickly native-speakers speak and how much vocabulary there is still to be learned. Just concentrate on a *small* extract – either a video/audio clip or a short article – and work through it till you have mastered it. In this way, you'll find that your command of Spanish increases steadily. See the **Taking it further** section on page 262 for information on sources of authentic Spanish, including newspapers, magazines, websites and organizations linked to the Spanish-speaking world.

The structure of this course

The course book contains

- an introductory unit
- 25 course units
- self-assessment tests and a reference section at the back of the book
- 2 CDs or cassettes (which you really do need to have if you are going to get maximum benefit from the course).

The course units

The course units can be divided roughly into the following categories, although of course there is a certain amount of overlap from one category to another.

Statement of aims

You will be told what you can expect to learn, mostly in terms of what you will be able to do in Spanish by the end of the unit.

Presentation of new language

You will find two or more dialogues which are recorded ▶ on the cassettes or CDs and also printed in the book. Some assistance with vocabulary is also given. The language is presented in manageable chunks, building carefully on what you have learned in earlier units. Transcripts of listening comprehension exercises are at the back of the book.

Key phrases and expressions

All new phrases and expressions with their English translation are listed in the **How do you say it?** section.

Description of language forms

In the **Grammar** section you learn about the forms of the language, thus enabling you to construct your own sentences correctly. For those who are daunted by grammar, assistance is given in various ways.

Pronunciation

The best way to acquire good pronunciation and intonation is to listen to native speakers and try to imitate them. But most people do not actually notice that certain sounds in Spanish are pronounced differently from their English counterparts, until this is pointed out to them. Specific advice on pronunciation is given in some of the units in the **Pronunciation** section.

Practice of the new language

In the **Practice** section you will be able to use the language that you have learned. Practice is graded, so that activities ('actividades' on the recording) which require mainly *recognition* normally come first. As you grow in confidence in manipulating language forms, you will be encouraged to *produce* both in writing and in speech.

Information on Spanish-speaking countries

At different stages in the course, you will find relevant information about aspects of life and customs in the Spanish speaking world. This information, found in the 🛈 section, is given in English in the first part of the course (Units 1–6), but later on in Spanish.

Testing yourself

A **Testing yourself** section, on pages 252–61, will help you to test what you have learnt in your Spanish course, and allow you to judge whether you have successfully mastered the language and if you are ready to move to a more advanced course.

Each activity in this section has references to the relevant units, so you can either do the tests at intervals, after every five units, or when you have worked your way through the course. If you are uncertain about how you perfomed with a particular test, you will be able to check your answers in the **Key to 'testing yourself'** section and revise that language point until you feel confident that you have mastered it.

Reference

At the end of the book there are sections that you can use for reference:

- a 'taking it further' section
- a glossary of grammatical terms
- a grammar summary
- a list of irregular verbs
- transcripts of the listening comprehension exercises
- a key to the activities in each unit
- a key to the 'testing yourself' exercises
- a Spanish–English vocabulary
- an English–Spanish vocabulary
- an index to the grammar

How to use this course

Make sure at the beginning of each course unit that you are clear about what you can expect to learn.

Read any background information that is provided. Then listen to the dialogues on the audio recordings. Try to get the gist of what is being said before you look at the printed text in the book. Refer to the printed text and the key vocabulary in order to study the dialogues in more detail. If you want an explanation of new language points at this stage, study the relevant paragraphs in the **Grammar** section. All the dialogues include listening and reading activities and you can check your answers in the **Key to the activities**.

Don't fall into the trap of thinking you have 'done that' when you have listened to the audio a couple of times and worked through the dialogues and activities in the book. You may *recognize* what you hear and read, but you almost certainly still have some way to go before you can *produce* the language of the dialogues correctly and fluently. This is why we recommend that you keep listening to the recordings at every opportunity – sitting on the train or bus, waiting at the dentist's or stuck in a traffic jam in the car, using what would otherwise be 'dead' time. Of course, you must also be internalizing what you hear and making sense of it – just playing it in the background without really paying attention is not enough!

After you have gone through the dialogues, check the **How do you say it?** section for key phrases and expressions. Try covering up the English translations and producing the English equivalents of the Spanish. If you find that relatively easy, go on to cover the Spanish sentences and produce the Spanish equivalents of the English. You will probably find this more difficult. Trying to recall the context in which words and phrases were used may help you learn them better.

You can then study the grammar explanations in the **Grammar** section in a systematic way. We have tried to make these as user-friendly as possible, since we recognize that many people find grammar daunting. But in the end, it is up to you just how much time you spend on studying and sorting out the grammar points. Some people find that they can do better by getting an ear for what sounds right, others need to know in detail how the language is put together. At this stage you may want to refer to the relevant sections of the **Glossary of grammatical terms** and the **Grammar summary** for clarification and further information.

You will then be ready to move on to the **Practice** section and work through the activities following the instructions that precede them. Some of the activities in this section are listen-only activities. The temptation may be to go straight to the transcriptions in the back of the book, but try not to do this. The whole point of listening exercises is to improve your listening skills. You will not do this by reading first. The transcriptions are there to help you if you get stuck.

As you work your way through the activities, check your answers carefully in the back of the book. It is easy to overlook your own mistakes. If you have a study buddy it's a good idea to check each other's answers. Most of the exercises have fixed answers, but some are a bit more open-ended, especially when we are asking you to talk about yourself. We then, in most cases, give you a model answer which you can adapt for your own purposes.

Before you move on to a new unit, go through the **How do you say it?** section once more to make sure that you know all the key language in the current unit.

Spanish in the modern world

Spanish, **el español**, also known as **el castellano**, is an international language and more than 300 million people speak it as their mother tongue. Outside Spain, Spanish is an official language in nineteen countries in Latin America. It is also spoken in parts of Africa, by many people in the Philippines, and by over 20 million people in the United States. Speakers from across Spain and places as far afield as Mexico and Chile share a common language, and the different accents and local words are no obstacle to communication.

Other languages

Alongside Spanish, other languages are spoken by a large number of Spaniards in their own country: **el catalán**, in Cataluña, Valencia and the Balearic Islands; **el gallego**, in Galicia; and **el vasco** or **el euskera**, in the Basque Country, each of them having an official status in the regions in which they are spoken. In Latin America, Spanish is used by millions of indigenous people alongside their own native languages. Spanish has borrowed a number of words from these indigenous languages, some of which have found their way into Peninsular Spanish and even other European languages.

What kind of Spanish am I going to learn?

The language we have chosen for your *Teach Yourself Spanish* course is standard Spanish, which will allow you to communicate with speakers anywhere in the Spanish-speaking world. The audio recordings have been done mostly by speakers from Spain, but to get you acquainted with other accents, a few have been recorded by Latin American people, mainly from Mexico, the largest Spanish-speaking country in the world. Differences between Peninsular and varieties of Latin American Spanish are explained in the course units – we refer to the Southern Cone countries (Argentina, Chile, Uruguay, Paraguay), the River Plate area, and individual countries.

We hope you enjoy working your way through *Teach Yourself Spanish*. Don't get discouraged. Mastering a new language does take time and perseverance and sometimes things can seem just too difficult. But then you'll come back to it another day and things will begin to make more sense again.

antes de empezar

before you start

In this unit you will learn
- how to greet people
- how to ask someone's name and say your name
- how to seek clarification and help
- how to say goodbye

▶A Greeting people

You will hear some people greeting each other. The first exchange is printed for you, the others are on the recording.

1 Look at the drawings, then listen to each greeting a few times, and repeat it after the speaker.

¡Hola!

Hola, buenos días.

Buenos días   Buenas tardes   Buenas noches

How do you say it?

Hola.	*Hello*.
Buenos días.	*Good morning*.
Buenas tardes.	*Good afternoon*.
Buenas noches.	*Good evening/night*.

2 Read the greetings above now, and try saying them yourself.

3 a At a party, you see your friend Rosa. Say hello to her.
   b You arrive in a hotel at 8.00 a.m. Greet the receptionist.
   c It's 2.00 p.m. and you go into a bank to change some money. Greet the bank clerk.
   d It's 9.00 p.m. and you go into a bar for a drink. Greet the waiter before placing your order.
   e As you go into your hotel late at night you see a Spanish acquaintance. Say hello to him/her, and add another greeting appropriate to the time of day.

▶ B Asking someone's name and saying your name

Sara meets José, and señor Salas meets señora Díaz.

1 Listen to each exchange several times, paying attention to how people ask someone's name and how they reply. You can check the **How do you say it?** and **ⓘ** sections below for meanings and usage.

Sara ¡Hola! ¿Cómo te llamas?
José José. ¿Y tú?
Sara Me llamo Sara.

Señor Salas Buenas tardes. Me llamo Carlos Salas. Y usted, ¿cómo se llama?
Señora Díaz Me llamo Julia Díaz.

How do you say it?

Asking someone's name and saying your name

Informal

– ¿Cómo te llamas?	*What's your name?*
– Me llamo ..., ¿y tú?	*My name is ... and yours?*

Formal

– ¿Cómo se llama (usted)?	*What's your name?*
– Me llamo ..., ¿y usted?	*My name is ... and yours?*

ⓘ Informal and formal ways of addressing people

Spanish makes a distinction between informal and formal address. The *familiar* word for *you* when addressing one person is **tú**, and the *formal* one is **usted**, abbreviated in writing to '**Vd.**' or '**Ud.**'.

Generally speaking, **usted** is used for talking to people one doesn't know, and to address the elderly and one's superiors.

Tú is used among friends, equals, for example colleagues, and generally among younger people, even if they haven't met before. Within the family, the prevalent form is **tú**.

Verb forms, and other words, change depending on whether you are using informal or formal address.

2 Now read the dialogues a few times until you feel confident with them, then play each one of the parts, using your own name where appropriate.

3 a At a party you meet a young Spanish person. Ask his/her name.
   b A Spanish-speaking person is visiting your company for the first time. Say your name and ask his/her name.

◼ C Seeking clarification and help

1 You will hear some key phrases for seeking clarification and help. Look up their meanings in the **How do you say it?** section below and repeat each phrase, trying to imitate the speakers on the recording.

How do you say it?

¿Qué significa ...?	*What does ... mean?*
¿Cómo dice?	*Pardon me?*
¿Puede repetir, por favor?	*Can you repeat, please?*
¡Perdón, no entiendo!	*I'm sorry, I don't understand.*
Más despacio, por favor.	*More slowly, please.*
¿Habla usted inglés?	*Do you speak English?*

2 What would you say in the following situations?

   a Your Spanish friend mentioned the word *dinero* but you don't know what it means.
   b The hotel receptionist is speaking too fast.

c A Spanish-speaking person is speaking to you but you didn't catch what he/she said.

d A cry for help! You need someone who speaks English.

▶ D Saying goodbye

1 You'll hear four people saying goodbye. Listen to each expression, and identify each picture below as you hear it.

How do you say it?

Goodbye

Adiós (formal and informal)
Adiós, buenos días/buenas tardes/buenas noches (more formal)
Chao (informal, Latin America)

See you later

Hasta luego (generally formal and informal, though in some Latin American countries it is considered formal)

2 a It's Friday evening and you are saying goodbye to your Spanish-speaking boss.
  b You'll be seeing your Spanish-speaking friend later on in the day. Say goodbye to him/her.
  c You are going back home after a holiday with some Spanish-speaking friends. Say goodbye to them.

▶ Check what you have learnt

On a flight home from Spain, Helen meets Enrique. Can you complete the missing parts of their conversation?

Enrique ¿Cómo se _____ usted?
Helen Me _____ Helen. Helen Thomas. ¿Y _____?
Enrique Enrique Ramírez.
Helen Perdón, no _____ ¿_____ repetir, por favor?
Enrique Enrique Ramírez.
Helen ¿_____ usted inglés?
Enrique No, sólo hablo español.

| **sólo hablo español** | *I only speak Spanish* |

01

hablo español
I speak Spanish

In this unit you will learn
- how to say where you are from
- how to say your nationality
- how to say what languages you speak

▶ 1 ¿De dónde eres?

At an international conference Ana meets Alfonso. They address each other using the informal form.

1.1 Listen to the conversation several times and, as you do, try filling in the gaps in the bubbles below, without looking at the printed dialogue. A key phrase here is **Soy de ...**, *I'm from ...*

Ana	¿De dónde eres?
Alfonso	Soy de Madrid. ¿Y tú?
Ana	Soy de Salamanca.

1.2 Now read the dialogue and find the Spanish equivalent for *Where are you from?*

▶ 2 Usted es español, ¿verdad?

Señor Arenas meets señor Medina. The language here is formal, so some of the expressions differ slightly from those in Dialogue 1.

2.1 Listen to the conversation a few times and say whether the following statements are true or false (**verdadero o falso**). Each time you hear the dialogue focus attention on a different point:

a Señor Arenas is Mexican. **c** Señor Medina is Spanish.
b He is from Mexico City. **d** He is from Guadalajara.

Señor Medina	Usted es español, ¿verdad?
Señor Arenas	Sí, soy español, de Málaga. Y usted, ¿de dónde es?
Señor Medina	Yo soy mexicano. Soy de Guadalajara.

2.2 Now read the dialogue and answer the following questions:

a How does señor Medina ask señor Arenas whether he's Spanish?

b How does señor Arenas ask señor Medina where he's from?

Compare his question with that used by Ana in Dialogue 1.

| usted es ... | you are ... (formal) |

▶ 3 ¿Habla usted inglés?

Señor Arenas was approached by Sarah, who is looking for someone who speaks English.

3.1 Listen to the conversation several times, each time focussing attention on a different point. The key word here is **hablar**, *to speak*.

a Does señor Arenas speak English?

b What languages does he speak?

Sarah	Perdone.
Señor Arenas	Sí, ¿dígame?
Sarah	¿Habla usted inglés?
Señor Arenas	No, lo siento, no hablo inglés. Sólo hablo español.

3.2 Now read the dialogue and find the Spanish equivalent for the following:

a Do you speak ...?   **b** I speak ...

sí, ¿dígame?	yes, can I help you?
lo siento	I'm sorry
sólo	only
inglés	English

4 Es de Barcelona

In a letter to a friend, Mercedes, from Perú, wrote about Eduardo, whom she met at the conference. What languages does Eduardo speak?

... se llama Eduardo y es catalán. Es de Barcelona. Habla catalán, español y un poco de inglés...

se llama...	*his name is...*	**un poco de**	*some*
catalán	*from Catalonia*		

How do you say it?

Asking people where they are from and replying

¿De dónde eres/es usted? (informal/formal)   *Where are you from?*

Soy de ...   *I'm from ...*

Asking someone's nationality and replying

¿Eres/es usted (informal/formal) español/española (man/woman)?   *Are you Spanish?*

Soy mexicano/mexicana (man/ woman).   *I'm Mexican*

Asking people whether they speak a certain language and replying

¿Hablas/Habla usted español/ inglés? (informal/formal)   *Do you speak Spanish/English?*

(No) hablo español/inglés.   *I (don't) speak Spanish/English.*

Giving similar information about others

Es (nationality).   *He/she is (nationality).*

Es de ...   *He/she is from ...*

Habla ...   *He/she speaks ...*

Grammar

1 Three types of verbs

If you look up verbs, that is words like **ser**, *to be*, **hablar**, *to speak*, in a Spanish dictionary, you'll see that they fall into three main categories according to their endings:

-ar	e.g. **hablar**	*to speak*
-er	**ser**	*to be*
-ir	**vivir**	*to live*

2 Regular and irregular verbs

The majority of Spanish verbs are 'regular', that is, they change in a fixed way, for example *for person* (e.g. *I, you*) or *for tense* (e.g. *present, past*), but others show some variation, and so are called 'irregular'. In this unit you will learn some of the present-tense forms of two important verbs: **hablar**, *to speak*, and **ser**, *to be*. The first one is regular, the second irregular.

	hablar *to speak*		**ser** *to be*	
(yo)	hablo	*I speak*	soy	*I am*
(tú)	hablas	*you speak* (inf.)	eres	*you are* (inf.)
(usted)	habla	*you speak* (form.)	es	*you are* (form.)
(él/ella)	habla	*he/she speaks*	es	*he/she/it is*

Note that the forms for **usted**, *you* (formal), **él**, *he*, and **ella**, *she*, are always identical. These same verb forms are used for **it**, as in 'it is', for which Spanish does not have a specific word, as the verb on its own is sufficient (see 3 below), e.g. **es español**, *it is Spanish*.

3 Yo, tú, él, ella ... *(I, you, he, she ...)*

As the ending of the verb normally indicates the person one is referring to (e.g. *I, you*), words like **yo**, *I*, **tú**, *you* (informal), **él**, *he*, **ella**, *she*, are usually omitted, except for emphasis or contrast.

Soy español.	*I'm Spanish.*
Yo soy mexicano.	*I am a Mexican.*

Usted, *you* (formal) is very often kept, as it adds more politeness. Like **él**, *he*, and **ella**, *she*, **usted** is sometimes kept in order to avoid ambiguity, as verb endings are the same for all three (see 2 above).

4 Asking questions

As in English, there are different ways of asking questions in Spanish.

- By using the same word order as in a statement.

  ¿Usted es de Madrid?   *Are you from Madrid?*
- By starting your sentence with the verb.

  ¿Habla usted inglés?   *Do you speak English?*
- By placing the word **¿verdad?** or **¿no?** at the end of the statement.

  Usted es español, ¿verdad?/¿no?   *You are Spanish, aren't you?*
- By using a question word.

  ¿Cómo te llamas?   *What's your name?*

Note that all questions in Spanish must carry two question marks, one at the beginning and one at the end of the sentence. Note, too, that all question words, e.g. **¿cómo?**, *how?*, **¿dónde?**, *where?*, carry a written accent.

5 Saying 'no'

To negate something in Spanish simply put the word **no** before the verb.

No soy español.   *I'm not Spanish.*
No hablo español.   *I don't speak Spanish.*

6 Masculine or feminine?

Words for nationality, like other words used for describing people, e.g. **guapo/a**, *good-looking (man/woman)*, have *masculine* and *feminine forms*.

- To form the feminine from a masculine word ending in **-o**, change the **-o** to **-a**.

  Soy británico/americano   *I'm British/American.*
  (man)
  Soy británica/americana   *I'm British/American.*
  (woman)

- To form the feminine from a masculine word ending in a consonant, add -a to the consonant.

    Soy español/inglés (man)   *I'm Spanish/English.*
    Soy española/inglesa (woman) *I'm Spanish/English.*

Note the omission of the accent in **inglesa** (see 'Accentuation', section 22 in the **Grammar summary**).

7 'México' or 'Méjico'?

Mexicans spell their country's name, *México*, and their nationality, *mexicano/a*, with an *x*, and this is the form adopted in this book. In Spain, you will sometimes find these spelled as *Méjico* and *mejicano*.

▶ Pronunciation

Spanish vowels: 'a', 'e', 'o'

Spanish vowels are different from English vowel sounds, as they are generally short and do not change their quality or length, as do English vowels. Each vowel corresponds to one sound only. References to English below are an approximation to how Spanish should sound.

a, as in 'Salamanca' like the 'a' in 'answer'
e, as in 'Mercedes' like the 'e' in 'yet'
o, as in 'Alfonso' like the 'o' in 'not'

Listen to your recording and practise these sounds by imitating the speakers.

    ¿Cómo te llamas?
    Me llamo Ana.
    Ana es de Salamanca, Eduardo es catalán.
    Es de Barcelona.

Practice

1 Palabra por palabra

How many of the countries listed on the next page can you recognize? Match each country with the corresponding nationality and language.

País	Nacionalidad (m/f)	Idioma
a Alemania	1 inglés/inglesa	A árabe
b Francia	2 egipcio/a	B portugués
c Rusia	3 brasileño/a	C inglés
d España	4 francés/francesa	D francés
e Inglaterra	5 ruso/rusa	E alemán
f Brasil	6 alemán/alemana	F ruso
g Egipto	7 español/a	G español

▶ 2 Soy española

Listen to Silvia, Cristóbal and Mario introducing themselves, and fill in the table below with the nationality, city and language corresponding to each person.

Nombre	Nacionalidad	Ciudad	Idioma(s)
a Silvia			
b Cristóbal			
c Mario			

3 Me llamo …

How would each of the following people introduce themselves? Follow the models in Activity 2, and look at the **How do you say it?** section and 6 in the **Grammar** section for other nationalities.

a Boris, Moscú.
b Paco, Granada.
c Ingrid, Berlín.

d Marguerite, París.
e Mark, Nueva York.
f Mª Ángeles, Monterrey, México

i María is a very common name in the Spanish-speaking countries, and is frequently used as the first part of a compound name (as in María Ángeles, above). Here María is abbreviated in writing to Mª.

4 Soy de Bogotá

In a letter to a correspondent, Ramiro, a student, gave some information about himself. Can you fill in the blanks with the missing verbs?

Querida Patricia:

_____ *Ramiro Fernández Salas y* _____
colombiano. _____ *de Bogotá. Aparte de español,*
_____ *inglés y un poco de francés.*

i **Querido**, *dear* (to a man), and **querida**, *dear* (to a woman), are used for close relationships only. Note also that Ramiro, like all Spanish-speaking people, has two surnames (**apellidos**): Fernández Salas. The first surname is his father's, while the second is his mother's. The second surname is used in more formal and in official situations.

5 Ahora tú

You are writing to a Spanish correspondent for the first time. Give similar information to that given by Ramiro in Activity 4.

6 ¿Cómo se llama?

During a visit to a trade fair in Barcelona, a visitor was asked to fill in this form, which is in Spanish and Catalan, the local language. How would you answer someone's questions about him?

a What's the visitor's surname?
b What's his first name?
c What city and country is he from?

Hora de su visita/Hora de la seva visita

☐ ☐ ☐ ☑ ☐ ☐

| Antes de las 8h. | De las 8h.a 11h. | De las 11h.a 14h. | De las 14h. a 17h. | De las 17h. a 20h. | Después de las 20h. |
| Avant de les 8h. | De les 8h.a 11h. | De les 11h.a 14h. | De les 14h. a 17h. | De les 17h. a 20h. | Després de les 20h. |

Fecha de su visita/Data de la seva visita: ... *23 de julio* ....

Datos personales (Facultativo)/Dades personals (Facultatiu)

Apellido/Cognom ... *Palma* .... Nombre/Nom *Guillermo* ....

Dirección/Adreça. *Calle de Linares, 25* ....

Ciudad/Ciutat. *Córdoba* .... País/País .. *España* ....

Gracias por depositar esta ficha en la urna
Mercès per depositar aquesta fitxa dins l'urna

| **el apellido** *surname* | **el nombre** *name* |
| **la ciudad** *city* | **el país** *country* |

7 Sólo hablo español

During a flight delay you talk to a Spanish-speaking person. Follow the guidelines below and complete your part of the conversation with him. He's using the polite form, so do likewise.

– *Ask his name.*
– Me llamo Antonio. ¿Y usted?
– *Reply, and ask where he's from.*
– Soy mexicano, de Veracruz. Y usted, ¿de dónde es?
– *Reply, and ask if he speaks English.*
– No, lo siento, sólo hablo español. No hablo nada de inglés. Pero usted sí habla español.
– *Say yes, you speak a little Spanish.*

no hablo nada de ...	*I don't speak any ...*
pero	*but*

02

¿cómo estás?

how are you?

In this unit you will learn
- how to introduce yourself and others
- how to ask people how they are and say how you are
- how to ask people where they live and say where you live
- how to ask for and give telephone numbers

▶ 1 Mucho gusto

Roberto has come to see señora Rivas at her office and he introduces himself to her. This is a formal introduction.

1.1 Listen to the conversation several times and try answering these questions:

a What do you think Roberto asks señora Rivas?
b What does the phrase **Sí, soy yo** mean in this context?

Try to work it out yourself first before checking the vocabulary.

Roberto	Perdone, ¿es usted la señora Rivas?
Señora Rivas	Sí, soy yo.
Roberto	Soy Roberto Muñoz, de La Coruña.
Señora Rivas	Mucho gusto.
Roberto	Encantado.

---

soy yo   *it's me*   **la**   *the* (fem.)

1.2 Now read the dialogue and find two expressions meaning 'Pleased to meet you'.

▶ 2 ¿Cómo estás?

Señora Rivas introduces Roberto to Felipe, a colleague of hers, **un compañero de trabajo**. The language here is informal.

2.1 Listen to the conversation and, as you do, try answering these questions:

a How does Felipe reply to the greeting **¿Cómo estás?** *How are you?*
b How does señora Rivas reply to the question **¿Y tú?**

Señora Rivas	¡Hola Felipe! ¿Cómo estás?
Felipe	Muy bien, ¿y tú?
Señora Rivas	Bien, gracias. Te presento a Roberto Muñoz, de La Coruña. Éste es Felipe, un compañero de trabajo.
Felipe	¡Hola! ¿Qué tal?
Roberto	¡Hola!

2.2 Read the dialogue now and find the expressions which mean the following:

a Let me introduce you to …
b This is Felipe.

éste   *this* (masc.)   **presentar**   *to introduce*
te   *to you* (informal)

---

i In a formal introduction men and women will normally shake hands and will do so also when saying goodbye. Younger people often dispense with this formality and will simply exchange informal greetings such as **hola**, *hello*, or **¿qué tal?**, *hi, how are you?*

▶ 3 ¿Dónde vives?

While visiting friends in Toledo, Roberto meets Cristina.

3.1 Listen to the conversation and answer the questions which follow. The key word here is **vivir**, *to live*.

a   Where does Roberto live?
b   Where does Cristina live?

Cristina   ¿Vives aquí en Toledo?
Roberto   No, vivo en La Coruña. Y tú, ¿dónde vives?
Cristina   En Madrid.

3.2 Now read the dialogue and find the Spanish for

a   Where do you live?
b   I live in …

▶ 4 ¿Qué número de teléfono tienes?

Cristina and Roberto exchange telephone numbers.

4.1 Look at numbers on page 26, then listen to the conversation several times and fill in the box below with their telephone numbers.

Nombre	Número de teléfono	
a Roberto	casa:	oficina:
b Cristina	casa:	oficina:

Cristina   ¿Qué número de teléfono tienes?
Roberto   El 712 6973.
Cristina   Y el teléfono de tu oficina, ¿cuál es?
Roberto   El 603 5823. ¿Qué teléfono tienes tú?
Cristina   No tengo teléfono en casa, pero el teléfono de mi oficina es el 520 1417.

4.2 What question does Cristina use to ask Roberto his telephone number? Read the dialogue and find out.

¿qué?	what?	¿cuál?	which?
tener	to have	la casa	house
de	of		

How do you say it?

Introducing yourself and others

(Yo) soy…	I am …
Éste es … (for a man)/Ésta es … (for a woman)	This is …
Te presento a …	Let me introduce you to … (informal)
Le presento a …	Let me introduce you to … (formal)
Mucho gusto/Encantado (man)/ Encantada (woman)	Pleased to meet you

Asking people how they are and saying how you are

¿Cómo estás/está?	How are you? (informal/formal)
(Estoy) bien/muy bien.	(I'm) fine/very well.

Asking people where they live and saying where you live

¿Dónde vives/vive?	Where do you live? (informal/formal)
Vivo en …	I live in …

Asking and giving telephone numbers

¿Que (número de) teléfono tienes/tiene?	What's your telephone number? (informal/formal)
El teléfono de mi casa/oficina es el …	My home/office telephone number is (number)

Grammar

1 Masculine or feminine?

a El, la (*the*)

Nouns are words which denote a person (e.g. **secretaria**, *secretary*), a thing (e.g. **teléfono**, *telephone*) or an abstraction (e.g. **gusto**, *pleasure*). In Spanish, all nouns are either masculine or feminine, and the word for 'the' is **el** for masculine nouns and **la** for feminine nouns. Nouns ending in **-o** are usually masculine, while nouns ending in **-a** are normally feminine.

| masculine | **el** número | *the number* |
| feminine | **la** oficina | *the office* |

b Nouns referring to males are masculine while those referring to females are feminine.

| masculine | **el** secretario | *male secretary* |
| feminine | **la** secretaria | *female secretary* |

Normally, nouns referring to females can be formed by changing the -o of the masculine form into -a, as above, or by adding -a to the consonant, but there are many exceptions.

| *masculine* | **el** señor | *the gentleman, Mr* |
| *feminine* | **la** señora | *the lady, Mrs* |

c The endings of some nouns do not indicate whether they are masculine or feminine, so it is advisable to learn each word with its corresponding article (**el** or **la**).

el nombre   *name*   **la calle**   *street*

2 El señor, la señora/señorita

Note the use of **el** before **señor**, and **la** before **señora/señorita**, in indirect address.

> ¿Es usted el señor Martínez/la señorita Miranda?

But:

> Buenas tardes, señora Vera.

In writing, **señor, señora** and **señorita** are often found in abbreviated form, **Sr., Sra.** and **Srta.**, respectively.

3 De (*of*)

Note the use of **de**, *of*, in

> el teléfono **de** mi oficina   *my office telephone number*
> el teléfono **de** Carmen   *Carmen's telephone number*

4 Al (*to the*), del (*of the*)

A + **el** becomes **al**, and de + **el** becomes **del**.

> Te presento **al** señor Lira.   *Let me introduce you to señor Lira.*
> El teléfono **del** señor Castro. *Señor Castro's telephone number.*

5 Un, una (a)

The Spanish equivalent of *a*, as in *a colleague*, *a secretary*, is **un** for masculine and **una** for feminine.

un compañero de trabajo   *a male colleague*
una secretaria   *a female secretary*

6 Mi, tu, su ... (my, your ...)

The Spanish equivalent of *my*, *your*, *his*, *her*, *its*, *their*, is:

mi marido/mujer	*my husband/wife*
tu casa	*your house* (informal)
su teléfono	*your telephone* (formal)
su comida	*his, her, its, their food*

7 'Ser' and 'estar' (to be)

There are two ways of saying *to be* in Spanish: **ser** and **estar**. Personal information such as where you are from, your nationality and who you are, are expressed with **ser**, e.g. **Soy Cristóbal**, *I'm Cristóbal* (Unit 1).

To ask people how they are and say how you are you need to use **estar**. **Estar** is an irregular verb, and its singular forms are:

(yo)	**estoy**	*I am*
(tú)	**estás**	*you are* (informal)
(usted)	**está**	*you are* (formal)
(él/ella)	**está**	*he/she/it is*

¿Cómo estás?   *How are you?*
(Estoy) bien.   *I'm fine.*

8 Tengo, tienes ... (I have, you have ...)

Tener, to have, is an irregular -er verb, whose singular forms are:

(yo)	**tengo**	*I have*
(tú)	**tienes**	*you have* (informal)
(usted)	**tiene**	*you have* (formal)
(él/ella)	**tiene**	*he/she/it has*

¿Que teléfono tienes?	*What is your telephone number?*
No tengo teléfono.	*I don't have a telephone.*

9 *-ir* verbs

The following are the singular present tense forms of **vivir**, *to live*, a regular -ir verb.

(yo)	vivo	*I live*
(tú)	vives	*you live* (informal)
(usted)	vive	*you live* (formal)
(él/ella)	vive	*he/she/it lives*

¿En qué barrio/calle vives?	*Which area/street do you live in?*
Vivo en el barrio/la calle de ...	*I live in (area)/(street)*

▶ Pronunciation

Spanish vowels 'i', 'u'

i as in 'oficina', is pronounced like the 'ee' in 'feet'.

u as in 'mucho gusto'. is pronounced like the 'oo' in 'good'.

ñ (n + tilde)

ñ, as in 'señora', is a separate letter of the Spanish alphabet and is pronounced nearly like the 'ni' in 'onion'.

Practise with:

¿Usted es la señora María Inés Rivas?
Soy el señor Roberto Muñoz, de La Coruña.
Mucho gusto.

Practice

▶ 1 ¿Ser o estar?

Alfredo meets Marisa, and señor Lira meets señorita Romero. Can you complete the conversations with the correct forms of **ser** and **estar**? The first exchange is informal and the other one formal.

a – Hola, ¿tú _____ Marisa Frías?
– Sí, _____ yo.
– Yo _____ Alfredo Ríos, de Sevilla.
– Hola, ¿cómo _____?
– Bien, gracias.

b – Buenos días. Usted _____ la señorita Romero, ¿verdad?
– Sí, soy Mercedes Romero. ¿Usted _____ Alfonso Lira?
– Sí, sí. ¿Cómo _____ usted?
– Muy bien. Y usted, ¿cómo _____?
– Bien, gracias. Mire, ésta _____ María, mi mujer.
– Encantada.

---

la mujer *wife*	**mire** *look*

▶ 2 ¿El o la? ¿Un o una?

Fill in the gaps with **el, la, un, una** where necessary.

Sr. Ibarra   Perdone a **a** _____ señora. ¿Usted es **b** _____ señora
                    Santos, **c** _____ secretaria del señor Martínez?
Sra. Santos   Sí, soy yo.
Sr. Ibarra   Yo soy **d** _____ señor Ibarra, de Transibérica.
Sra. Santos   Mucho gusto **e** _____ señor Ibarra.
Sr. Ibarra   Le presento a Carmen, **f** _____ compañera de
                    trabajo. Y éste es Alfonso, **g** _____ amigo.
Sra. Santos   Encantada.

3 Una presentación

Señor Barrios is visiting your place of work, and you and your colleague John have been asked to meet him at reception. Follow the guidelines and fill in your part of the conversation, using the formal form.

– *Ask whether he is señor Barrios.*
– Sí, soy yo.
– *Say who you are.*
– Mucho gusto.
– *Say you are pleased to meet him and introduce your colleague to him.*

---

una presentación   *an introduction*

4 Ahora tú

How would you introduce the following people to a friend? Look up the words in the **Vocabulary** and choose as appropriate, using the informal expression **Te presento a ...**

a	tu marido/mujer	**c**	tu padre/madre
b	tu novio/novia	**d**	tu hermano/hermana

Now introduce each of the following people, using the expression **Éste/Ésta es ...**, as appropriate.

e Gloria, una compañera de trabajo **g** Carlos, un amigo
f Paul, un compañero de clase **h** Laura, una vecina

▶ 5 ¿Dónde vive?

You'll hear three conversations in which people are being asked where they live. Can you complete each sentence with information from the appropriate map below? One of the speakers is Mexican.

a Francisco vive en ...
b Julio vive en ...
c Silvia vive en ...

▶ 6 Los números (*numbers*) 0–20

Listen and repeat each number as you hear it.

0	cero	4	cuatro	8	ocho	12	doce	16 dieciséis
1	uno	5	cinco	9	nueve	13	trece	17 diecisiete
2	dos	6	seis	10	diez	14	catorce	18 dieciocho
3	tres	7	siete	11	once	15	quince	19 diecinueve
								20 veinte

Note that **uno** becomes **un** before a masculine noun, e.g. **un amigo,** *a/one friend.*

▶ 7 ¿Qué número desea?

You will hear two conversations in which people request telephone numbers. Listen and write each number as you hear it.

a

┌─────────────────────┐
│ **Hotel Sancho**   │
│ **Teléfono ...**   │
└─────────────────────┘

┌─────────────────────┐
│ **Sr. Martín Ramos**│
│ **Teléfono ...**   │
└─────────────────────┘

b

i Telephone numbers in Spanish can be read out in single or double figures. For example, the telephone number 719 2015 can be read out as:

siete-uno-nueve-dos-cero-uno-cinco *or*
siete-diecinueve-veinte-quince.

8 Ahora tú

a ¿Dónde vives?
b ¿En qué barrio vives?
c ¿En qué calle?
d ¿Qué número de teléfono tienes?
e ¿Tienes teléfono en tu oficina/trabajo?
f ¿Cuál es el número?
g ¿Tienes extensión?
h ¿Cuál es el número?

9 Crucigrama

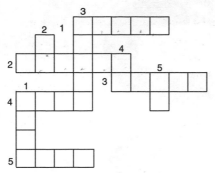

Horizontales
1 ¿Qué número de teléfono _____ usted?
2 ¿Tú _____ teléfono en casa?
3 Buenas tardes, señor Bravo, ¿cómo está _____?
4 (Yo) _____ en la Calle de la Rosa.
5 ¿(Tú) _____ Gonzalo Martínez?

Verticales
1 Raquel _____ en Sevilla, en el barrio de Santa Cruz.
2 Te presento a _____ marido.
3 (Yo) no _____ teléfono en casa.
4 Perdone, señora, el teléfono de _____ oficina, ¿cuál es?
5 Y _____ extensión, Mónica, ¿cuál es?

el marido   *husband*

03

quiero una habitación, por favor

I want a room, please

In this unit you will learn
- how to ask for a room in a hotel
- how to spell your name
- how to ask where something can be done

▶ 1 ¿Para cuántas personas?

Victoria is booking into a hotel.

1.1 Listen to the conversation several times. At each hearing tick the right information in one of the boxes below. Key words here are **quiero** *I want*, **para** *for*, **con** *with*, **sin** *without*.

Victoria quiere una habitación …

☐ para una persona ☐ para dos personas
☐ para una noche ☐ para seis noches
☐ con desayuno ☐ sin desayuno
☐ con baño ☐ sin baño

Recepcionista	Buenas tardes.
Victoria	Buenas tardes. Quiero una habitación, por favor.
Recepcionista	¿Para cuántas personas?
Victoria	Para una.
Recepcionista	¿Y para cuántas noches?
Victoria	Para seis noches. Hasta el veintiocho.
Recepcionista	¿Con desayuno?
Victoria	No, sin desayuno. ¿Tiene baño la habitación?
Recepcionista	Sí, sí, todas las habitaciones tienen baño.
Victoria	Vale.
Recepcionista	Su carnet de identidad, por favor.

1.2 Now read the dialogue and find the phrases which mean the following:

a For how many nights?
b Until the 28th.
c All rooms have a bathroom.
d Your identity card, please.

¿cuántas?	*how many?*	**el baño**	*bathroom*
el desayuno	*breakfast*	**noches**	*nights*

ℹ Identity cards are compulsory for all adults in Spain and Latin American countries, and these carry information such as the person's name, date and place of birth, and occupation. Hotels require some form of identification from their guests, normally an identity card (**el carnet de identidad**) for nationals and a passport (**el pasaporte**) for foreigners.

▶ 2 Tenemos una habitación reservada

Guillermo and Laura from Barcelona have booked a room at a hotel in Mexico.

2.1 Listen to the conversation a few times and fill in the gaps in the box below with the appropriate information. You may need to check numbers on page 34.

Tipo de habitación:	
Número de la habitación:	

Recepcionista	Buenas noches. ¿Qué desean?
Guillermo	Buenas noches. Tenemos una habitación reservada. Una habitación doble.
Recepcionista	¿A qué nombre?
Guillermo	Guillermo Torrens.
Recepcionista	¿Cómo se escribe su apellido, por favor?
Guillermo	T-o-r-r-e-n-s. Torrens.
Recepcionista	Sí, sus pasaportes, por favor.
Guillermo	Aquí tiene.
Recepcionista	Gracias. Su habitación es la número treinta y cinco. Aquí tienen la llave.
Guillermo	¿Dónde se puede cambiar dinero, por favor?
Recepcionista	Pueden cambiar aquí mismo.

2.2 Now read the dialogue and answer these questions:

a   How does Guillermo say that they have a room booked?
b   How does the hotel receptionist ask Guillermo to spell his surname?
c   How does Guillermo ask where money can be changed?

¿qué desean?	*what would you like?, can I help you?*
¿a qué nombre?	*in what name?*
reservada	*booked*
la llave	*key*
¿dónde se puede...?	*where can one/you...?*
pueden	*you can* (plural)

How do you say it?

Asking for a room in a hotel

Quiero una habitación
individual/para una persona.

¿Tiene una habitación doble/
para dos personas?

*I want a single room/
a room for one person.*

*Have you got a double
room/a room for two?*

Asking someone to spell a name

¿Cómo se escribe su nombre/
apellido?

*How do you spell your name/
surname?*

Asking where something can be done and responding

¿Dónde se puede cambiar
dinero/cenar?

Pueden cambiar/cenar aquí
mismo.

*Where can we/one change
money/have dinner?*

*You can change/have
dinner right here.*

Grammar

1 More than one

Most words form the plural by adding an -s. Nouns ending in a consonant add -es.

una persona   *one person*   cuatro personas *four people*
una habitación *a room*   dos habitaciones *two rooms*

Note that the written accent on the vowel disappears after adding -es.

2 Los, las (*the*, plural)

The plural of **el** and **la** (*the*, sing.) are **los** and **las**, respectively:

el hotel   *the hotel*   **los** hoteles   *the hotels*
la llave   *the key*   **las** llaves   *the keys*

3 Mis, tus, sus ... (*my, your ...*)

When the object possessed is more than one, **mi, tu, su** (see Unit 2) add an -s.

su habitación   *your* (formal) */his/her/their room*
sus habitaciones   *your* (formal) */his/her/their rooms*

4 ¿Cuántos? (*how many?*), todos (*all*)

¿Cuántos? *how many?*, becomes ¿cuántas? before a feminine word.

| el día | ¿Cuántos días? | *How many days?* |
| la noche | ¿Cuántas noches? | *How many nights?* |

With singular nouns, use ¿cuánto/a?

¿Cuánto dinero?   *How much money?*

Todos, *all*, changes into **todas** before a feminine word.

| el hotel | Todos los hoteles. | *All hotels.* |
| la habitación | Todas las habitaciones. | *All rooms.* |

With singular nouns, use todo/a.

Todo el tiempo   *All the/the whole time*

5 Querer (*to want*), poder (*can, to be able to*)

a Radical-changing verbs

Some verbs undergo a vowel change in the stem in certain forms, but their endings remain the same as for regular verbs.

- Some, like **querer**, change the -e of the stem (**quer-**) into -ie.
- Others, like **poder**, change -o into -ue.

Such verbs are known as radical-changing verbs. The symbol > next to a verb has been used to signal a vowel change in a stem-changing verb, e.g. **querer** (e > ie).

b Present tense forms

The following are the present tense forms of **querer** and **poder**, including the plural forms for

nosotros/as, *we* (masc./fem.),
vosotros/as, *you* (informal. masc./fem.),
ustedes, *you* (formal),
ellos, ellas, *they* (masc./fem.).

Latin Americans do not use **vosotros/as**, *you* (informal), and the forms which go with this. Instead they will use **ustedes** in both formal and informal address.

Note that the stem does not change in the first and second person plural, **nosotros/as** *we* and **vosotros/as** *you* (informal).

	querer	poder
yo	quiero	puedo
tú	quieres	puedes
usted	quiere	puede
él, ella	quiere	puede
nosotros/as	queremos	podemos
vosotros/as	queréis	podéis
ellos/as	quieren	pueden

Quiero una habitación doble. *I want a double room.*
Queremos el desayuno en *We want breakfast in our room.*
  la habitación.
¿Podemos pasar? *Can we come/go in?*
Sí, pueden pasar. *Yes, you can come/go in.*

In requests, you may sometimes hear **quisiera** *I'd like*, instead of **querio**, for extra politeness. The corresponding form for **nosotros** is **quisiéramos**.

6 Impersonal sentences

To say *you* or *one*, as in *How do you spell it? Where can you/one change money?* you need to use **se** followed by the third person of the verb.

▶¿Cómo **se escribe** tu nombre? *How do you spell your name?*
¿Dónde **se puede** aparcar? *Where can you/one park?*

Pronunciation

The pronunciation of **ll**, as in '**apellido, calle**', varies from region to region, but it is pronounced by most Spanish speakers like the 'y' in 'yacht'.

Practise with:

El Hotel del Valle en Valladolid es un hotel de tres estrellas y está en la calle de Mallorca.

¿Cómo te llamas?
Me llamo Estrella.
¿Y cómo te apellidas?
Ulloa. Estrella Ulloa.

Practice

▶ 1 Los números del 21 al 100

Listen and repeat each number as you hear it, and fill in the blanks with the missing ones.

21 veintiuno	30 treinta	59	_____
22 veintidós	31 treinta y uno	60	sesenta
23 veintitrés	32 treinta y dos	64	_____
24 veinticuatro	36 _____	70	setenta
25 veinticinco	40 cuarenta	76	_____
26 veintiséis	42 cuarenta y dos	80	ochenta
27 veintisiete	45 _____	88	_____
28 veintiocho	50 cincuenta	90	noventa
29 veintinueve	53 cincuenta y tres	93	_____
		100	cien

▶ 2 ¿La habitación del señor Luis García, por favor?

Listen to these brief conversations and fill in the box with the room or office number of each of the people mentioned.

	Nombre	Habitación	Oficina
a	Sr. García		
b	Srta. Sáez		
c	Sres. Silva		

3 Palabra por palabra

On the next page is a list of some of the facilities you might find in certain hotels. Can you match them with the drawings below?

a la ducha
b el lavabo
c la calefacción

d el hilo musical
e el ascensor
f la piscina

4 Un moderno hotel a su servicio

Your boss is travelling to a Spanish-speaking country. He has seen the following hotel advertisement and has asked you to list all facilities and services for him in English.

PLAYA DORADA
Hotel *VICTORIA RESORT* Primera
Playa Dorada – Puerto Plata – Tel. (508) 586 12 00

Una edificación tropical, situada en el corazón de Playa Dorada, considerada como uno de los edificios más bellos de la costa norte, rodeado de un lago poblado de exuberantes jardines. Todas las habitaciones con terraza y baño privado, aire condicionado central, T.V. a color por cable y teléfono. Dispone de Club de Playa, piscina y jacuzzi. Restaurante, piano-bar y night club.

Programa completo de actividades desde clases de buceo hasta excursiones en bicicleta, caballos, tenis, wind-surfing, etc. Acceso directo al campo de golf.

Suplemento habitación individual por noche: 12 euros.

una edificación	*building*	**un lago**	*a lake*
un edificio	*building*	**poblado**	*full*
rodeado	*surrounded*		

5 En un país de habla española

You and a travelling companion have just arrived in a hotel in a Spanish-speaking country. Complete the following requests and questions by filling in the gaps with the correct form of **querer** and **poder**, as appropriate.

a Q - - r - m - s dos habitaciones individuales.
b ¿Q - - - r - n ustedes media pensión o pensión completa?
c ¿Dónde p - d - m - s cambiar dinero?
d ¿P - - d - usted lavar esta ropa para mañana?
e ¿Dónde se p - - d - alquilar un coche?

la media pensión	half board
la pensión completa	full board
lavar	to wash
alquilar	to hire

6 Hoteles y servicios

Read this passage about hotels and services in Spain and Latin America, then consider the statements below and say whether they are true or false (**verdadero o falso**). Some of the words will be familiar to you from this or previous units, while others you will be able to guess from the context.

a Todos los hostales tienen baño privado.
b El desayuno es normalmente aparte.
c Los paradores nacionales son hoteles muy exclusivos.
d Los paradores no están normalmente en la ciudad.

En España y en Latinoamérica hay una enorme variedad de hoteles y servicios, desde grandes y lujosos hoteles de cinco estrellas hasta hostales y pensiones o casas de huéspedes. En España los hostales pueden ser de una, dos o tres estrellas y, dependiendo de la categoría, las habitaciones pueden tener baño, ducha o sólo lavabo. Las pensiones o casas de huéspedes son más económicas y generalmente no tienen baño privado. El desayuno, normalmente, no está incluido en el precio de la habitación.

Los paradores nacionales, en España, son hoteles de primera categoría, situados generalmente en las afueras de las ciudades. Para los jóvenes existen los albergues juveniles, informales y económicos, pero con todos los servicios básicos.

hay	there are	las afueras	outskirts
desde ... hasta	from ... to	los jóvenes	the young
primera categoría	first class	el albergue juvenil	youth hostel

7 ¿Qué servicios tienen?

Now look at the table opposite, which lists all the services you can expect to find in the different categories of hotels.

a What services would you find in a 3-star hotel?
b What extra service would you find in a 4-star hotel?
c Where would you find a safe-deposit box? And a fire exit?

Lo que tienen que tener					
	5★	4★	3★	2★	1★
Aire acondicionado	●	●	●(1)	–	–
Teléfono en habitación	●	●	●	●	–
Bar	●	●	●	–	–
Salidas de incendios	●	●	●	●	●
Suites	●	–	–	–	–
Caja fuerte individual	●	●	–	–	–
Superficies mínimas por habitación (en metros cuadrados)					
Doble	17	16	15	14	12
Individual	10	9	8	7	7
(1) En salón, comedor y bar					

▶ 8 El alfabeto

Listen to the letters of the Spanish alphabet and try saying each
as you hear them. See page 279 for more on 'ch' and 'll'.

a	a	Ana	n	ene	no
b	be	Bilbao	ñ	eñe	mañana
c	ce	Cuba, gracias	o	o	Colombia
d	de	día	p	pe	Perú
e	e	Elena	q	cu	que, quinto
f	efe	Francia	r	erre	París, Río, perro
g	ge	Gloria, Algeciras	s	ese	Susana
h	hache	hasta	t	te	Tarragona
i	i	Isabel	u	u	Murcia
j	jota	Juan	v	uve	Venezuela
k	ca	kilo	w	uve doble	Washington
l	ele	Londres	x	equis	taxi
ll	elle	calle	y	i griega	yo, Paraguay
m	eme	María	z	zeta	Cádiz

9 ¿Cómo se escribe?

A group of Spanish speakers arrive at your place of work and
you need to spell their surnames to a Spanish person.

a Aguirre
b Fernández
c Arredondo

d Bravo
e Collado
f Julián

10 Ahora tú

Can you spell the following words?

tu nombre, tu apellido
el nombre de tu barrio
el nombre de tu calle

el nombre y apellido de tu jefe/a
el nombre y apellido de tu profesor/a.

04

¿dónde está?

where is it?

In this unit you will learn
- how to ask and say if there is a certain place nearby
- how to ask and say where a place is
- how to ask and say how far away a place is

▶ 1 ¿Hay una oficina de cambio por aquí cerca?

On *calle Agustinas* and *San Martín*, Carmen stops a passer-by to ask for directions. She is facing *calle Morandé*.

1.1 Listen to the dialogue several times, each time focusing attention on different information, while you try to follow directions on the map below. Key words here are:

hay *there is* **derecha** *right* **izquierda** *left*

a   What word does Carmen use to draw the passer-by's attention?
b   Which of the following is Carmen looking for? Tick the correct boxes.

☐ una estación   ☐ una oficina de turismo   ☐ una plaza

☐ un banco   ☐ una oficina de cambio   ☐ un hotel

c   How does Carmen ask about the places she is looking for? Complete her sentences:

¿ ... por aquí cerca? ¿Y ... por aquí?

d   What expressions are used in the dialogue for *on the left, on the right*?

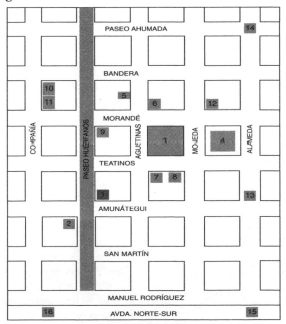

1 oficina de cambio
2 museo
3 plaza
4 aparcamiento
5 restaurante
6 banco

7 hotel
8 iglesia
9 hotel
10 banco
11 oficina de turismo
12 Correos

Carmen   Perdone, ¿hay una oficina de cambio por aquí cerca?

Señor   Hay una en la calle Amunátegui, la primera calle a la izquierda.

Carmen   ¿Y hay un hotel por aquí?

Señor   Sí, hay uno en esta calle, la calle Agustinas, a la derecha, al lado de una iglesia. Hay otro en la calle Morandé, la tercera a la izquierda, en la primera esquina.

Carmen   Muchas gracias.

Señor   De nada.

1.2 Now read the dialogue while you follow directions on the map and try to spot the numbers for the places Carmen is looking for. You can check that you were right by looking at the map references.

1.3 Now use the map and the conversation above as a model to make up similar dialogues.

por aquí cerca	*nearby*	**al lado de**	*next to*
primero/a	*first*	**tercero/a**	*third*

▶ 2 ¿Dónde está?

Pablo has just arrived in a Spanish town and he is asking for directions. He is outside the post office, on calle Moneda and Morandé (see map in Dialogue 1 above).

2.1 Listen to the conversation several times while you follow directions on the map, and try to answer the questions which follow. Key words here are   **¿dónde?**   *where?*

                  estar   *to be*

a   What place is Pablo looking for?
b   What do you think the first person means by **no lo sé**?
c   Can you spot the number for the place he is looking for, on the map?

Pablo	Por favor, ¿sabe usted dónde está la oficina de turismo?
Señora	Lo siento, no lo sé. No conozco muy bien la ciudad.
Pablo	La oficina de turismo, por favor, ¿está muy lejos?
Policía	Está al final de esta calle, a la derecha, a cinco minutos de aquí.
Pablo	Muchas gracias.

2.2 Now read the dialogue and find the Spanish for

a   It's at the end of this street.
b   (It's) five minutes from here.

2.3 Now use the map and the conversation above as a model to make up similar dialogues.

saber	*to know*	**lo siento**	*I'm sorry*
conocer	*to know*	**lejos**	*far*

ℹ️ In most Spanish towns you will find a tourist information office, **una Oficina de Información y Turismo**, where you can get free plans, **planos**, maps, **mapas**, lists of hotels, **listas de hoteles**, and brochures, **folletos**. To get any of these you can say:

Por favor, ¿tiene un plano de la ciudad/una lista de hoteles?
Do you have a plan of the town/a list of hotels?

Alternatively, you can use **querer**, *to want*:

Por favor, quiero un folleto de Valencia.
I want a brochure of Valencia, please.

▶ 3 Están en el primer piso

Ignacio is looking for the toilets in a restaurant. Listen, and then read the dialogue and answer these questions:

a How does he ask for **los servicios**?
b What do you think the answer means?

Ignacio	Por favor, ¿dónde están los servicios?
Camarero	Están en el primer piso, al final del pasillo.
Ignacio	Gracias.

el piso	*floor*	**el pasillo**	*corridor*

How do you say it?

Asking and saying if there is a certain place nearby

¿Hay una oficina de cambio/ un hotel por aquí (cerca)?	*Is there a bureau de change/ hotel nearby?*
Hay una/uno en …/esta calle.	*There is one in …/in this street.*

Asking and saying where a place is

¿Dónde está/están …?	*Where is/are …?*
Está/Están …	*It is/They are …*
al (otro) lado de …	*next to/on the other side of …*
enfrente de …	*opposite …*
al final de …	*at the end of …*
delante de …/detrás de …	*in front of…/behind …*
entre … y …	*between … and …*
a la derecha/izquierda	*on the right/left*
en la esquina	*on the corner*
en el primer/segundo piso	*on the first/second floor*

Asking and saying how far a place is

¿Está cerca/lejos?	*Is it near/far?*
Está (bastante/muy) cerca/ lejos (de aquí).	*It's (quite/very) near/far (from here).*
Está a … minutos / … metros /… calles de aquí.	*It's … minutes / … metres /… streets from here.*

Grammar

1 Hay (*there is, there are*)

a To say *there is/are* and *is/are there?* use the single word **hay**:

¿Hay un banco por aquí?	*Is there a bank nearby?*
Hay uno en la esquina.	*There is one at the corner.*
¿Hay teléfonos aquí?	*Are there any telephones here?*
No hay.	*There aren't any.*

b To ask where you can find something if you are not sure it exists, use the expression **¿dónde hay ...?**

¿Dónde hay un aparcamiento?	*Where's a car park?*
¿Dónde hay una estación de metro?	*Where's a metro station?*

2 ¿Dónde está? (*where is it?*)

To ask and say where a place is, use **estar**, *to be* (for its forms and other uses see Unit 2).

¿Dónde está el mercado?	*Where is the market?*
Está detrás de la estación.	*It's behind the station.*
¿Dónde están los teléfonos?	*Where are the telephones?*
Están en el primer piso.	*They are on the first floor.*

3 Está a cinco minutos (*it's five minutes away*)

a To say how far away a place is you use **estar** followed by **a** and an expression of distance.

Está a cinco minutos de aquí.	*It's five minutes from here.*
Está a cien metros de la estación.	*It's a hundred metres from the station.*

b To ask how far it is to a place you can say:

¿A qué distancia está/están?	*How far is it/are they?*

Or simply:

¿Está/están cerca/lejos?	*Is it/are they near/far?*

4 Otro, otros (*another, others*)

Otro agrees in number (sing. or pl.) and gender (masc. or fem.) with the noun it refers to.

otro banco	*another bank*
otra oficina de cambio	*another bureau de change*
otros bancos	*other banks*

Otro, otros can replace a noun when this is understood:

Hay un banco en la esquina	*There's a bank at the corner*
y otro enfrente del mercado.	*and another one opposite*
	the market.

5 'Saber' and 'conocer' (*to know*)

There are two ways of saying 'to know' in Spanish: **saber** and **conocer**. **Saber** is used to refer to *knowledge of a fact* and *ability to do something*, while **conocer** is used to refer to *acquaintance with something*, *a person or a place*. Both are irregular in the first person singular of the present tense.

saber	conocer
sé	conozco
sabes	conoces
sabe	conoce
sabemos	conocemos
sabéis	conocéis
saben	conocen

¿Sabe usted dónde está	*Do you know where the*
el museo?	*museum is?*
No sé dónde está.	*I don't know where it is.*
No (lo) sé.	*I don't know.*
No conozco este barrio.	*I don't know this area.*

6 Ordinal numbers

1st primero	5th quinto	8th octavo
2nd segundo	6th sexto	9th noveno
3rd tercero	7th séptimo/sétimo	10th décimo
4th cuarto		

Ordinal numbers must agree in gender (masc. or fem.) and number (sing. or pl.) with the noun they refer to.

el segundo piso	*the second floor*
la segunda calle	*the second street*
las primeras dos calles	*the first two streets*

Before a singular masculine noun, **primero** and **tercero** become **primer** and **tercer** respectively:

el primer/tercer piso   *the first/third floor*

▶ Pronunciation

c, before a, o, u, as in 'casa, conozco, Cuba', is pronounced like the 'c' in 'coast'.

c, before e, i, as in 'cerca, cinco', is pronounced like the 'th' in 'thin'.

z, as in plaza, izquierda, is also pronounced like the 'th' in 'thin'.

Practise with:

¿Conoce usted la ciudad? No, no la conozco.

¿Hay una oficina de cambio por aquí cerca? Hay una en la plaza de Cádiz, a la izquierda, entre la oficina de turismo y la estación de metro.

Latin American pronunciation

c, before e, i, as in cerca, cinco, is pronounced like the 's' in 'sale'.
z, as in plaza, izquierda, is also pronounced like the 's' in 'sale'.

Practice

▶ 1 ¿Hay o está?

Fill in the gaps in these conversations with **hay** and **está(n)**, as appropriate.

a ¿Dónde _____ una panadería, por favor?
   La más cercana es la Modelo, a dos calles de aquí.
b Perdone, ¿la Telefónica _____ muy lejos?
   A unos cinco minutos en coche.
c Oiga, perdone, ¿ _____ una lavandería por aquí cerca?
   Sí, en la calle de Zamora, la tercera a la izquierda.
d Perdone, ¿sabe dónde _____ el mercado central?
   Lo siento, no lo sé. No conozco bien este barrio.
e Los teléfonos, por favor, ¿dónde _____?
   En la planta baja.

f ¿Dónde _____ un camping, por favor?
En la Avenida del Mar, la segunda a la derecha.

la planta baja	*ground floor*

2 Ahora tú

You are spending a few days in a Spanish city and you need to find your way around. How would you ask if there is one of the following nearby?

a un restaurante
b una librería

c una tienda de ropa
d una tienda de comestibles

And how would you ask where the following places are?

e la estación de autobuses
f la iglesia

g la biblioteca
h la Plaza Mayor

una librería	*bookshop*	**la biblioteca**	*library*

▶ 3 ¿Saber o conocer?

Martín has just arrived in a Spanish town and is trying to find a **hostal**. Fill in the gaps in the conversation with **saber** and **conocer**, as appropriate. Note that the speakers are using the informal form.

Martín Perdona, ¿_____ (tú) dónde hay un hostal por aquí cerca?

Chica No (lo) _____. No _____ este barrio. _____ un hostal, pero está un poco lejos de aquí, en la calle de Los Olivos. ¿_____ (tú) la calle de Los Olivos?

Martín No soy de aquí. No _____ la ciudad.

4 Entre el banco y la papelería

You are working in a Spanish-speaking country and have been asked to look after some visitors who don't know your area. Study the map opposite and answer their questions, using expressions from the following. First, look at the example.

al lado (de)
a la derecha/izquierda
al final (de)
enfrente (de)

detrás (de)
delante (de)
entre
en la esquina

Ejemplo: ¿Hay un restaurante por aquí?

Hay dos, uno enfrente y otro cerca de la parada de autobuses, entre el banco y la papelería.

a ¿Hay un aparcamiento por aquí cerca?
b ¿Dónde hay un banco?
c ¿Dónde está Correos?
d ¿Dónde hay un quiosco de periódicos?
e La parada de autobuses, ¿dónde está?
f ¿Dónde hay una agencia de viajes?
g ¿Hay una papelería por aquí?
h La Plaza de la Luz, ¿dónde está?

▶ 5 ¿Dónde están?

A travel guide in Mexico is giving information in Spanish about the location of certain places in a town. Listen to the questions and answers several times, each time focusing attention on a different place, and make a note of each location in your own language.

a la avenida del Mar   c Correos
b la playa   d el museo

> **la cuadra**   *block* (Latin Am.)

6 Ahora tú

a ¿En qué calle está tu casa? ¿Y en qué barrio está?
b ¿Hay una parada de autobús o estación (de metro) cerca de tu casa? ¿A qué distancia está?
c ¿Qué tiendas hay en tu barrio?
d ¿Qué sitios importantes hay?

05

¿qué van a tomar?

what are you going to have?

In this unit you will learn
- how to order food and drinks
- how to ask what there is to eat or to drink
- how to say what you prefer

▶ 1 Queremos el menú del día

Marisol and Antonio are having lunch in a restaurant. Here's a typical day's menu in a Spanish restaurant. How many of the words can you guess? Look up the rest of the vocabulary before you listen to the conversations which follow.

RESTAURANTE SANTA MARIA
Menú del día

Sopa
Gazpacho
Ensalada mixta
Guisantes con jamón

*****

Paella
Merluza a la plancha con ensalada
Pollo con patatas
Cordero asado

*****

Pan, vino, helado, flan, fruta

1.1 Listen to the conversation several times and, as you do so, try to find the answers to the following questions:

a What is Marisol having for lunch?
b What is Antonio having?
c What drink does Marisol order?
c What does Antonio prefer to drink?

Camarero	¿Qué van a tomar?
Marisol	Queremos el menú del día. Para mí, gazpacho de primero, y de segundo quiero merluza a la plancha con ensalada.
Camarero	¿Y para usted?
Antonio	Yo, guisantes con jamón, y de segundo pollo con patatas fritas.
Camarero	¿Y para beber?
Marisol	Agua mineral sin gas.
Antonio	Yo prefiero vino tinto.

1.2 Now read the dialogue and find the Spanish equivalent for the following:

a We want the day's menu
b For me …
c as a first/second course
d I prefer …

¿qué van a tomar?	*what are you going to have?*
beber	*to drink*
patatas fritas	*chips*

▶ 2 ¿Me trae otra agua mineral, por favor?

Antonio calls the waiter to order something else.

2.1 What is each person ordering? Listen and find out.

Antonio   Por favor, ¿nos trae un poco más de pan?
Marisol   ¿Y me trae otra agua mineral, por favor?
Camarero   Muy bien.
(*Antonio and Marisol order a dessert.*)
Marisol   ¿Qué tienen de postre?
Camarero   Hay flan, helados y fruta.
Marisol   Un helado de chocolate para mí.
Antonio   Yo quiero un flan.

2.2 Now read the dialogue and say how the following is expressed.

a Will you bring us …?
b Will you bring me …?

2.3 Use the menu on page 49 and the conversation you have just heard as a model to make up similar dialogues.

---

traer	*to bring*	un poco más de	*some more*
el postre	*dessert*	el flan	*creme caramel*
el helado	*ice cream*		

---

i Eating habits have changed substantially in Spain and in large Latin American cities in the last few years. Many working people no longer enjoy the traditional leisurely lunch, **la comida o almuerzo** at home during the week, opting instead for **el menú del día** in a restaurant near their office, or for a quick meal, **una comida rápida** in a fast-food place. Many restaurants serve **el menú del día**, known as **la comida corrida** in Mexico, at reasonable prices, with **vino** or an alternative drink, **una bebida**, normally included in it. In smaller towns, though, people still go home for lunch, and at weekends the majority have the traditional family lunch.

How do you say it?

Ordering food and drinks

¿Qué van a tomar?	*What are you going to have?*
Para mí/Yo, ensalada/ guisantes con jamón.	*Salad/peas with ham for me.*
Quiero merluza a la plancha/ pollo con patatas.	*I'd like grilled hake/chicken with potatoes.*
¿Me/Nos trae (un poco) más (de) pan/agua?	*Will you bring me/us (some) more bread/water?*

Asking what there is to eat or to drink

¿Qué tienen de postre/ de segundo/ para beber?	*What do you have for dessert/ as a second course/to drink?*

Saying what you prefer

Prefiero melón/flan.	*I prefer melon/creme caramel.*

Grammar

1 Prepositions

Words like **para, con, sin, de,** are called *prepositions*. As in English, Spanish prepositions can have several uses and different meanings.

Para mí, una sopa.	*Soup for me.*
¿Y **para** usted (*formal*)/ ti (*informal*)?	*And for you?*
¿Y **para** beber?	*And to drink?*
De segundo quiero merluza **a** la plancha.	*I want grilled hake as a second course.*

Yo, cordero asado **con** patatas.   *Roast lamb with potatoes for me.*

Un agua mineral **con/sin** gas.   *A sparkling/still mineral water.*

2 ¿Me/nos trae ...? (Will you bring me/us ...?)

To request something in a polite way use the third person present tense of the verb preceded by **me** *(to) me*, or **nos** *(to) us*.

¿Me trae una botella de vino?   *Will you bring me a bottle of wine?*

Por favor, ¿me trae una taza de té?   *Will you bring me a cup of tea, please?*

¿Nos trae dos cafés con leche?   *Will you bring us two white coffees?*

¿Nos trae la cuenta, por favor?   *Will you bring us the bill, please?*

3 Preferir (to prefer)

To say what you or others prefer, use **preferir**, an **-ir** radical-changing verb, whose stem changes from **e** to **ie**, like **querer**, *to want* (see Unit 3). The following are its present tense forms.

prefiero	preferimos
prefieres (*informal*)	preferís (*informal*)
prefiere	prefieren

¿Qué prefieres?   *What do you prefer?*

Prefiero un té con limón.   *I prefer a lemon tea.*

¿Prefieren cerveza o vino?   *Do you prefer beer or wine?*

Preferimos vino blanco.   *We prefer white wine.*

4 Same word, different meaning

Note that just as in English, words referring to food and meals can have different meanings in some regions. The standard word for *breakfast* is **el desayuno**, for *lunch*, **el almuerzo** or **la comida**, and for the *evening meal*, **la cena**. But **el almuerzo** is also mid-morning snack in some places (e.g. Barcelona, Mexico City), while **la comida** refers to the evening meal in some Latin American countries. **Un sandwich**, in Spain, is a sandwich made from a tin loaf, and **un bocadillo** is one made with French bread. Most Latin American countries use the word **sandwich**, without making a distinction between the two types of bread. In Mexico, a **torta** is made with French bread and they are very popular.

▶ Pronunciation

j, as in 'jamón, ajo', is pronounced like a strong 'h', or like the Scottish 'ch' in 'loch'.

g, before e, i, as in '**li**gero, **Gi**braltar', is pronounced like Spanish **j** (see above).

g, before a, o, u, as in '**gas**, se**gu**ndo', is pronounced like the 'g' in 'government'.

g, in the combination **gue** and **gui**, as in **Guer**nica, **gui**sante, is also pronounced like the 'g' in 'government'. Here the 'u' remains silent.

Practise with:

Para mí un sandwich de jamón y un agua con gas. Para Jaime un gazpacho, y de segundo pollo con guisantes y judías verdes.

Practice

▶ 1 Una comida

Raquel and Francisca are having lunch together. Can you fill in the gaps in the conversation with one of these words: **a, con, de, sin, para?**

– ¿Qué van a tomar?
– _____ mí, sopa de verduras, _____ primero, y _____ segundo quiero cordero asado _____ arroz.
– ¿Y _____ usted?
– Yo, pescado _____ la plancha _____ puré.
– ¿Y _____ beber?
– Dos aguas minerales.
– ¿ _____ o _____ gas?
– Una _____ gas y la otra _____ gas.

▶ 2 ¿Tú o usted?

You are going to hear some people asking for things. Which of the requests are informal and which formal? Classify them accordingly, using **tú** for informal and **usted** for formal.

a _____   c _____   e _____
b _____   d _____   f _____

la servilleta *napkin*	**el azúcar** *sugar*
la sal *salt*	

3 Ahora tú

You are in the Restaurante Santa María. Choose from the menu board on page 49 and fill in your part of this conversation with the waitress.

Camarera	Tú
¿Qué va a tomar?	_____
¿De segundo qué quiere?	_____
¿Y para beber? ¿Vino blanco, tinto, cerveza, agua ...?	_____
Muy bien.	*Ask her what she has for dessert.*
Hay helado, flan y fresas con nata.	_____
	Now ask for a coffee and the bill.
Sí, un momento, por favor.	

▶ 4 En un bar

What snacks do they serve in this Spanish bar? First, study the words in the menu board below, then listen to Ramón, Silvia and Clara placing their order. What is each one having? Fill in the table below with each order.

BAR LAS GAVIOTAS

<u>Tapas</u>	<u>Bocadillos</u>
champiñones	jamón
gambas	queso
calamares	chorizo
tortilla de patatas	salchichón

	Para comer	Para beber
Silvia		
Clara		
Ramón		

5 ¿Qué restaurante prefieres?

During a visit to Chile you and a colleague spot a couple of restaurant ads in a local magazine. Which one would you choose for your dinner? Consider the following:

FICHA:

Restaurante Montealpino
Ubicación: Camino El Bajo 16.749, con Pastor Fernández, a pocos metros de la Plaza San Enrique.
Horario: Martes a sábado, 20 a 00:00 horas.
Domingo: almuerzo.
Comida: centroeuropea, incluye suiza, alemana, francesa e italiana.
Modalidad: A la carta.
Dos comen por: $ 24.000 aproximadamente.
Cómo ir: de sport o formal.
Otros: En otros horarios se abre para eventos de empresas.

FICHA:

Restaurante Salvaje
Dirección: *Providencia 1177*
Fono reservas: *235 25 15*
Horario: *de 12:00 a 01:00 horas (incluso domingos y festivos durante todo el año).*
Viernes y sábado hasta las 02:00
Capacidad: *240 personas*
Especialidad: *comida internacional*
Modalidad: *a la carta*
Dos comen por: *9 mil pesos aproximadamente*
Cómo ir: *informal*
Importante: *hay estacionamiento propio.*

a   What sort of food does each restaurant serve?
b   What does each charge? (Prices are in Chilean pesos.)
c   What is the dress code in each restaurant?
d   Which one offers parking facilities?
e   Which one would you choose if you wanted to go for dinner on Sunday?

6 Palabra por palabra

Here are some common words related to food and eating. Look them up and list them under the appropriate headings below.

cuchillo	lechugas	uvas	merluza	cerdo
piñas	pollo	manzanas	cordero	tenedor
atún	cuchara	ajos	cebollas	plato

Pescado, Carne, Verdura, Fruta, Utensilio

Can you add other words to each list?

7 Buen provecho

Read the following passage which describes the main meals in Spain and Latin America, and find out how these compare with those in your country. Then read the statements below and say whether they are true or false (**verdadero o falso**).

En España y en Latinoamérica hay tres comidas principales: el desayuno, la comida o el almuerzo, y la cena.

En España, el desayuno es una comida ligera, consistente normalmente en café y tostadas, pero en algunos países latinoamericanos, México por ejemplo, el desayuno es generalmente abundante. Aparte de café, un desayuno mexicano puede incluir frutas, huevos, y algún plato típico de la región.

La comida o el almuerzo es la comida principal, se toma entre la una y las tres y consiste normalmente en dos platos, postre y café. El plato principal o segundo plato, generalmente lleva carne o pescado. A la hora de la comida, españoles y latinoamericanos consumen muchas legumbres, verduras y frutas frescas.

La cena se toma entre las nueve y las diez y es normalmente una comida ligera.

a   En España se toma un desayuno muy abundante.
b   En México se toma un desayuno ligero.
c   La comida principal en España y Latinoamérica es la comida o almuerzo.
d   El primer plato normalmente lleva pescado o carne.

buen provecho	*bon appetit*	**la legumbre**	*pulse*
ligero	*light*	**la verdura**	*vegetables*

06

¿a qué hora llega?

what time does it arrive?

In this unit you will learn

- how to ask and tell the time
- how to ask about travel times
- how to buy tickets and ask how much they cost
- how to ask the way to somewhere by public transport

▶ 1 ¿Qué hora es?

1.1 Listen to some people asking and telling the time and, as you do, look at the clock faces only and repeat each question and answer after the speakers several times. Note the two alternative questions.

¿Qué hora es? (*What time is it?*) /¿Tiene hora? (*Have you got the time?*)

a Es la una (en punto) **b** Son las cuatro y diez **c** Son las seis y cuarto

d Son las siete y media   **e** Son las diez
menos cinco

f Son las doce
menos cuarto

1.2 Listen again several times while you read the phrases under each clock and say them aloud until you feel confident that you have learned them. Then look at the clock faces only, and practise asking and saying the time. You can then practise in a similar way with other times.

---

en punto *sharp, on the dot*

▶ 2 Deme un billete de ida y vuelta

Señor Molina from Mexico is at a railway station in Spain, buying a ticket. Note that official times are given with the 24-hour clock, with 1.00 becoming **las trece horas**, and fractions of time like 6.45 p.m. expressed as **las dieciocho cuarenta y cinco**.

2.1 Listen to the conversation several times, each time focusing attention on a different point. Two key words in this dialogue are **salir** *to leave*, and **llegar** *to arrive*.

a Where does señor Molina want to travel to?
b Does he get a single ticket, **un billete de ida,** or a return ticket, **un billete de ida y vuelta?**
c Is he travelling first or second class, **primera o segunda clase?**
d Does he ask for a smoker, **fumador,** or non-smoker carriage, **no fumador?**

Sr. Molina	Buenos días. Quiero reservar un asiento para Barcelona para el domingo.
Empleada	Pues, hay un tren a las once y media de la mañana, otro a las dieciséis quince …
Sr. Molina	¿A qué hora llega el tren de las dieciséis quince a Barcelona?
Empleada	A las veinte cuarenta y cinco.
Sr. Molina	Muy bien, deme un billete de ida y vuelta, por favor.
Empleada	¿Primera o segunda clase?
Sr. Molina	Segunda. ¿Cuánto cuesta?
Empleada	Sesenta euros. ¿Fumador o no fumador?
Sr. Molina	No fumador.

2.2 Now read the dialogue and find the equivalent for the following times:

a las nueve menos cuarto (de la noche)
b las cuatro y cuarto (de la tarde)

2.3 Make up similar conversations by varying the destinations, days of the week and times. The days of the week are given on page 62.

deme	*give me*	**domingo**	*Sunday*
un asiento	*seat*		

▶ 3 ¿Qué línea tengo que tomar?

Pilar will be visiting Toledo and she asks her friend Raúl how to get to the railway station at Atocha. She's staying near **estación de metro** Ópera in Madrid (see map overleaf).

3.1 Listen to the conversation several times and say whether the statements which follow are true or false (**verdadero o falso**). Key words here are **tomar** *to take,* **cambiar** *to change,* **la línea** *line.*

Pilar tiene que … (*Pilar has to …*)

a tomar la línea dos en Sol
b cambiar en Ópera
c tomar el metro en dirección a Portazgo

Pilar ¿Qué línea tengo que tomar para ir a Atocha?
Raúl Tienes que tomar la línea dos en Ópera, cambias en Sol, tomas la línea uno en dirección a Portazgo y te bajas en Atocha. La estación está allí mismo.
Pilar Vale.

tener que *to have to*	**bajarse** *to get off*

3.2 Now read the dialogue and find the expressions which mean the following:

a What line do I have to take?
b You have to take …
c You get off at …
d It is right there.

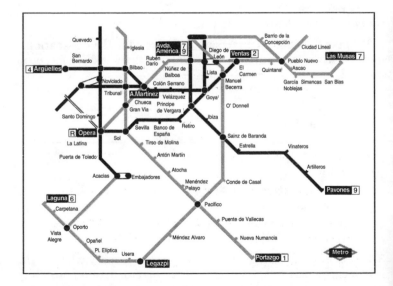

3.3 Use the map of the Madrid metro and the conversation on the previous page as a model to make up similar dialogues.

i Large Spanish cities like Madrid, Barcelona, Valencia and Seville, have a modern and relatively cheap transport system. Madrid, Barcelona and Seville have an underground system, **el metro**, and buses, **los autobuses**, cover most areas of the city. The *Red Nacional de los Ferrocarriles Españoles*, the Spanish national railway system, operate a wide range of services, including modern, fast intercity trains like *el Talgo*, the high-speed *el AVE*, between Madrid and Seville, stopping trains like *el electrotrén*, the not-so-fast night *expreso*, and commuter services, covered by *los trenes de cercanía*.

How do you say it?

Asking and telling the time

¿Qué hora es?	*What time is it?*
¿Tiene/s hora?	*Have you got the time?*
Es la una.	*It's one o'clock.*
Son las diez menos cuarto.	*It's a quarter to ten.*
Son las doce y cuarto/media.	*It's a quarter/half past twelve.*

Asking about travel times

¿A qué hora sale/llega?	*What time does it leave/arrive?*
Sale/llega a las …	*It leaves/arrives at …*

Buying tickets and asking how much they cost

Quiero reservar un asiento/ hacer una reserva para …	*I want to book a seat/make a reservation for …*
Deme/quiero un billete de ida/ de ida y vuelta.	*Give me/I want a single/ return ticket.*
¿Cuánto cuesta/vale? Cuesta/ Vale …	*How much does it cost? It costs …*

Asking how to get to a place by public transport and responding

¿Qué línea/autobús tengo que tomar/coger?	*What line/bus do I have to take?*
Toma(s)/Coge(s) (*formal/inf.*) la línea …/el autobús número …	*You take line number …/ bus number …*
Cambia(s) (*formal/inf.*) a la línea …	*You change onto line …*
Se baja/te bajas en … (*formal/inf.*)	*You get off at …*

Grammar

1 Telling the time

To tell the time use **ser** *to be*: **es** for one o'clock, midday and midnight, and **son** for all other times.

Es mediodía/medianoche.	*It's midday/midnight.*
Es la una y cuarto.	*It is a quarter past one.*
Son las nueve y veinticinco.	*It is nine twenty-five.*
Son las once y dieciocho minutos.	*It is eighteen minutes past eleven.*
Son las seis menos cuarto.	*It is a quarter to six.*

Some Latin American countries use expressions like **es un cuarto para las seis**, *it's a quarter to six*, **son diez para las ocho**, *it's ten to eight*, instead of **son las seis menos cuarto, son las ocho menos diez**.

2 Los días de la semana (*days of the week*)

lunes	martes	miércoles	jueves	viernes	sábado	domingo
Monday	*Tuesday*	*Wednesday*	*Thursday*	*Friday*	*Saturday*	*Sunday*

Days are masculine in Spanish, and are normally written with a small letter.

el lunes	*on Monday*
los martes	*on Tuesdays*
para el miércoles	*for Wednesday*

3 More prepositions

para
- destination: para Málaga, *for Malaga*
- In time phrases: para el sábado, *for Saturday*

por
- with parts of the day:

por la mañana/tarde	*in the morning/afternoon*
por la noche	*at night*
el jueves por la mañana	*on Thursday morning*

de
- with parts of the day, when the time is specified:

Sale/Llega a las 3.00 de la tarde.	*It leaves/arrives at 3.00 in the afternoon.*

- with **salir** *to leave*:

Sale de Madrid a las 6.00.	*It leaves Madrid at 6.00.*

a

- with **llegar** *to arrive*:

Llega a Sevilla a las 9.00.	*It arrives in Seville at 9.00.*

4 Que (*that, which*)

To say 'that' or 'which' as in *There is a train which/that leaves Barcelona at midday*, use the word **que:** Hay un tren **que** sale de Barcelona al mediodía.

5 Telling someone what transport to take

a The present tense:

Tomas/Coges un tren.	*You take a train.* (informal)
Toma/Coge un autobús.	*You take a bus.* (formal)
Cambias en Sol.	*You change at Sol.* (informal)
Cambia a la línea 2.	*You change on to line two.* (formal)

Latin Americans normally use **tomar** *to take*, with means of transport, instead of **coger**, which is more common in Spain, and which is a taboo word in some Latin American countries. **Tomar** will be understood and accepted everywhere.

b **Tener que,** *to have to*

Tienes que cambiar en Sol.	*You have to change at Sol.* (informal)
Para ir de Valencia a Mallorca tiene que tomar un avión o un barco.	*To go from Valencia to Mallorca you have to take a plane or a boat.* (formal)

▶ Pronunciation

q occurs only in the combination **que** and **qui,** and is pronounced like [ke] and [ki].

Practise with:

¿A qué hora sale el avión para Quito?
Quiero un billete para el tren que sale a las quince treinta.
Queremos cambiar quinientos euros.

Practice

1 La hora en el mundo

You need to make some international phone calls from Chile, where you have been sent by your company. How would you ask the operator what the time is in the following cities, and how would she/he reply? Look at the table below and ask and answer using the twelve-hour clock and expressions like **de la mañana/de la tarde.**

LA HORA	
Cuando en Chile es mediodía en el resto del mundo es:	
N. York	12.00
Madrid	18.00
Londres	17.00
Roma	18.00
Tokio	01.00
San Fco	09.00
México	10.00
Sao Paulo	13.00
París	18.00
Sidney	02.00

a Madrid
b Londres
c Tokio
d San Francisco
e Sao Paulo
f Nueva York

2 De Sevilla a Málaga

You are now in Spain with a travelling companion and you want to take a train from Sevilla to Málaga. Check the time-table and answer your partner's questions using the 12-hour clock.

ORIGEN				
SEVILLA STA. JUSTA	7,50	12,20	17,30	18,40
La Salud	–	12,28	–	–
Dos Hermanas	8,01	12,35	17,41	18,51
Utrera (LL)	8,13	12,47	17,53	19,03
Utrera (S)	8,15	12,50	17,55	19,05
El Arahal	–	13,07	–	–
Marchena	8,39	13,18	18,19	19,29
Osuna	9,05	13,45	18,44	19,55
Pedrera	9,34	14,12	19,08	–
La Roda Andalucía	9,47	14,26	19,21	20,36
Fuente Piedra	–	14,37	–	–
Bobadilla (LL)	10,05	14,46	19,42	21,00
Bobadilla (S)	10,09	15,04	–	21,01
MALAGA (LL)	10,58	16,17	–	22,03

a ¿A qué hora hay trenes para Málaga?
b ¿A qué hora llegan a Málaga?

▶ **3 Un recado**

María Luisa is being sent by her company overseas and her travel agent leaves *a message*, **un recado**, on her answerphone with details of her flight. Can you fill in the box below with the appropriate information?

Destino	Salida	Llegada	Presentación en aeropuerto
- - - - -	- - - - -	- - - - -	- - - - -

la salida *departure*	**la llegada** *arrival*

▶ **4 Números**

Listen, tick the numbers that you hear, and then try learning them all.

100	cien	800	ochocientos
101	ciento uno	900	novecientos
200	doscientos	1 000	mil
299	doscientos noventa y nueve	2 000	dos mil
300	trescientos	3 500	tres mil quinientos
400	cuatrocientos	10 000	diez mil
500	quinientos	100 000	cien mil
600	seiscientos	1 000 000	un millón
700	setecientos	2 000 000	dos millones

Note that **-cientos** becomes **-cientas** before a feminine plural noun

| doscientos euros | *two hundred euros* |
| doscientas libras | *two hundred pounds* |

The plural of **millón** is **millones,** and the word loses the accent.

Years are read in the following way:

1985	mil novecientos ochenta y cinco
1999	mil novecientos noventa y nueve
2004	dos mil cuatro

5 Ahora tú

You have seen the following holiday advertisement in a Spanish paper, and you phone a Spanish friend to tell him/her about it. How would you read the following prices?

EUROPA

AMSTERDAM. 3 días
Hotel 2*   desde **318,00 €**

MALTA. 3 días
Hotel 3*   desde **376,00 €**

CAPITALES DE RUSIA. 7 días
Hotel 4*   desde **900,00 €**
Visitando Moscú y San Petersburgo.

AFRICA

TWENDE (KENIA). 10 días
Hotel 4*   desde **1.977,00 €**
Visitando Nairobi, Samburu, Treetops, Lago Nakuru, Massai Mara.

ASIA

BANGKOK-BALI. 10 días
Hotel 5*   desde **933,00 €**
Visitando Bangkok y Bali

INDIA. 8 días
Hotel 4/5*   desde **1.206,00 €**
Visitando Delhi, Jaipur, Sariska, Fatehpur, Sikri, Agra.

MALDIVAS. 10 días
Hotel 4*   desde **1.418,00 €**

CHINA MILENARIA + GUILIN. 15 días
Hoteles 5*   desde **1.693,00 €**
Visitando Shanghai, Suzhou, Hangzhou, Guilin, Xian, Pekín.

▶ 6 El vuelo dura una hora

While on business in Bogotá, Colombia, you decide to spend a couple of days in the colonial town of Cartagena de Indias. Follow the guidelines and fill in your part in the conversation with the travel agent.

– Buenos días.
– *Answer the greeting and ask how much is a return ticket to Cartagena by plane.*
– Doscientos cuarenta dólares.
– *Say you want to book a ticket for Friday morning and ask what time there are flights.*
– Hay un vuelo a las ocho y cuarto y otro a las once y media.
– *Say you prefer the 8.15 flight. Ask what time it arrives in Cartagena.*
– El vuelo dura una hora aproximadamente. Llega a Cartagena a las nueve y veinte.
– *Say that's all right.*

durar	*to last*

7 Tienes que tomar la línea 2

You are now in Madrid and you want to get from Sol to Lista on the metro (see page 60).

a How would you ask what line you have to take?
b The instructions you were given are wrong. Can you correct them?

Tienes que tomar la línea dos en Sol, en dirección a Ventas, cambias en Príncipe de Vergara y tomas un tren en dirección a Núñez de Balboa. Lista está una estación antes de Núñez de Balboa.

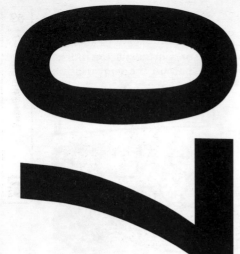

07

¿cuánto cuestan?

how much do they cost?

In this unit you will learn
- how to say what food you want and how much
- how to say what clothes you want
- how to find out how much things cost

▶ 1 ¿Cuánto cuestan los plátanos?

Lola is doing her shopping in a Spanish market.

1.1 First, look at the list of fruit and vegetables below. How many of them can you guess? Look up the words you don't know.

Frutas

el albaricoque/damasco (L.Am.)
la fresa/frutilla (Southern Cone)
el limón
la manzana
el melocotón/durazno (L.Am.)
el melón
la naranja
la piña/ananá (River Plate area)
el plátano/banana (Perú, River Plate area)
la uva

Verduras

el ajo	el pepino
la cebolla	el perejil
la coliflor	el pimiento (verde/rojo)
la lechuga	el tomate/jitomate (Méx.)
la patata/papa (L.Am.)	la zanahoria

1.2 Now listen to the dialogue several times. Can you say what and how much Lola is buying?

Dependiente	Buenos días. ¿Qué le pongo?
Lola	Quería un kilo y medio de naranjas.
Dependiente	¿Algo más?
Lola	¿Cuánto cuestan los plátanos?
Dependiente	Un euro con cuarenta céntimos el kilo.
Lola	Quiero un kilo.
Dependiente	¿Qué más?
Lola	Los tomates, ¿cuánto valen?
Dependiente	Un euro el kilo.
Lola	¿Me da dos kilos? Y deme una lechuga y dos kilos de patatas, también.
Dependiente	¿Algo más?
Lola	Nada más. ¿Cuánto es?
Dependiente	Son seis euros con ochenta céntimos.

1.3 Now read the dialogue and find another word or expression meaning:

a Deme   **b** ¿Cuánto cuestan?   **c** ¿Qué más?

1.4 Practise what you have learned now by playing the customer's role. Replace the words for fruit and vegetables in the dialogue by other words from the list above, and use expressions like **un cuarto de kilo, medio kilo, un kilo (y medio)**, etc.

¿qué le pongo?	*what would you like?* (in a market)
quería	*I wanted*
dar	*to give*

▶ 2 ¿Puedo probármelos?

Listen to Agustín buying clothes for himself. Here, you will learn to say what colour and size clothes you want, and you will also learn the Spanish for words such as *these* and *those*.

2.1 First, match the words and the items below, then listen to the conversation several times and say which of these items Agustín is buying.

1 una chaqueta
2 un par de calcetines
3 un par de zapatos
4 un jersey/un suéter (L.Am.)
5 unos pantalones
6 una camisa

a.
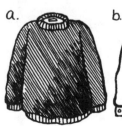

b.

c.

d.

e.

f.

2.2 What colour is each item Agustín is buying? Listen again. You will find the words for colours on page 74.

Dependienta	Buenos días. ¿Qué desea?
Agustín	Quisiera ver esos pantalones que están en el escaparate, por favor.
Dependienta	¿Éstos?
Agustín	Sí, ésos.
Dependienta	¿Qué talla tiene?
Agustín	La cuarenta y seis.
Dependienta	¿De qué color los quiere?
Agustín	Negros. ¿Son de algodón?
Dependienta	Sí, de algodón.
Agustín	¿Puedo probármelos?
Dependienta	Sí, sí, el probador está por aquí.
Agustín	Gracias.
Dependienta	¿Cómo le quedan?
Agustín	Me quedan muy bien. Me los llevo.
Dependienta	¿Desea algo más?
Agustín	Sí, quisiera ver esa camisa blanca.

2.3 Now read the dialogue and find the expressions meaning

a Can I try them on?
b How do they fit?
c They fit me very well.
d I'll take them.

2.4 Now practise what you have learned by playing the customer's role in the dialogue, replacing words for clothing and colours by other words of the same category. You may need to check the **Grammar** section for words such as 'this, that, it, them', etc.

quisiera	I would like	**quedar**	to fit
el algodón	cotton	**llevar**	to take
el probador	fitting-room	**éstos/ésos**	these/those (masc.)

How do you say it?

Saying what food you want and how much

Quiero/Quería/Deme un kilo/ un kilo y medio de ...

I want/wanted/Give me one kg/one and a half kg of ...

¿Me da medio kilo de ...?

Will you give me half a kg of ...?

Saying what clothes you want

Quisiera ver ..., de la talla ...   *I'd like to see ..., size ...*
Lo/La quiero en (blanco/negro). *I want it (masc./fem.) in*
(white/black).
¿Es/Son de algodón/lana?   *Is it/Are they cotton/wool?*

Asking whether you can try something on

¿Puedo probármelo(s)/la(s)?   *Can I try it/them on?*
(masc./fem.)

Asking and saying how clothes fit

¿Cómo te/le queda(n)?   *How does it/do they fit you?*
(informal/formal)
Me queda(n) bien.   *It fits/They fit well.*
Me queda(n) largos(s)/corto(s). *It is/They are too long/short.*

Finding out how much things cost

¿Cuánto cuestan/valen las   *How much are the lettuces/*
lechugas/esos zapatos?   *those trousers?*
¿Cuánto es?   *How much is it?*

Grammar

1 Este ..., ese ... (*this ..., that ...*)

Este, *this*, and ese, *that*, change for number (singular or plural)
and gender (masculine or feminine) depending on the noun they
refer to.

	Singular		Plural	
masc.	este traje	*this suit*	estos pantalones	*these trousers*
fem.	esta camisa	*this shirt*	estas chaquetas	*these jackets*
masc.	ese melón	*that melon*	esos limones	*those lemons*
fem.	esa fruta	*that fruit*	esas verduras	*those vegetables*

Note that these words can stand in place of a noun, in which
case they are normally written with accents.

esta corbata *this tie*	**esos pantalones** *those trousers*
ésta *this one*	**ésos** *those ones*

2 Lo, los (*it, them*)

To say 'it' or 'them' as in *What colour do you want it/them? I'll take it/them*, use **lo** when reference is to a masculine word, and **la** for feminine. In the plural use **los** and **las**.

¿De qué color quiere el vestido? *What colour do you want the dress?*
Lo quiero en negro. *I want it in black.*
¿Y la blusa? *And the blouse?*
La quiero en blanco. *I want it in white.*
Me los llevo. *I'll take them.*

These words are known as *direct object pronouns*, and they normally come before the verb. If you want more information on their use see Unit 8 and 5.2 in the **Grammar summary**.

3 Me quedan muy bien (*They fit me very well*)

Me, *me*, has various uses in Spanish, as you'll see from sentences such as these:

¿Me da una piña? *Will you give me a pineapple?*
Me queda estrecho. *It's too tight for me.*
Me lo llevo. *I'll take it (with me).*

When reference is to *you*, use **te** in informal address, and **le** in formal address.

¿Cómo te queda? *How does it fit you?*
¿Le queda un poco largo? *It is a bit long for you?*

Le also stands for *him* and *her*.

Los zapatos le quedan *The shoes are too big for*
grandes. *him/her.*

Words such as these are known as *indirect object pronouns*. If you want more information on their use see Units 8 and 12 and 5.2 in the **Grammar summary**.

4 Colours

Los colores *colours* are masculine, e.g. **el negro es elegante**, *black is elegant*.

Colours ending in -o change for feminine and plural:

	singular	*plural*
masc.	cinturón negro *black belt*	guantes negros *black gloves*
fem.	chaqueta negra *black jacket*	blusas negras *black blouses*

Colours ending in consonant or -e do not change for masculine and feminine:

> *masc./fem.* corbata (*fem.*) marrón *brown tie*
> zapatos (*masc.*) marrones *brown shoes*

Colours ending in -a are usually invariable:

> abrigo (*masc. sing.*) naranja *orange coat*
> camisas (*fem. pl.*) rosa *pink shirts*

negro	black	**blanco**	white
marrón	brown	**azul**	blue
naranja	orange	**rosa**	pink
rojo	red	**amarillo**	yellow
gris	grey	**verde**	green
violeta	violet	**malva**	mauve

▶ Pronunciation

Spanish does not make a distinction between the pronunciation of **b** and **v**. The 'b' in Colombia and the 'v' in 'Valencia' are pronounced in the same way, nearly like an English 'b', as in 'big'. More frequently, in other positions, as between vowels, e.g. Sevilla, La Habana, they sound softer.

Practise with:

¿Cuánto vale ese vestido blanco?
Quisiera probarme esa blusa verde.
¿Dónde está el probador?
Me queda muy bien. Me la llevo.

Practice

1 Una lista de compras

You and a Spanish-speaking friend are spending a few days in a small town. It is your turn to buy some food today and you need to prepare a shopping list. Complete each of the phrases which follow with the name of the appropriate product opposite.

1 un kilo de ...
2 una lata de ...
3 una barra de ...
4 medio litro de ...
5 media docena de ...
6 una botella de ...

a

b

c

d

e

f

▶ 2 Ahora tú

You are in a Spanish market doing some shopping. Follow the
guidelines below, and fill in your part of the conversation with
the stallholder.

Dependiente/a	Tú
¿Qué le pongo?	*Say you wanted one and a half kilos of tomatoes.*
¿Qué más?	*Ask how much the strawberries are.*
Dos euros el kilo.	*Ask him/her to give you one kilo.*
¿Algo más?	*Ask if he/she has green peppers.*
Sí, ¿cuántos quiere?	*Say you want four.*
¿Quiere algo más?	*Yes, you want some parsley too.*
¿Qué más?	*Nothing else, thank you.*

3 Palabra por palabra

Each row below contains a word which is unrelated to the rest. Can you spot it?

a camisa, falda, harina, vaqueros, abrigo, camiseta
b algodón, aguacate, lana, pana, lino, seda
c marrón, galleta, amarillo, rojo, verde, azul

▶ 4 Quisiera ver ...

Here is a brief exchange between a customer and a shop assistant. Write similar dialogues using the remaining words in the following list. Note that words which describe things, for example **negro** *black*, **estrecho** *tight*, must agree in gender (masc./ fem.) and number (sing./pl.) with the noun they refer to, e.g. **el** sombre**ro** blan**co**, *the white hat*, **las** camis**as** blanc**as**, *the white shirts*.

Artículo	Color	Característica
botas	negro	estrecho
zapatos	marrón	grande
camiseta	amarillo	ancho
abrigo	gris	largo

Clienta	Por favor, quisiera ver esas botas negras.
Dependiente	¿Éstas?
Clienta	Sí, ésas. ¿Puedo probármelas?
Dependiente	Sí, por supuesto. ¿Cómo le quedan?
Clienta	Me quedan estrechas.

las botas *boots*	**por supuesto** *of course*	

5 Ahora tú

You are buying some clothes. How would you express the following?

a I'd like to see (name the item).
b How much is it/are they?
c I want it/them in size ... (your size)
d I prefer it/them in ... (colour).
e Can I try it/them on?
f It/they fit me well.
g It/they are too short.
h I'll take it/them.

i This section, dealing with aspects of Hispanic culture, has been in English so far. Starting with this unit, this will be in Spanish. Try getting the gist of what the passages say with the help of the key words given to you. There are no follow-up questions, but some of the texts carry prompts in English to help you get more out of them. The text which follows tells you a little about shopping habits among Spanish and Latin American people. Where do you think they prefer to buy their food? Do you think the opening hours are the same as in your country? Read and find out.

De compras

En España y en Latinoamérica la mayoría de la gente compra los alimentos en pequeñas tiendas y mercados. Esta costumbre es mucho más evidente en pueblos y ciudades pequeñas donde no hay supermercados. Pero aún en ciudades grandes, como Barcelona o Madrid, donde hay muchos supermercados, la gente prefiere el contacto directo con el dependiente o el tendero.

Las tiendas, en España y en Latinoamérica, normalmente abren entre 9.00 y 10.00, cierran al mediodía y abren nuevamente a las 3.00 o 4.00 de la tarde. En ciudades grandes, muchas tiendas, especialmente los grandes almacenes, están abiertas todo el día.

aún	*even*	**cerrar**	*to close*
el tendero	*shopkeeper*	**abrir**	*to open*
nuevamente	*again*		

08

quisiera cambiar dinero

I'd like to change some money

In this unit you will learn
- how to change money
- how to give your address
- how to hire a car

▶ 1 En el banco

Alonso, from Mexico, who is on business in Spain, is changing some money at the bank.

1.1 First, look at the key words below, then listen to the dialogue several times and, as you do so, say whether the statements below are true or false (**verdadero o falso**).

a   Alonso quiere cambiar euros a dólares.
b   El cambio está a un euro con diez céntimos.
c   Alonso quiere cambiar doscientos cincuenta euros.

Alonso	Buenos días. Quisiera cambiar doscientos cincuenta dólares a euros. ¿A cuánto está el cambio? Tengo cheques de viaje.
Empleada	Está a un euro con diez céntimos. ¿Me da su pasaporte, por favor?
Alonso	Aquí tiene.
Empleada	Bien. Puede firmarlos. ¿Qué dirección tiene aquí en Madrid?
Alonso	Calle Salvador Nº 26, 2º, 4ª.

1.2 Now read the dialogue and find the Spanish for

a   I'd like to change ...
b   What's the rate of exchange?
c   What's your address?

---

cambiar	*to change*
el cheque de viaje	*traveller's cheque*
el cambio	*change*
firmar	*to sign*

ℹ Addresses in Spanish

Addresses in Spanish do not follow the same pattern as in English. Read this passage and find out what makes them different.

Observa esta dirección: **Salvador Nº 26, 2º, 4ª.** Salvador corresponde a la calle (*street*), 26 indica el número de la casa o edificio (*house or building number*), **2º**, segundo, corresponde al piso (*floor*) y **4ª**, cuarta, indica la puerta (*the door or flat number*). En **Avenida del Mar nº 150, quinto, B**, 'B' indica la puerta B. En **Calle Rosas nº 40, sexto, derecha**, 'derecha' indica la puerta derecha. **En Paseo de la Castellana nº 379, quinto, izquierda**, 'izquierda' indica la puerta izquierda.

En cartas, las direcciones se utilizan normalmente en forma abreviada: C/ = calle; Avda. = avenida; P° = paseo; dcha. = derecha; izq. o izda. = izquierda.

▶ 2 Queríamos alquilar un coche

Pilar and Luis, her husband, want to hire a car.

2.1 First, look at the key words, then listen to the dialogue several times and, as you do so, say whether the statements below are true or false (**verdadero o falso**).

a Pilar y Luis quieren un coche para una semana.

b Quieren un coche mediano.

c El seguro obligatorio está incluido en el precio.

d Los impuestos también están incluidos.

2.2 Listen again a few times and fill in the gap in the following table and dialogue with the car rate.

		KMS. ILIMITADOS		
Grupo	Modelo Model	1–2 Días Por día/ Per day	3–6 Días Por día/ Per day	7+ Días Por día/ Per day
A	Ford Fiesta 1.1 Renault Clio		33.80 €	32 €
C	R. 19RL/Megane 1.4 A/C – Radio	66 €	42 €	40 €
D	Ford Escort 1.6 A/C – Radio	73 €	52 €	50 €
F	Seat Toledo 1.8 A/C – Radio	86.50 €	64 €	58 €
P	Renault Espace A/C 7 Pax. – Radio	117 €	100 €	87 €

Empleado	¿Dígame?
Pilar	Queríamos alquilar un coche mediano para el fin de semana. ¿Qué nos recomienda?
Empleado	Pues, les recomiendo el Ford Fiesta.
Pilar	¿Cuánto vale el alquiler?

Empleado	Para uno o dos días vale _____ euros por día. El seguro obligatorio está incluido, pero los impuestos no.
Pilar	Vale. ¿Y podemos pagar con tarjeta de crédito?
Empleado	Sí, por supuesto.

2.3 Read the dialogue and find the Spanish for:

a What do you recommend?
b Can we pay with a credit card?

2.4 Now look at the car rental information again and vary the dialogue above, using other types of cars, rental periods and rates. The words **pequeño** *small* and **grande** *big* could be used to describe the sort of car you want.

| **mediano** | *medium size* | **los impuestos** | *taxes* |
| **el seguro** | *insurance* | | |

How do you say it?

Changing money

| Quisiera/Quiero cambiar dólares/libras a euros. | *I'd like/I want to change dollars/pounds into euros.* |
| ¿A cuánto está el cambio? | *What's the rate of exchange?* |

Asking someone's address and giving your address

¿Qué dirección tienes/ tiene Vd.?	*What's your address?*
¿Cuál es tu/su dirección?	*What's your address?*
(Vivo en la) calle/avenida … número …	*(I live at) number … (name of street) …*

Hiring a car

Queríamos/Queremos alquilar un coche.	*We wanted/want to hire a car.*
¿Cuánto cuesta/vale el alquiler?	*How much is the rental?*
¿Está incluido el seguro/ IVA (masc.)?	*Is insurance/vat included?*
¿Está incluida la gasolina (fem.)?	*Is petrol included?*

Grammar

1 ¿A cuánto está el cambio?
(*What's the rate of exchange?*)

Note the use of **estar** *to be* in this expression. **Estar** is used for expressing cost when rates or prices fluctuate, as in rates of exchange.

La libra está a un euro con   *The rate for the pound is*
cincuenta y cinco céntimos   *1.55 euros.*

2 Queríamos (*we wanted*), quisiéramos (*we'd like*)

In Unit 7 you became familiar with the use of **quería** *I wanted*, and **quisiera**, *I would like*, both from **querer** *to want*. In the first person plural, these become **queríamos** and **quisiéramos,** respectively.

Queríamos alquilar un coche. *We wanted to hire a car.*
Quisiéramos llevarlo ahora   *We'd like to take it right now.*
mismo.

3 ¿Qué nos recomienda?
(*What do you recommend?*)

In Unit 7 you learned the use of such words as **me** *(to) me*, **te** *(to) you* (fam.), and **le** *(to) him, her, you* (formal, sing.), e.g.

¿Cómo le quedan?   *How do they fit you?*
Me quedan muy bien.   *They fit me very well.*

Dialogue 3 of this unit brings in **nos** *(to) us*, and **les** *(to) you* (formal, pl.).

¿Qué coche nos recomienda? *What car do you recommend*
                               (to us)?
Les recomiendo el Ford Fiesta. *I recommend (to you) the*
                                Ford Fiesta.

To address more than one person in an informal way, use **os**.

Os recomiendo este hotel.   *I recommend this hotel (to you).*

You'll find more on the use of these words in Unit 12 and in section 5 in the **Grammar summary.**

4 **Puede firmarlos** (*You can sign them*)

Note that **los** *them*, here is attached to **firmar** *to sign*, which is an infinitive. In a sentence such as this, pronouns like 'me, te, lo, la, le', etc. can be placed either before the main verb, here **puede** *you can*, or after the infinitive. Here are some other examples.

¿Puede recomendar**me** uno? *or*
¿**Me** puede recomendar uno? *Can you recommend one (to me)?*
¿Quiere llevar**lo** ahora? *or*
¿**Lo** quiere llevar ahora? *Do you want to take it now?*

Note that if there is no infinitive, the pronoun must come before the verb.

¿**Me** da su pasaporte? *Will you give me your passport?*

Practice

▶ 1 **Quisiera cambiar ...**

You'll hear three people changing money into euros. What is the rate for each currency and how much is each person changing? Fill in the grid below with the appropriate information. Note the use of the word **céntimo** for *cent*.

Moneda	Cambio	Cantidad
libras		
francos suizos		
coronas suecas		

la moneda	*currency*	**la corona sueca**	*Swedish crown*
la cantidad	*amount*		

2 En una casa de cambio

You are at a bureau de change in Chile changing some money. Fill in the gaps in the conversation between you and the employee, using rates from the table overleaf, ignoring decimals. You are staying at *Calle Vergara 640, 6°, C.*

Tú _____ dólares americanos a pesos. ¿ _____?
Empleado/a ¿Tiene billetes?
Tú No, tengo cheques _____ .

Empleado/a	Está a _____
	¿Cuánto quiere _____?
Tú	(*Say you want to change two hundred dollars*)
Empleado/a	Muy bien.
Tú	Y el cambio de la libra, ¿_____?
Empleado/a	La libra está a _____ ¿_____ libras quiere _____?
Tú	(*Say you want to change a hundred and eighty pounds*)
Empleado/a	¿Cuál es su dirección en Santiago?
Tú	_____ .

---

los billetes	*banknotes*
la casa de cambio	*bureau de change* (L.Am.)
EE.UU. = Estados Unidos	*United States*

Monedas extranjeras

TIPO DE CAMBIO	$
corona sueca	65,20
dólar australiano	351,06
dólar canadiense	422,80
dólar EE.UU.	670,30
euro	601,82
franco suizo	407,20
libra esterlina	976,20
nuevo sol peruano	194,52
peso colombiano	0,30
peso mexicano	73,00
real brasileño	281,55

▶ 3 Ahora tú

During your stay in Santiago you exchange addresses with a Chilean.

– *Ask his/her address.*
– Vivo en la avenida Santa María 45, departamento 22. ¿Y tú?
– *Give your home address.*
– ¿Y la dirección de tu oficina?
– *Give the address of your place of work.*

▶ 4 Con cheque

Fill in the gaps in this conversation with one of the following pronouns: **lo, me, le**. Then listen to the recording.

Clienta Quería alquilar un coche pequeño. ¿Cuál _____ recomienda Vd.?

Empleado _____ recomiendo éste. Es pequeño y económico. ¿Para cuándo _____ quiere Vd.?

Clienta Quisiera llevar_____ mañana a ser posible. ¿Puedo pagar el alquiler con cheque?

Empleado Sí, puede pagar_____ con cheque, con tarjeta de crédito o en efectivo.

pequeño	*small*	**en efectivo**	*cash*
cuándo	*when*	**el alquiler**	*hire*
a ser posible	*if possible*		

5 Ahora tú

You and your travelling companions want to hire a car. What questions would you ask to get the following replies?

a El alquiler del Ford Escort cuesta setenta y tres euros por día.
b Sí, el seguro obligatorio está incluido.
c No, los impuestos no están incluidos.
d No, la gasolina tampoco.
e Por supuesto. Pueden pagar con tarjeta de crédito.
f Sí, sí, pueden llevarlo ahora mismo.

tampoco	*nor, neither*

6 Crucigrama

Horizontales

1 Puede pagar con cheque o en _____ .
2 Queremos _____ un coche.
3 (Yo) _____ llevarlo mañana.
4 ¿Puedo pagar con _____ de crédito?
5 El seguro y los impuestos no están _____ .
6 La _____ no está incluida en el precio.
7 Le _____ este coche. Es estupendo.

Verticales

1 ¿Cuánto cuesta el _____ de este coche?
2 ¿A _____ está el cambio del dólar?
3 ¿Puede _____ los cheques, por favor?
4 Quería _____ cien libras.
5 ¿Tiene cheques o _____?
6 ¿Puedo pagar con cheques de _____?
7 ¿Hay una _____ de cambio por aquí? (L.Am.)

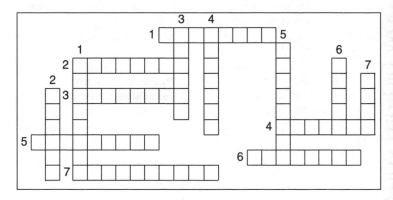

09

¿cuántos años tienes?

how old are you?

In this unit you will learn
- how to talk about yourself and your family
- how to say how old you are
- how to describe your house and your neighbourhood
- how to make comparisons

▶ 1 Tengo dos hijos

María has taken on a new job. She and her colleague Pablo talk about their families.

1.1 Listen to the conversation several times and say whether the statements which follow are true or false (**verdadero o falso**). Note that age is expressed in Spanish with **tener** *to have*.

a María tiene una hija de ocho años y un hijo de seis.
b Pablo está soltero (*single*).
c Pablo vive con su familia.
d Pablo es el menor de dos hermanos.

Pablo	Estás casada, ¿verdad?
María	Sí, tengo dos hijos.
Pablo	¿Cuántos años tienen?
María	El mayor, Gonzalo, tiene ocho años, y la menor, Laura, tiene seis. ¿Tú estás soltero?
Pablo	Sí, y vivo con mis padres y mis hermanos.
María	Eres muy joven. ¿Cuántos años tienes?
Pablo	Tengo veintidós años.
María	¿Cuántos hermanos tienes?
Pablo	Dos. Un hermano y una hermana. Yo soy el más pequeño.

1.2 Now read the dialogue and say how the following are expressed:

a You're married, aren't you?   c I'm twenty-two years old.
b Are you single?   d the eldest/the youngest

▶ 2 ¿Qué tal tu nuevo piso?

María and Pablo talk about their homes and neighbourhoods.

2.1 Listen to the conversation a few times, each time focusing attention on a different point. Two key words here are **el piso** *flat* (used in Spain), and **el barrio** *area or neighbourhood*.

a How does María describe her new flat?
b How does she describe the area where she lives?
c How does Pablo describe his own flat?

Pablo	¿Qué tal tu nuevo piso?
María	No está mal. Tiene cuatro habitaciones, un gran salón, cocina equipada, dos baños, y mucho sol.
Pablo	¿Y qué tal el barrio?
María	Es muy bueno y es más tranquilo que el centro.

Pablo Nosotros vivimos en un piso en la calle Génova. No es tan grande como tu piso, pero es muy cómodo. Tiene tres habitaciones, el salón, la cocina, el baño, y calefacción individual. Pero el barrio es bastante ruidoso.

2.2 Now read the dialogue and say which of the flats advertised below fits in:

a María's description,
b Pablo's.

el barrio	area
ruidoso	noisy
buenos acabados	high finish
la cocina equipada	fitted kitchen
reformado	converted
más tranquilo que	quieter than
tan grande como	as big as
la calefacción	heating
el aseo	toilet
jto. (junto a)	next to

**GENOVA
V. MONTSERRAT**

Luminoso, sol, 3 hab. salón, cocina equip. baño nuevo, calef. indiv. buenos acabados.
150.000 €

**GRACIA
T. VIDALET**

Todo reformado, alto, mucho sol, gran salón, 4 hab. cocina equip. y 2 baños.
210.000 €

**RONDA SAN
ANTONIO**

2 hab. salón, cocina y aseo.
75.000 €

**COLLBLANCH
JTO METRO**

Muy tranquilo, sol, 3 hab. gran salón, coc. y baño completo.
90.500 €

How do you say it?

Talking about yourself and your family

¿Estás soltero(a) o casado(a)? *Are you single or married?*
(masc./fem.)

Estoy soltero(a)/casado(a).   *I'm single/married.*
¿Cuántos hijos/hermanos   *How many children/brothers*
tienes?   *and sisters do you have?*
Tengo (dos) hijos/hermanos. *I have (two) children/brothers*
                                      and sisters.

Asking and saying how old someone is

¿Cuántos años tienes/tienen? *How old are you/they?*
Tengo/Tiene … años.   *I am/he/she is … years old.*

Describing your house and your neighbourhood

¿Qué tal el piso/la casa/   *What's the flat/house/*
el barrio?   *area like?*
Tiene tres habitaciones/   *It has three rooms/bedrooms.*
dormitorios.
Es un piso cómodo/   *It's a comfortable flat/*
un barrio bueno.   *a good area.*

Making comparisons

Es más tranquilo que el centro. *It's quieter than the centre.*
No es tan grande como tu piso. *It's not as large as your flat.*

Grammar

1 Expressing marital status

Marital status is usually expressed with **estar**. Note that **soltero** *single*, and **casado** *married*, change from **-o** to **-a** for feminine and to **-os** for plural.

Pablo está soltero.   *Pablo is single.*
María está casada.   *María is married.*
Estamos divorciados.   *We're divorced.*

In this context, Latin Americans tend to use **ser** rather than **estar**.

¿Es usted soltero(a) o casado(a)? *Are you single or married?*

2 Words for relatives

The masculine plural form of words referring to people such as **el padre** *father*, **el hijo** *son*, **el hermano** *brother*, can refer to members of both sexes.

Tengo dos hijos.	*I have two children.*
Vivo con mis padres y mis hermanos.	*I live with my parents and my brothers and sisters.*

3 Making comparisons

a More ... than

To say that something is cheaper, more expensive, etc. than something else, use the construction **más ... que**.

Este barrio es más barato que el centro.	*This area is cheaper than the centre.*
Los alquileres son más caros (que aquí).	*Rents are more expensive (than here).*

b Irregular comparisons

bueno	*good*	mejor	*better*
malo	*bad*	peor	*worse*
grande	*big*	mayor	*older*
pequeño	*small*	menor	*younger*

Más grande and **más pequeño** are normally used with reference to size, but sometimes also with reference to age.

Mi apartamento/departamento (L.Am.) es mejor	*My flat is better.*
Soy menor que Antonia.	*I'm younger than Antonia.*

c As ... as

To say that something is (not) as expensive as, (not) as comfortable as something else, etc., use the expression **tan ... como**.

Este piso no es tan caro como el otro.	*This flat is not as expensive as the other one.*
Mi habitación es tan cómoda como la de Pepe.	*My room is as comfortable as Pepe's.*

d The most ...

To say that someone is the youngest or something is the biggest, the most pleasant, etc., use the construction **el, la, los** or **las + más +** adjective.

Soy el más pequeño.   I'm the youngest.
Es la casa más grande.   It's the biggest house.
Son los barrios más   They're the most pleasant
agradables.   areas.

Más is not needed with irregular forms:

Ella es la menor de todas.   She is the youngest of all.
Este coche es el mejor.   This car is the best.

◖ Pronunciation

rr, as in 'barrio, perro', is strongly rolled.
r, after n, l, and s, for example 'Enrique, alrededor (*around*),
Israel', and at the beginning of a word, for example 'Ronda,
rosa', is also strongly rolled, and is pronounced like **rr**.
r, between vowels, as in 'caro, pero', is much softer and closer
to the English 'r' in 'very'.

Practise with:

Enrique y Rosa viven en un barrio muy caro de Tarragona.
Sara vive en Gerona.
Ramón y Carmen tienen un apartamento en las afueras de
Sanlúcar de Barrameda.

Practice

1 Yo y mi familia

In his first letter to a correspondent Ricardo wrote about
himself and his family. Can you fill in the gaps with the missing
words?

Querida Pat:

*¡Hola! Como ésta es mi primera carta, quiero contarte algo
sobre mí y mi familia. Me (a) _____ Ricardo Gutiérrez,
(b) _____ veintiún años, (c) _____ soltero, y (d) _____ con
mi madre, mis tres hermanos y mi abuela. Mis (e) _____
están divorciados. Yo soy el (f) _____ de los cuatro
hermanos. El segundo se (g) _____ Javier y (h) _____
diecinueve años, después viene Carmen, (i) _____ tiene
dieciséis, y la (j) _____ es mi hermana Isabel, que va a
cumplir catorce.*

contar	to tell	después	then
sobre	about	venir	to come
la abuela	grandmother	va a cumplir	she's going to be

2 Ricardo y su familia

How would you tell someone else about Ricardo? Begin like this: *Se llama Ricardo Gutiérrez …*

3 Me llamo Luisa …

Look at this family tree. How would Luisa write about herself and her family?

▶ 4 Una entrevista personal

In the course of a formal interview, señor Bravo had to provide some personal information. Listen and fill in the form below with his details. The interviewer uses the word **esposa** for *wife*.

Nombre:	
Edad:	
Estado civil:	
Nombre de su mujer:	
Edad de su mujer:	
N° de hijos:	

la edad	age	la mujer	wife
el estado civil	marital status	la esposa	wife

5 Ahora tú

¿Cómo te llamas? ¿Cuántos años tienes? ¿Estás casado(a) o soltero(a)? ¿Cómo se llama tu marido/mujer? ¿Cuántos años tiene? ¿Tienes hijos/hermanos? ¿Cómo se llaman? ¿Cuántos años tienen?

6 Un nuevo piso

Elena has moved into a new flat and, in a letter, she describes it to her friend Roberto. Read this extract from her letter and then answer the questions which follow.

Querido Roberto:

¡No te imaginas lo contenta que estoy! Tengo un nuevo piso. Es estupendo, mucho mejor que el anterior y más barato. Tiene dos dormitorios y un salón bastante grande, con mucha luz. Es exterior y da a una pequeña plaza. El barrio es muy tranquilo y la calle donde vivo no tiene mucho tráfico. Además, tiene calefacción y aparcamiento, pero no tiene terraza. ¡Una lástima! Pero está muy cerca del metro. Tienes que venir. Es muy fácil llegar aquí ...

a ¿Cuántos dormitorios tiene el piso de Elena?
b ¿Qué tal es?
c ¿Cómo es el barrio?
d ¿Qué servicios tiene?

el dormitorio	bedroom	exterior	facing the street
el salón	sitting-room	da a	it faces

7 Alquileres

You've been posted to a Spanish-speaking country and are looking for accommodation. Which of the following features would you find in each flat in the advertisements below? Look up the words you don't know and tick the appropriate boxes.

<table>
<tr><td>a</td><td>PS. CARLOS I. Amueblado, 130 m², cocina office, 4 hab., baño, aseo, parket, parking, gas natural, calefac., piscina com. 1800 € Ref. 3320. Tel 451 14 72.</td></tr>
<tr><td>b</td><td>Pº VALLDAURA. Amueblado, 75 m², 2 hab., baño, teléf., gas natural, exterior. 600 €. Ref. 3343. Tel. 451 14 72.</td></tr>
<tr><td>c</td><td>PL LESSEPS. Sin muebles, 85 m², 3 hab., baño, aseo, coc. office, parket, teléf., parking opc., gas natural, calefac. 1080 €. Ref. 3427. Tel. 451 14 72.</td></tr>
</table>

		a	b	c
1	Furnished	☐	☐	☐
2	Unfurnished	☐	☐	☐
3	Facing street	☐	☐	☐
4	Kitchen with pantry	☐	☐	☐
5	Extra toilet	☐	☐	☐
6	Car park	☐	☐	☐
7	Heating	☐	☐	☐
8	Telephone	☐	☐	☐
9	Swimming pool	☐	☐	☐

d ¿Cuál piso es más grande y cuántas habitaciones tiene?

com. (común) *communal*	**los muebles** *furniture*

8 ¿Cuál es el mejor?

You've made notes about two other flats you've seen, rating them from 0 to 5, with 5 being the most convenient. Write sentences comparing the two flats, using the words in brackets. The first one has been done for you.

	calle Lorca	avenida Salvador
precio	1	3
tamaño	5	3
situación	2	5
comodidad	4	4
seguridad	2	0
tranquilidad	3	3

a (barato) El piso de la avenida Salvador es *más barato que* el de la calle Lorca.

b (grande)

c (céntrico)

d (cómodo)

e (seguro)

f (tranquilo)

9 Ahora tú

Can you describe the place where you live and your neighbourhood? Use the letter in Activity 6 as a model.

i The following extract provides an interesting insight into recent trends in relation with marriage, number of children per family and life expectancy in Spanish society. Consider the following questions with regard to your own country, then read the text and compare the situation with that of Spain.

a Do people tend to marry young in your country? Around what age?
b What would you say the average number of children per family is nowadays?
c People live much longer now. What would you say the average life expectancy is for men and women in your country?

Los españoles no se casan tan jóvenes. Los hombres suelen casarse entre los 25 y los 29 años; las mujeres se casan alrededor de los 25 y suelen tener el primer hijo a los 28 años.

España tiene la tasa de natalidad más baja del mundo, con 1,23 hijos por mujer. Como consecuencia de la caída de la natalidad y del incremento de la esperanza de vida, la población española envejece. El 11 por ciento de los españoles tiene más de 65 años y una esperanza de vida de 75 años los hombres y 81 las mujeres.

soler (o > ue)	*to be accustomed to, usually (do, etc.)*
la esperanza de vida	*life expectancy*
la caída	*fall, drop*
la tasa de natalidad	*birth rate*

10

¿a qué te dedicas?

what do you do?

In this unit you will learn
- how to say what your occupation is
- how to say how long you have been doing something (1)
- how to say what hours and days you work and what holidays you have

▶ 1 ¿Qué haces?

At a party Patricia meets Ramón and they talk about each other's occupations.

1.1 Listen to the conversation several times and, as you do so, say whether the following statements are true or false (**verdadero o falso**). The key words below will help you to understand.

a Ramón es estudiante.
b Estudia arquitectura en un colegio de Madrid.
c Patricia es bibliotecaria.
d Trabaja en la biblioteca de la Universidad de Granada.

Patricia ¿Qué haces? ¿Trabajas o estudias?
Ramón Soy estudiante. Estudio arquitectura en la universidad de Granada. Y tú, ¿a qué te dedicas?
Patricia Soy bibliotecaria. Trabajo en la biblioteca de un colegio de Madrid.
Ramón ¿Cuánto tiempo hace que trabajas allí?
Patricia Desde hace un año solamente.

1.2 How does Ramón ask Patricia how long she has been working there? Read the dialogue and find out. How does she reply?

| **trabajar** *to work* | **el/la bibliotecario/a** *librarian* |
| **estudiar** *to study* | |

▶ 2 Trabajo de 8.00 a 3.00

Ramón asks Patricia about her working hours.

2.1 Listen to the dialogue a few times and, as you do so, fill in the gaps in the sentences which follow. Look at the key words below if you have difficulty in understanding.

a Patricia trabaja _____ horas al día.
b Trabaja de _____ de la _____ a _____ de la _____.
c Trabaja de lunes a _____.
d Tiene _____ semanas de vacaciones al _____.

Ramón	¿Cuántas horas trabajas al día?
Patricia	Siete horas.
Ramón	¿Qué horario tienes?
Patricia	De ocho de la mañana a tres de la tarde, de lunes a viernes. Los sábados no trabajo.
Ramón	¿Y cuántas semanas de vacaciones tienes al año?
Patricia	Tengo tres semanas solamente.

2.2 Now read the dialogue several times until you feel confident with it, then listen again and try playing Patricia's part in the conversation.

al día	*per day*	**al año**	*per year*
el horario	*working hours*		

How do you say it?

Asking people what they do for a living and saying what you do

¿Qué haces?	*What do you do?*
¿A qué te dedicas/se dedica Vd.?	*What do you do for a living?*
Soy …	*I'm (occupation).*
Estudio …/Trabajo en …	*I'm studying/work in (place).*

Asking people how long they have been doing something, and giving similar information about yourself

¿Cuánto tiempo hace que trabajas/estudias?	*How long have you been working/studying?*
(Trabajo/estudio) desde hace un año/mucho tiempo.	*(I've been working/studying) for a year/a long time.*

Saying what hours and days you work and what holidays you have

Trabajo siete horas al día/treinta y cinco horas a la semana.	*I work seven hours a day/thirty-five hours a week.*
Trabajo de 9.00/lunes a 5.00/viernes.	*I work from 9.00/Monday to 5.00/Friday.*
Tengo … días/semanas de vacaciones al año.	*I have … days/weeks holiday a year.*

Grammar

1 Omission of 'a', with professions

To say what your job is you need the verb **ser** *to be*, followed directly by the occupation or profession. The Spanish for 'a', as in 'a plumber', is not used in this context.

Soy fontanero/plomero (L.Am.).	*I'm a plumber.*
Soy pintor/a.	*I'm a painter.*
Soy fotógrafo/a.	*I'm a photographer.*

2 Asking people how long they have been doing something

To ask people how long they have been doing something, use either of the expressions below:

- **¿Cuánto tiempo hace que?** + present tense verb

  ¿Cuánto tiempo hace que estás aquí? — *How long have you been here?*

- **¿Desde cuándo?** + present tense verb

  ¿Desde cuándo vive Vd. en España? — *Since when have you been living in Spain?*

3 Saying how long you have been doing something

To say how long you have been doing something, choose from the following expressions:

- Present tense verb + **desde hace** + time phrase

  Estoy aquí desde hace bastante tiempo. — *I've been here for quite a long time.*

- **Hace** + time phrase + **que** + present tense verb

  Hace varios años que vivo en España. — *I've been living in Spain for several years.*

- Short replies

desde hace mucho tiempo	*for a long time*
desde 1980	*since 1980*
desde la edad de 25 años	*since I was 25*

4 More prepositions

Note the use of these prepositions, and their English translation in:

siete horas **al** día/**a** la semana	*seven hours per day/week*
de 10.00/lunes **a** 1.00/sábado	*from 10.00/Monday to 1.00/Saturday*
desde las 11.00 **de** la mañana **hasta** las 4.00 **de** la tarde.	*from 11.00 in the morning till 4.00 in the afternoon.*
desde hace mucho tiempo	*for a long time*
en la biblioteca **de** un colegio **de** Madrid	*at the library of a school in Madrid*

▶ Pronunciation

h, as in 'hace', is silent.
ch, as in 'ocho', is pronounced like the 'ch' in 'chair'.

Practise with:

Hace ocho años que Charo trabaja en Chile. Hernán trabaja desde las ocho de la mañana hasta las nueve de la noche.

Practice

1 Palabra por palabra

Can you match each occupation with the most likely activity?

a	Soy enfermero/a.	1	Enseño en un colegio.
b	Soy azafata.	2	Tengo una industria.
c	Soy conductor/a.	3	Escribo artículos para una revista.
d	Soy profesor/a.	4	Trabajo en un hospital.
e	Soy dependiente/a.	5	Hago muebles.
f	Soy cartero/a.	6	Conduzco camiones.
g	Soy periodista	7	Reparto cartas.
h	Soy abogado/a.	8	Vendo ropa en una tienda.
i	Soy carpintero/a.	9	Trabajo en una línea aérea.
j	Soy empresario/a.	10	Trabajo en los tribunales.

2 ¿A qué se dedica?

What would the following people say with regard to their work? Match the drawing with the sentences below.

1 Soy muy rico y no necesito trabajar.
2 Estoy jubilada (*retired*).
3 Soy ama de casa.
4 Estoy sin trabajo.

▶ 3 ¿Qué hace Ema?

Now listen to Ema, from Chile, talking about her occupation and fill in the table below with the information she gives. Note that she says **en la mañana/tarde** instead of **por la mañana/tarde**, *in the morning/afternoon*. The first usage is Latin American.

Profesión		
Trabaja en		
Desde hace		
Horario	**Mañana**	**Tarde**
Vacaciones	Semana Santa Invierno Verano	

la Semana Santa	*Easter*	**el verano**	*summer*
el invierno	*winter*	**alrededor**	*around*

4 Busco trabajo

Look at these advertisements placed by people offering their services. Who wants to do the following work? Give their names or telephone number.

- Profesora de EGB, con título de inglés a nivel Proficiency, da clases particulares y traduce artículos. Eugenia. (91) 543 03 92. Madrid

- Busco trabajo cuidando niños por las mañanas. Llamar a partir de las 21 horas. M.ª Ángeles. (91) 945 33 52. Madrid

- Tengo 20 años y busco trabajo sólo por las mañanas o por las tardes como recepcionista, mecanógrafa o puesto similar. Mónica. (93) 209 36 48. Barcelona.

- Licenciada en psicología, en la especialidad industrial, trabajaría preferentemente en una empresa. En cualquier lugar de España. Victoria. (986) 85 67 33. Pontevedra.

- Tengo 17 años y estudio COU nocturno. Me gustaría encontrar trabajo por las mañanas, tengo experiencia como dependienta. Mónica. (93) 787 61 70. Badalona, Barcelona.

- Auxiliar administrativa se ofrece para trabajar en oficina o como recepcionista. (94) 637 96 35. Vizcaya.

| **EGB (Educación General Básica)** | *primary education* |
| **COU (Curso de Orientación Universitaria)** | *pre-university course* |

a   receptionist or typist
b   company psychologist
c   childminder

d   office clerk or receptionist
e   teacher and translator
f   shop assistant

5 Ahora tú

Can you write an advertisement offering your services or expertise? Use as a model one of the advertisements in Activity 4. Note the key phrases:

Busco trabajo como…	*I'm looking for work as…*
(tu profesión)	*(your profession)*
se ofrece para trabajar en …	*seeks employment in …*
/ como …	*as …*

6 ¿Cuánto tiempo hace?

Your friend Paul has just introduced you to Carmen, who is studying English in your country and is living in your area. How would you ask her how long she has been doing each of the following, and how would she reply? Use the phrases below.

actividad	*período de tiempo*
a estar aquí	dos meses y medio
b estudiar inglés	dos meses
c vivir en este barrio	tres semanas
d conocer a Paul	un año y medio

▶ **7 Ahora tú**

a ¿Cómo te llamas? ¿A qué te dedicas? ¿Dónde trabajas? ¿Cuánto tiempo hace que trabajas allí? ¿Cuántas horas al día trabajas? ¿Qué horario tienes? ¿Trabajas los fines de semana? ¿Cuántas vacaciones tienes al año?

b ¿Cuánto tiempo hace que estudias español? ¿Estudias por tu cuenta o estudias en un colegio o universidad? ¿Qué horario de clases tienes? ¿Qué días tienes clases?

i In what sector of the economy do you think most Spanish people work? What percentage of women do you think are employed as opposed to men? Do you think many of them reach senior positions in public administration or get to be company directors or managers? Read the following text and find out and, as you do so, check the information in the tables on the next page.

Del total de españoles con trabajo, la mayor parte trabaja en el sector servicios. El segundo lugar lo ocupa el sector industrial. El tercero lo ocupa el sector agrícola, seguido muy de cerca por la construcción. Las mujeres trabajan preferentemente en el sector servicios y en menor número en la agricultura y la industria. En la construcción, la mayoría de los trabajadores son hombres. Del total de españoles con trabajo, el 66 por ciento son hombres y sólo el 34 por ciento mujeres. En España, como en otros países, el desempleo afecta principalmente a las mujeres y a los jóvenes que buscan por primera vez un puesto de trabajo. El número de mujeres que ocupa puestos directivos en la administración pública y en las empresas, es muy inferior al de los hombres.

los hombres	*men*
seguido por	*followed by*
la población activa	*working population*
las mujeres	*women*
el desempleo	*unemployment*
el puesto directivo	*executive job*

PERSONAL DIRECTIVO DE ÓRGANOS DE LA ADMINISTRACIÓN PÚBLICA, DIRECTORES/AS y GERENTES DE EMPRESAS

	Número	%
MUJERES	28.900	12,7
HOMBRES	199.200	87,3
TOTAL	228.100	100

POBLACIÓN ACTIVA

	Total población activa ocupada por sector	% Hombres	% Mujeres
Sector agrícola	1.181.700	73,2	26,8
Sector industrial	2.485.000	78,4	21,6
Sector construcción	1.040.500	96,4	3,6
Sector servicios	7.016.300	56	44
Total población activa ocupada	11.723.500	66	34

11

empiezo a las nueve
I start at nine

In this unit you will learn
- how to talk about your daily routine
- how to say what you do in your spare time
- how to say how often you do certain things

Mónica, who works in an office, tells Joaquín about her daily routine.

1.1 Listen to the conversation several times and, as you do, try completing the information in the box. You may need to look up the key words overleaf before you listen to the dialogue.

Joaquín	¿A qué hora te levantas?
Mónica	Normalmente me levanto a las siete menos cuarto.
Joaquín	¡Muy temprano! ¿A qué hora empiezas a trabajar?
Mónica	Empiezo a las nueve, y siempre tardo casi una hora en llegar a la oficina. A esa hora el tráfico es fatal.
Joaquín	¿Cómo vas al trabajo? ¿En coche?
Mónica	No, ¡qué va! Voy en autobús.
Joaquín	¿Y dónde comes?
Mónica	Pues, hay un restaurante enfrente de la oficina que no está nada mal. Normalmente como allí.
Joaquín	¿A qué hora sales?
Mónica	Salgo de la oficina a las siete y suelo volver a casa sobre las ocho.

Mónica . . .

a se levanta a las _____
b empieza a trabajar a las _____
c va al trabajo en _____
d tarda _____
e come en _____
f sale de la oficina a las _____
g suele volver a casa sobre las _____

Joaquín se levanta a las 7:00

1.2 Now read the dialogue and find in it the missing forms of the verbs below.

levantarse *to get up*	(yo) _____	(tú) te levantas
empezar *to begin*	(yo) empiezo	(tú) _____
tardar *to take time*	(yo) _____	(tú) tardas
ir *to go*	(yo) _____	(tú) vas
comer *to eat*	(yo) como	(tú) _____
salir *to leave, finish*	(yo) _____	(tú) sales

1.3 Now play Mónica's part in the conversation, first as it stands, then trying to adapt the answers to your own situation.

levantarse	*to get up*
empezar (e > ie)	*to begin*
va	*she goes*
¡qué va!	*certainly not*
tardar	*to take (time)*
suele (from **soler**) **volver**	*she usually comes back*

▶ 2 ¿Te acuestas muy tarde?

Mónica tells Joaquín about what she does in her spare time.

2.1 Listen to the dialogue several times and find out what Mónica does in the evenings and at the weekends. Tick the right activities in the boxes below as they come up.

Por la noche, Mónica . . .

a lee novelas ☐
b lee el periódico ☐
c visita a sus amigos ☐
d ve televisión ☐
e friega los platos ☐
f prepara la cena ☐
g escucha música ☐

Los fines de semana, ella . . .

h sale con amigos ☐
i hace la compra ☐
j va al cine ☐
k toma unas copas con amigos ☐
l va a bailar ☐
m limpia la casa ☐
n lava la ropa ☐

Joaquín ¿Qué haces por la noche?
Mónica Pues, en casa cenamos sobre las nueve y después de cenar a veces veo la televisión o leo el periódico y escucho música.
Joaquín ¿Te acuestas muy tarde?
Mónica Nunca me acuesto antes de las once y media o doce.
Joaquín Y los fines de semana, ¿qué haces normalmente?
Mónica Pues, hago la compra, lavo la ropa, a veces salgo con amigos, vamos a tomar unas copas o vamos a bailar a alguna discoteca.

2.2 Now read the dialogue and find the Spanish equivalent of

a about nine
b after having dinner
c I sometimes watch television
d I never go to bed before 11.30

ver	*to watch, to see*	**la compra**	*shopping*
leer	*to read*	**lavar**	*to wash*
escuchar	*to listen to*	**una copa**	*a drink*

How do you say it?

Talking about daily activities

¿A qué hora te levantas/ empiezas a trabajar/sales?	*What time do you get up/start work/finish?*
Me levanto/empiezo/ salgo a las siete.	*I get up/start/finish at seven.*
¿Cómo vas al trabajo/ a clases?	*How do you go to work/ school?*
Voy al trabajo/a clases en coche/autobús/metro.	*I go to work/school by car/ bus/on the metro.*
¿Dónde comes/sueles comer?	*Where do you eat/usually eat?*
Como/suelo comer en un restaurante.	*I eat/usually eat lunch in a restaurant.*

Talking about spare time activities

¿Qué haces por la noche/los fines de semana?	*What do you do in the evenings/the weekends?*
Hago la compra, lavo la ropa, salgo con amigos …	*I do the shopping, I do the washing, I go out with friends*

Saying how often you do certain things

Normalmente veo la televisión/escucho música.	*I normally watch television/ listen to music.*
A veces salgo con amigos/ vamos a tomar unas copas.	*Sometimes I go out with friends/ we go and have a few drinks.*
Siempre/Nunca me acuesto antes de las 11.30.	*I always/never go to bed before 11.30.*

Grammar

1 Talking about daily activities

a The present tense

To talk about things you do regularly you use the present tense, which you already know from previous units. Here you will have a chance to review all its forms and to practise them in the context of daily routines. Below is the present tense of three regular verbs: lav**ar**, *to wash*, com**er** *to eat, to have lunch*, viv**ir** *to live*.

Lavo la ropa	*I wash my clothes.*
Como en un bar.	*I eat in a bar.*
Vivo lejos de la oficina.	*I live far from the office.*

-ar verbs	-er verbs	-ir verbs
lavo	como	vivo
lavas	comes	vives
lava	come	vive
lavamos	comemos	vivimos
laváis	coméis	vivís
lavan	comen	viven

b Soler + infinitive

You can also talk about habitual actions by using **soler** (o > ue), '*to usually do something*', followed by an infinitive.

¿Qué **sueles hacer** por la noche?

What do you usually do in the evening?

Suelo estudiar.

I usually study.

2 Radical-changing verbs

The dialogues and previous sections in this unit contain some radical-changing verbs, that is, verbs that undergo a vowel change in the stem in all forms of the present tense, *except* the first person plural, **nosotros/as**, and the second person plural, **vosotros/as** (see Unit 3). Their endings are the same as for regular verbs.

- e changes into **ie**
  empezar *to begin*:   empiezo, empiezas ...
  fregar *to wash up*:   friego, friegas ...

- o changes into **ue**
  acostarse *to go to bed*:   me acuesto, te acuestas ...
  almorzar *to have lunch*:   almuerzo, almuerzas ...
  volver *to come back*:   vuelvo, vuelves ...
  soler *to usually do something*: suelo, sueles ...

Empiezo a trabajar a las nueve. *I start work at nine.*
Vuelvo a casa sobre las seis.   *I return home about six.*

Nunca me acuesto tarde.   *I never go to bed late.*

3 Irregular verbs

a The *first person singular* of the present tense of **salir** *to leave*, **ver** *to see, to watch*, and **hacer** *to do, to make*, is irregular. The rest of the forms are regular.

Salgo del trabajo a las seis.	*I leave/finish work at six.*
Por la noche **veo** la televisión.	*In the evening I watch television.*
Los fines de semana **hago** la compra.	*At weekends I do the shopping.*

b **Ir** *to go* is completely irregular.

Singular		Plural	
voy	*I go*	vamos	*we go*
vas	*you go* (inf.)	vais	*you go* (inf.)
va	*you go* (formal)	van	*you go* (formal)
	he, she, it goes		*they go*

4 Reflexive verbs

Levantarse *to get up*, like a number of other verbs, carries the particle **se**, literally *oneself*, attached to it. Forms like 'I get up, you get up', carry the Spanish equivalent of words like 'myself, yourself', etc.

Usage does not always correspond to that of English. There are many verbs which function as reflexives in Spanish, but which are used without a reflexive pronoun in English; others use the reflexive pronoun in both English and Spanish:

acostarse	*to go to bed*
llamarse	*to be called*
quedarse	*to stay*
divertirse	*to enjoy oneself*
dedicarse	*to devote oneself to*

The endings of such verbs are the same as for regular verbs and only the addition of **me** *myself*, **te** *yourself*, etc., makes them different. Below are the present tense forms of **levantarse**:

(yo)	me levanto	*I get up*
(tú)	te levantas	*you get up* (inf.)
(Vd./él/ella)	se levanta	*you get up, he/she gets up*
(nosotros/as)	nos levantamos	*we get up*
(vosotros/as)	os levantáis	*you get up* (inf.)
(Vds./ellos/as)	se levantan	*you/they get up*

¿A qué hora te levantas?	*What time do you get up?*
Me levanto a las seis y media.	*I get up at half past six.*

▶ Pronunciation

y, as in 'yo', is pronounced like the 'y' in 'yes', but in some regions it is stronger and nearly like the 's' in 'pleasure'. In many areas too, 'y' is pronounced like the 'll' in 'calle'. 'Y', *and*, is pronounced like 'e' in 'be'.

Practice with:

yo, yoga, yogur, desayuno, mayo
Yo desayuno en un bar de la calle dos de Mayo.
Yolanda hace yoga.

Practice

1 Palabra por palabra

Below are some key verbs related to daily activities. Look them up and classify them into the following categories:

a personal hygiene **b** personal appearance **c** getting dressed

1 ponerse la ropa	**4** peinarse	**7** afeitarse
2 bañarse	**5** vestirse	**8** lavarse
3 maquillarse	**6** ducharse	**9** lavarse los dientes

Note that **vestirse** is a radical-changing verb, with **e** changing into **i**, e.g. me visto. **Ponerse** is irregular in the first person singular of the present tense, me **pongo**.

2 La rutina de Ramiro

Ramiro is a very methodical man. Every morning he follows exactly the same routine. How would Ramiro tell someone what he does? Use the pictures to write a description. One of them has been done for you.

Me levanto a las seis.

▶ **3 Mi rutina diaria**

Listen to Ema, from Chile, talking about her daily routine.

3.1 Can you match her activities with the times?

	Actividad		*Hora*
a	Se levanta	1	a las 6.00
b	Llega al trabajo	2	a las 7.00
c	Almuerza	3	a las 9.00
d	Regresa	4	a la 1.00

3.2 Look at the first column again. Can you find the equivalent of **vuelve** and **come**?

> **tomar desayuno (desayunar)**   *to have breakfast* (L.Am.)

4 ¿A qué hora…?

You have been asked to interview Delia, a school teacher, and ask her about her daily activities. Here are her answers. What were your questions? Choose an appropriate question word from the following: **¿dónde? ¿qué? ¿a qué hora? ¿cuánto tiempo? ¿cómo?** and use the informal form.

a   Me levanto a las siete y media.
b   Voy al colegio en coche.
c   Tardo media hora en llegar.
d   Empiezo las clases a las 9.30.
e   Almuerzo en la cafetería del colegio.
f   Salgo a las 3.00.
g   Vuelvo a casa sobre las 3.30.
h   Por la noche ceno algo ligero, y ayudo a mis hijos con sus deberes.
i   Los fines de semana me dedico a mi familia.

> **ayudar**   *to help*   **los deberes**   *homework*

5 Ahora tú

You have been asked to describe your own daily activities. Give as much information as possible, using as a model the activities above, and the introductory dialogues.

6 Un día en la vida de Plácido Domingo

Plácido Domingo, the famous Spanish tenor, talked to a journalist about some of his habits. As you read the interview try answering the following questions. The key words below will help you to understand.

a What does the tenor normally do before a performance?
b What does he eat when he has a performance?
c How many hours does he sleep at night?
d Where does he normally spend his summer holidays?

¿Cómo es un día de Plácido Domingo antes de una función?
Completamente tranquilo, trato de no aceptar ningún compromiso, no hacer absolutamente nada. Me quedo en casa, repaso, estudio, leo, y trato de estar en silencio.
¿Algún régimen especial?
Como una comida muy ligera, puede ser un poquito de pollo a la parrilla, o un poco de ternera y algo de sopa.
¿Cuántas horas duerme en la noche?
En días normales ocho horas. El día de la función trato de dormir hasta once.
¿Dónde veranea Plácido Domingo?
Depende, en la playa la mayoría de las veces.

la función	performance	**quedarse**	to stay
tratar de	to try to	**repasar**	to rehearse
el compromiso	engagement	**a la parrilla**	grilled

i The following article looks at reading habits among Spanish people. Think of reading habits in your own country before you read the text.

What percentage of Spaniards never read? What are the most popular newspapers and magazines? Do reading habits differ between men and women? Read and find out.

Los españoles leen poco

En España, con alrededor de cuarenta millones de habitantes, casi la mitad de los españoles mayores de 18 años no lee nunca, y el 63 por ciento no compra libros. Lo que más se lee son los periódicos deportivos y las revistas del corazón, la más popular de ellas ¡Hola!. De los periódicos serios, el más vendido es *El País*, con 400.000 ejemplares al día.

los españoles leen poco

Sólo doce millones de españoles leen periódicos, dieciocho millones leen revistas, treinta millones de personas ven televisión y sólo dos millones van al cine.

El hombre lee el doble de periódicos que la mujer; la mujer lee más revistas semanales. El hombre prefiere escuchar radio, pero hombres y mujeres ven por igual la televisión.

la mitad	*half*
la revista del corazón	*true romance magazine*
el ejemplar	*copy*
por igual	*equally*

12

I like it

me gusta

In this unit you will learn
- how to ask people what they like and say what you like or dislike
- how to talk about your interests and preferences
- how to say what you like or dislike about your job

▶ 1 ¿Te gusta?

Margarita and Victoria, from Spain, and Jorge, from Mexico, talk about what they like to do in their spare time.

1.1 Listen to the dialogue several times, each time focusing attention on a different point. Key words here are **gustar** *to like*, **encantar** and **fascinar**, *to like a lot*, **interesar** *to interest*, and **preferir** *to prefer*.

a   What does Margarita like to do in her spare time?
b   What television programmes does Victoria like?
c   What television programmes does Margarita prefer?
d   What does Margarita's husband like to watch on television?

Victoria	¿Qué te gusta hacer en tu tiempo libre, Margarita?
Margarita	Me gusta tocar la guitarra y cantar. Me encanta la literatura, y me gusta mucho el cine.
Jorge	A mí también me gusta el cine. Las películas españolas me gustan mucho. ¿Te gusta el cine, Victoria?
Victoria	A mí, la verdad, el cine no me interesa mucho. Prefiero ver la televisión. Me fascinan las telenovelas.
Jorge	A mí no me gustan nada.
Margarita	A mí tampoco. Las detesto. Prefiero los documentales y los programas deportivos. A mi marido le encanta el fútbol. Y a ti Jorge, ¿te gusta el fútbol?
Jorge	Sí, pero prefiero el tenis.

1.2 Now read the dialogue and, as you do so, fill in the gaps in these sentences with the missing words.

a   A Margarita le gusta _____ Le encanta _____ y le gusta mucho _____

b   A Victoria no le interesa mucho _____ Prefiere _____ Le fascinan ___

c   A Jorge le gusta _____ Las _____ le gustan mucho. Las _____ no le gustan nada.

d   Al marido de Margarita le encanta _____

la película	*film*
la telenovela	*soap opera*
el documental	*documentary*
el programa deportivo	*sports programme*

▶ 2 ¿Qué tal tu trabajo?

Jorge and Margarita talk about the things they like about their jobs and what they like to do on their holidays.

2.1 First, look at some of the things people like to do on their holidays. Can you match the pictures to the sentences below?

Me gusta ...

1 ir de camping/acampar (L.Am.)   **4** dormir hasta muy tarde
2 viajar al extranjero   **5** nadar
3 montar en bicicleta   **6** tomar el sol

2.2 Now listen to the dialogue several times, each time focusing attention on specific information:

a Why does Margarita like her job?
b Which of the activities above does Margarita like to do on her holidays?
c Which does Jorge like to do?

Jorge	¿Qué tal tu trabajo, Margarita? ¿Te gusta?
Margarita	Estupendo, me gusta mucho. El sueldo no está mal, tengo un horario muy bueno, y el ambiente es excelente. Me encanta. Pero el

sitio en que está no me gusta nada. Es horrible.

Jorge ¿Y qué te gusta hacer en las vacaciones?

Margarita Me gusta ir a la playa, nadar, tomar el sol y dormir hasta muy tarde.

Jorge A mí me gusta ir de camping, montar en bicicleta, viajar al extranjero. Me encanta Nueva York.

2.3 Now read the dialogue and find the Spanish for

a How do you like your job?　　　**b** It's not bad

---

el sueldo *salary*　　　　　**el ambiente** *atmosphere*

　　el sitio *place*

How do you say it?

Asking people what they like and saying what you like or dislike

¿Qué te gusta? *What do you like?*

Me gusta/encanta/fascina *I like/love cinema/*
　el cine/ver televisión. 　*watching television.*

Me gustan (mucho) las *I like films/documentaries*
　películas/los documentales. *(very much).*

¿Te gustan las telenovelas? *Do you like soap operas?*

No me gustan (nada). *I don't like them (at all).*
　Las detesto. 　*I detest them.*

Talking about your interests and preferences

La televisión (no) me interesa *I'm (not) very interested*
　mucho. 　*in television.*

Prefiero los programas *I prefer sports programmes/*
　deportivos/ver vídeos. *to watch videos.*

Saying what you like or dislike about your job

No/me gusta (mucho) *I like/don't like my job*
　mi trabajo. 　*(very much).*

Me gusta el ambiente/mi jefe/a. *I like the atmosphere/my boss.*

El horario no me gusta *I don't like the working hours*
　(nada). 　*(at all).*

Grammar

1 Me gusta, te gusta ... (*I like it, you like it ...*)

To say that one likes or dislikes something, Spanish uses the verb **gustar**, meaning *to please*. This must be preceded by a word such as **me** *me*, **te** *you* (informal), **le** *you* (formal)/*him/her*, words that you learned to use in contexts such as **me quedan bien** (Unit 7), **le recomiendo este coche** (Unit 8).

You only need the third person singular, **gusta**, or the plural, **gustan**. The first is used with an infinitive, e.g. **escuchar** *to listen*, to say what you like doing, and with singular nouns, e.g. **el cine** *cinema*. The second is used with plural nouns, e.g. **las telenovelas** *soap operas*.

Me gusta tocar la guitarra.	*I like playing the guitar.* *(Playing the guitar pleases me.)*
¿Te gusta el cine?	*Do you like cinema?* *(Does cinema please you?)*
Le gustan las telenovelas.	*He/she likes soap operas.* *(Soap operas please him/her.)*

To say you don't like something, simply place the word **no** before the construction with **gustar**.

No me gusta.	*I don't like it.*
No me gustan (nada).	*I don't like them (at all).*

Among other verbs which follow this pattern we find **encantar** and **fascinar** *to like a lot*, **interesar** *to interest*, **parecer** *to seem*. Practise forming questions and statements with these verbs, using the following construction.

me gusta/n	*I like it/them*
te gusta/n	*you like it/them (informal)*
le gusta/n	*you like it/them (formal)*
	he/she likes it/them
nos gusta/n	*we like it/them*
os gusta/n	*you like it/them (informal)*
les gusta/n	*you like it them (formal)*
	they like it/them

2 A él/ella le gusta (*he/she likes it*)

Note the ambiguity of phrases such as the following:

Le gusta.	*You like it* (formal, sing.), *he/she likes it.*
Les gusta.	*You like it* (formal, pl.), *they like it.*

The context may make it clear who you are referring to, but if it doesn't, you can be more specific by using the following construction with the preposition 'a', with exactly the same meaning as above:

Singular			Plural		
A	usted él ella	le gusta/n.	A	ustedes ellos ellas	les gusta/n.

Note that you still need **le** and **les**.

You also need the preposition 'a' when you use a person's name:

A Antonio le gusta el ajedrez. *Antonio likes chess.*
A Carmen y Sandra les gusta *Carmen and Sandra like*
   jugar a las cartas   *playing cards.*

3 A mí me gusta (*I like it*), a ti te gusta (*you like it*)

You can also use the construction in 2 above for emphasis, or to express contrast between your likes and interests and someone else's. For **yo** *I* and **tú** *you* (informal), you need **mí** and **ti**, respectively.

A mí me gustan los deportes. *I like sports.*
A ti no te gustan, ¿verdad?   *You don't like them, do you?*

For **nosotros/as** *we*, and **vosotros/as** *you* (informal pl.) use these same words:

A nosotros nos encanta   *We love opera.*
   la ópera.
¿**A vosotros** también   *You like it too?*
   os gusta?

4 Short questions and replies

You will need to use the construction in sections 2 and 3 above in short questions and replies, as shown in the following dialogue:

Carlos	A mí me fascina el jazz.	*I love jazz.*
Ana	A mí también. ¿Y a ti, María?	*So do I. And what about you, María?*
María	A mí no.	*I don't.*
Ignacio	A mí tampoco.	*Neither do I.*
María	A Victoria tampoco.	*Neither does Victoria.*

▶ Pronunciation

d is pronounced approximately like the English 'd' in 'day' in the following positions: after 'l', e.g. 'sueldo', after 'n', e.g. 'andar', and at the beginning of a word, when this is preceded by a pause, e.g. 'deporte'. In other positions, **d** is pronounced like the 'th' in 'that'.

Practise with:

A David le gusta hacer deportes, andar y sobre todo ver vídeos, pero detesta las tareas domésticas.

El sueldo de Delia no está mal y las condiciones de trabajo son estupendas.

Practice

1 ¿Qué te gusta hacer?

A group of people were asked what they like to do in their spare time. Study their answers, which are placed in order of preference, in the following list. Which ones do you like or dislike? Fill in each column below with your answers, as appropriate.

Me encanta	Me gusta	No me gusta (nada)	Detesto

¿Qué te gusta hacer en tu tiempo libre?

1 ver TV/cable/vídeo
2 hacer deportes
3 escuchar música
4 realizar tareas domésticas
5 salir con amigos/ir a fiestas
6 leer
7 viajar
8 andar
9 ir al cine
10 trabajar/estudiar
11 ir al teatro/conciertos
12 asistir a cursos

me encanta planchar

i What would you say is the main leisure activity in your country? What do you think Spanish and Latin American people prefer to do? Read and find out.

Los españoles y latinoamericanos son grandes adictos a la televisión. Sólo turcos, ingleses e italianos ven más televisión que los españoles. Cada español ve una media de tres horas y treinta y un minutos de televisión al día. Los programas más populares son las películas y teleseries, y en segundo lugar los deportivos.

Entre los deportes, lejos el más popular es el fútbol, aunque en los últimos años se aprecia un mayor interés por otros deportes, especialmente el tenis.

una media	*average*	**aunque**	*although*

▶ **2 ¿Qué le gusta hacer a Hortensia?**

Hortensia, from Perú, talks about the things she likes to do in her spare time.

2.1 Which of the following does she mention? Tick the right boxes.

a	ir a conciertos	☐	**e**	ver televisión	☐
b	leer	☐	**f**	viajar	☐
c	hacer deportes	☐	**g**	escuchar música	☐
d	salir de paseo	☐	**h**	trabajar en el jardín	☐

2.2 What television programmes does she like?

el jardín *garden*

3 Pasatiempos

Four people looking for correspondents wrote to a magazine and listed their hobbies. Use your dictionary or the **Vocabulary** at the back of the book to look up the words you don't know.

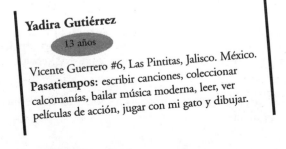

Yadira Gutiérrez

13 años

Vicente Guerrero #6, Las Pintitas, Jalisco. México.
Pasatiempos: escribir canciones, coleccionar calcomanías, bailar música moderna, leer, ver películas de acción, jugar con mi gato y dibujar.

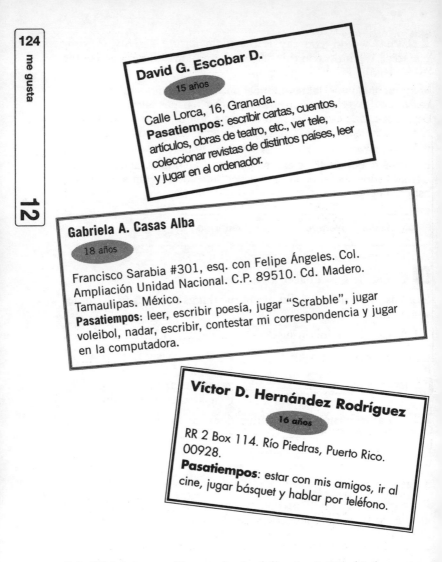

David G. Escobar D.

15 años

Calle Lorca, 16, Granada.
Pasatiempos: escribir cartas, cuentos, artículos, obras de teatro, etc., ver tele, coleccionar revistas de distintos países, leer y jugar en el ordenador.

Gabriela A. Casas Alba

18 años

Francisco Sarabia #301, esq. con Felipe Ángeles. Col. Ampliación Unidad Nacional. C.P. 89510. Cd. Madero. Tamaulipas. México.
Pasatiempos: leer, escribir poesía, jugar "Scrabble", jugar voleibol, nadar, escribir, contestar mi correspondencia y jugar en la computadora.

Víctor D. Hernández Rodríguez

16 años

RR 2 Box 114. Río Piedras, Puerto Rico. 00928.
Pasatiempos: estar con mis amigos, ir al cine, jugar básquet y hablar por teléfono.

3.1 Which person likes to do the following? Give his/her name.

a write plays
b write poetry
c play with his/her cat

d watch action movies
e write short stories
f play basketball

3.2 Use the advertisements above as a model to write one listing your own interests.

4 ¿Qué te gusta?

Consider each of the following, and say which you like, and which you don't. Use phrases like the following:

Me gustan/encantan/fascinan los concursos.
Las películas del Oeste no me gustan (nada).
Detesto las teleseries.

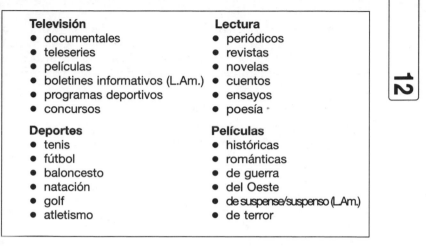

Televisión
- documentales
- teleseries
- películas
- boletines informativos (L.Am.)
- programas deportivos
- concursos

Lectura
- periódicos
- revistas
- novelas
- cuentos
- ensayos
- poesía

Deportes
- tenis
- fútbol
- baloncesto
- natación
- golf
- atletismo

Películas
- históricas
- románticas
- de guerra
- del Oeste
- de suspense/suspenso (L.Am.)
- de terror

▶ 5 Me encanta guisar

Lola talked to a magazine about her likes and interests.

Can you complete the text with the correct form of the verbs in brackets?

A mí (gustar) estar con mi familia, mis amigos y mis dos perros. (Encantar) guisar y arreglar la casa, pero (detestar) fregar los platos y planchar. (Interesar) la lectura, especialmente la novela y la poesía, y también (gustar) la fotografía y la pintura.

Los fines de semana (preferir) desayunar en la cama y levantarme tarde, y salir de compras con Antonio, mi marido.

En las vacaciones, Antonio y yo (preferir) ir a la playa. A él y a mí (encantar) nadar y tomar el sol. En invierno a Antonio y a mí (gustar) esquiar.

el perro	*dog*	**arreglar**	*to tidy up*
guisar (cocinar)	*to cook*	**planchar**	*to iron*

6 Ahora tú

You are writing to a correspondent about your likes and interests. Don't forget to mention your interest in Spanish and other languages! Follow the model above, and use words from this and previous activities.

▶ 7 Me interesa mucho la pintura

A Spanish-speaking person is visiting your place of work and you have been asked to entertain her. Before making plans you decide to ask her about her preferences. How would you ask the following? Use the guidelines below to fill in your part of the conversation.

– *Ask what sort of food she likes.*
– Me gusta todo tipo de comida, pero prefiero la francesa.
– *Say you also like it. Ask if she likes the theatre.*
– Sí, me encanta el teatro.
– *Say you do too. You love English theatre. Ask whether she does too.*
– Sí, a mí también. Y el cine también me gusta mucho.
– *Ask whether she is interested in painting. There is an excellent art gallery* (galería de arte) *in town.*
– Sí, me interesa mucho la pintura, pero la pintura abstracta no me gusta nada.
– *Say you don't (like it) either.*

8 ¿Qué te gusta o no te gusta de tu trabajo?

In a survey, Enrique was asked to rate the sort of things he liked and disliked about his job, using the following scale:

5 me encanta/n
4 me gusta/n
3 no me gusta/n
2 no me gusta/n nada
1 detesto

Study his answers, then fill in the column on the right with your own rating and write one sentence for each entry, e.g. Me encanta mi trabajo.

¿Qué te gusta o no te gusta de tu trabajo?	Enrique	Tú
tu trabajo	4	
tu jefe/jefa	2	
tus compañeros de trabajo	5	
las condiciones de trabajo (e.g. el sueldo)	3	
el ambiente de trabajo	4	
el horario	2	
trabajar horas extras	1	
escribir cartas/informes	2	
hablar por teléfono	5	
asistir a reuniones	1	

▶ 9 ¿Qué tal tu trabajo?

Angélica, from Spain, and Cristóbal, from Mexico, talked about their jobs. Listen and make a note in Spanish of what each likes or dislikes.

13

¿qué vas a hacer?

what are you going to do?

In this unit you will learn
- how to say what you are going to do
- how to say what you intend to do
- how to say what you want and hope to do

▶ 1 ¿Qué vas a hacer mañana por la noche?

Miguel and Nieves, from Spain, and Eduardo, from Mexico, talk about their plans for tomorrow night, **mañana por la noche.**

1.1 Listen to the conversation several times, each time listening for specific information. Look at the key words if you need help with new vocabulary.

a What is each person going to do? Listen and match the names with the drawings, inserting the appropriate numbers in the boxes below.

Nieves ☐   Miguel ☐   Eduardo ☐

b What film is on at the Princesa cinema?
c Has Eduardo got any special plans for tomorrow?
d Why isn't he going out?

Miguel	¿Qué vas a hacer mañana por la noche, Nieves?
Nieves	Voy a ir al cine con José María.
Miguel	¿Qué película pensáis ver?
Nieves	Flamenco, de Saura. La ponen en el cine Princesa. Y tú Miguel, ¿qué piensas hacer?
Miguel	Voy a cenar con Almudena y después vamos a ir a una discoteca.
Nieves	Y tú Eduardo, ¿tienes algún plan para mañana?
Eduardo	No, ninguno. Estoy muy cansado y quiero quedarme en casa. Voy a ver el tenis en la televisión.

1.2 Now read the dialogue and find the Spanish for:

a What are you going to do?   **c** I'm going to the cinema.
b What are you thinking of doing? **d** I'm going to have dinner.

pensar	*to think*	**ninguno**	*none*
poner	*to put on (film)*	**cansado/a**	*tired*

▶ 2 Espero ir a la universidad

Nieves and Miguel talk about their plans for *next year*, **el año que viene**.

2.1 Listen to the dialogue a few times and say who is going to do the following, Nieves or Miguel. The key words below will help you to understand.

a estudiar empresariales
b buscar otro trabajo
c ir a la universidad
d dedicarse al diseño o
  a la publicidad

espero ir a la universidad

Nieves	¿Qué planes tienes para el año viene?
Miguel	Pienso buscar otro trabajo. Estoy harto del sitio donde estoy. Quiero dedicarme al diseño o a la publicidad. Me interesan mucho más. ¿Qué vas a hacer tú?
Nieves	Espero ir a la universidad.
Miguel	¿Qué piensas estudiar?
Nieves	Quiero estudiar empresariales.

2.2 Now read the dialogue until you feel confident with it, then try playing first Nieves' part, then Miguel's, covering the corresponding part of the text.

buscar	*to look for*	**el diseño**	*design*
harto de	*fed up with.*	**esperar**	*to hope*

How do you say it?

Asking and answering questions about future plans

¿Qué vas a hacer mañana/el año que viene?	*What are you going to do tomorrow/next year?*
Voy a cenar con .../ir a una discoteca.	*I am going to have dinner with ... /go to a disco.*
¿Qué planes tienes?	*What plans have you got?*
¿Tienes algún plan?	*Have you got any plans?*
No tengo ningún plan.	*I have no plans.*

Asking and answering questions regarding intentions

¿Qué piensas hacer/ver?	*What are you thinking of doing/seeing?*
Pienso ir al cine/ver televisión.	*I am thinking of going to the cinema/watching television.*

Saying what you want or hope to do

Quiero quedarme en casa/ver el tenis.	*I want to stay at home/ watch tennis.*
Espero ir a la universidad /estudiar empresariales.	*I hope to go to university /do business studies.*

Grammar

1 Talking about future plans and intentions

To talk about future plans and intentions you can use the following constructions:

a *present tense of* **ir** + **a** + *infinitive*. (For the present tense of **ir** see Unit 11.)

¿Qué vas a hacer (tú)?	*What are you going to do?*
Voy a comer con Isabel.	*I'm going to have lunch with Isabel.*
Vamos a mudarnos de casa.	*We are going to move house.*
¿Vosotros vais a volver pronto?	*You are going to come back soon?*

b **pensar** (**e > ie**) + *infinitive*

¿Qué piensa hacer Vd.?	*What are you thinking of doing?*
Pienso cambiar de trabajo.	*I'm thinking of changing jobs.*
Pensamos ir de vacaciones al Caribe.	*We're thinking of going on holiday to the Caribbean.*

2 Saying what you want and hope to do

a **querer** (**e > ie**) + *infinitive*

Use this construction to say what you *want* to do:

¿Qué quieres hacer (tú)?	*What do you want to do?*
Quiero descansar un rato.	*I want to rest for a while.*
Queremos tomar dos días de descanso.	*We want to take two days off.*

b esperar + *infinitive*

Use this construction to say what you *hope* to do:

Este año espero ir a Sevilla en el AVE.	*This year I hope to go to Seville on the AVE (high-speed Spanish train).*
Esperan comprar un nuevo apartamento.	*They hope to buy a new apartment.*

3 Alguno (*some, any*), ninguno (*no, not any, none*)

a Alguno changes for number (singular and plural) and gender (masculine and feminine) depending on the noun it refers to. It can be used with an accompanying noun, or on its own, in place of a noun. Before a singular masculine noun **alguno** becomes **algún**.

¿Tenéis algún plan?	*Have you any plans?*
Tenemos algunos (planes).	*We have some (plans).*
¿Tienes alguna idea?	*Have you any idea?*

b ninguno (masc.) and **ninguna** (fem.) can also be used with an accompanying noun or on their own, in place of a noun. **Ninguno** becomes **ningún** before a singular masculine noun.

No tengo ningún plan.	*I have no plans.*
No tengo ninguno.	*I have none.*
No tengo ninguna idea.	*I have no idea.*

Madame Raquin

de Emile Zola con
Julia Gutiérrez Caba, Manuel Tejada,
Paula Sebastián, Juan A. Quintana

TEATRE APOLO
Dirección Colbas, S.A.
Av. Paral·lel, 59
Tel. 93 441 90 07

Enrique y Alain Cornejo
presentan

DEL 16 ENERO
AL 10 FEBRERO

Funciones
Lunes – No hay función
Martes 21:00 Miércoles 21:00
Jueves 21:00 Viernes 19:30 y 22:30
Sábado 19:30 y 22:30 Domingo 18:00

Note the word *teatre*, Catalan for *teatro*, and the raised point in Paral·lel.

Practice

1 Al teatro

It is Sunday night and you are going to the theatre. Your friend Victor phones to ask what plans you have. Look at the programme on the previous page and answer his questions.

a ¿Qué piensas hacer esta noche?   c ¿Dónde la ponen?
b ¿Qué obra vas a ver?   d ¿A qué hora es la función?

la obra	*play*	**la entrada**	*ticket*
la función	*performance*		

▶ 2 Un viaje de negocios

Ana is being sent to South America by her company and she's giving details of her journey to her secretary. Listen to what she says and, as you do, fill in the grid below with the appropriate information.

Destino 1	
Día y hora de salida	
Días de estancia	
Hotel y teléfono	
Destino 2	
Día y hora de salida	
Días de estancia	
Hotel y teléfono	

los negocios	*business*

3 Una nota

Mario left a note for Silvia on her desk. Can you put the infinitives in brackets in the appropriate form?

Silvia:

¿Tienes algún plan para este fin de semana? Carmen y yo (ir) a pasar el fin de semana en Cuenca. (Pensar) salir el viernes por la noche y regresar el domingo por la tarde. (¿Querer) venir con nosotros? (Ir) a ir en el coche.

Mario

4 De vacaciones

Elena and Pablo have booked the second of the two Cuban holidays below. How would they reply to someone's questions about their plans? Look at the ad below and answer for them. You'll need the **nosotros** form of the verb.

Oferta Especial

Precios Unicos

con cosmo

La Habana Varadero 1

- 04 noches Brisas del Caribe Régimen Todo Incluído
- 03 noches Comodoro La Habana Régimen media pensión

La Habana Varadero 2

- 05 noches Sol Palmeras Varadero
- 02 noches Copacabana La Habana Régimen media pensión Habana y Varadero
- City Tour La Habana

Los programas incluyen:
- Ticket aéreo vía Cubana de Aviación
- Valor en base a habitación doble
- Atención personalizada
- Solicite valor noche adicional

Consulte a su Agencia de Viajes

Programas 8 días/7 noches
Salidas : 10 – 11 febrero

US$ 1.199

OPERADOR INTERNACIONAL DE TURISMO

Tel.: 341 5095 – Fax: 225 0764

a ¿Adónde pensáis ir de vacaciones?
b ¿Qué ciudades vais a visitar?
c ¿Cuántos días vais a estar en total?
d ¿En qué hoteles vais a quedaros?
e ¿Vais a tomar la pensión completa?
f ¿En qué línea aérea vais a viajar?

¿adónde?   *where to?*

5 Ahora tú

How would you tell a Spanish-speaking colleague about your own plans for *a weekend*, **el fin de semana**, *the summer*, **el verano**, or *a business trip*, **un viaje de negocios**? You can use Dialogue 1 and Activities 2 and 4 as a model.

6 Los planes de tu amigo/a

How would you ask a Spanish-speaking friend about his/her own travel plans? Ask the following:

a what he/she is going to do this summer
b where he/she is going to go
c how long he/she is going to stay
d where he/she is going to stay
e when he/she is thinking of leaving
f when he/she is coming back

7 Buenos propósitos

Fernando and his friends Tina and Paco have made some resolutions. What are their plans? Look up the verbs below and use them to complete the sentences which follow, making changes where necessary:

mudarse, viajar, ahorrar, seguir, conseguir, casarse

Nombres	Propósitos	
Fernando	espero _____	un trabajo por las tardes
	quiero _____	estudiando
	pienso _____	de casa
Tina y Paco	vamos a _____	dinero
	esperamos _____	pronto.
	pensamos _____	al Oriente

8 ¿Qué piensan hacer?

How would you tell someone else about:

a Fernando's plans?
b Tina and Paco's plans?

9 ¿Alguno o ninguno?

Fill in the gaps in these sentences with the appropriate form of **alguno** or **ninguno**.

a '¿Tienes _____ compromiso para mañana? – No, _____ .'
b Héctor y yo tenemos _____ proyectos que _____ día esperamos realizar.
c '¿Hay _____ película interesante en la televisión? – No, _____ .'

el compromiso	*engagement*	**el proyecto**	*project*
realizar	*to fulfil*		

10 Ahora tú

¿Tienes algún plan para el año que viene? ¿Vas a continuar con el español? ¿Qué planes tienes en relación con tu trabajo o tus estudios? ¿Piensas cambiar de trabajo? ¿Tienes algún otro plan importante para el futuro? ¿Qué esperas hacer?

You can use Activity 7 and Dialogue 2 as a model.

14

¿dígame?

hello?

In this unit you will learn

- how to ask to speak to someone on the phone
- how to take and leave messages
- how to make appointments on the phone
- how to say what you or others are doing

▶ 1 Necesito hablar con él

María Ángeles Castillo telephones señor Ruiz at a Spanish firm.

1.1 Listen to the dialogue several times, each time focusing attention on specific information:

a Why can't señor Ruiz come to the phone? Choose the right activity from the drawings below.

b What does the secretary offer to do?

c What does señora Castillo ask the secretary to tell her boss?

Secretaria	Agrohispana, ¿dígame?
M. Ángeles	¿Está el señor Ruiz, por favor?
Secretaria	¿De parte de quién?
M. Ángeles	De María Ángeles Castillo, de Sevilla.
Secretaria	El señor Ruiz no puede ponerse en este momento. Está hablando por otra línea. ¿Quiere dejarle algún recado?
M. Ángeles	Por favor, dígale que voy a llamar más tarde. Necesito hablar con él.
Secretaria	Muy bien, le daré su recado.

1.2 Now read the dialogue and find the Spanish for

a Who's calling?

b He can't come to the phone at this moment.

c Please tell him that . . .

dejar	*to leave*
más tarde	*later*
le daré su recado	*I'll give him your message*

▶ 2 En seguida le pongo

Luis phones a friend at work.

2.1 Listen to the conversation several times and, as you do so, try filling in the gaps in these sentences.

a _____ Gloria Araya, por favor. c _____ 368.
b Su extensión _____ d _____ se pone.

Voz 1 Ibertour, ¿diga?
Luis Quisiera hablar con Gloria Araya, por favor.
Voz 1 Se ha equivocado. Su extensión no es ésta. Es la 368. No cuelgue, en seguida le pongo.
Luis Gracias.
Voz 1 Oiga, un momento, por favor. Está comunicando.
Voz 2 Sí, ¿diga?
Luis ¿Me puede poner con Gloria Araya, por favor?
Voz 2 Sí, ahora mismo se pone.

2.2 Now read the dialogue and find the Spanish for the following expressions. If you have difficulty with them you can check the *How do you say it?* section.

a You've got the wrong number. c It's engaged.
b I'll put you through right away. d Can you put me through to …?

2.3 There are several important expressions for the use of the phone in this conversation, so listen and read the dialogue again a few times. Then try playing each one of the parts.

no cuelgue	*don't hang up*	**poner**	*to put through*
comunicando	*engaged*		

▶ 3 Un momentito, por favor

Sandra, a graphic designer, has seen the job advertisements below and she telephones to ask for an interview.

Diseñadora Gráfica
Súper despierta y con la mejor disposición.
Necesita
Agencia de Publicidad
Llamar por entrevista al fono: **246 08 17**

DISEÑADOR GRÁFICO
Ambiente Macintosh, 3 años
Conocimientos:
Page Maker 6.0,
Freehand, Photoshop,
Disponibilidad inmediata.
Solicitar entrevista:
Lunes 14 ☎ 555.00.68
Depto. Publicidad

3.1 Listen to the dialogue several times and, as you do, try answering these questions.

a How does Sandra express the purpose of her call? Listen and find out.
b When is her appointment for? Listen again and make a note of this.

Voz	¿Dígame?
Sandra	Llamo por el anuncio para el puesto de diseñadora gráfica. Quería solicitar una entrevista.
Voz	Un momentito, por favor. ¿Puede usted venir el lunes a las nueve y media?
Sandra	Sí, a las nueve y media me va bien.
Voz	Bueno, dígame por favor su nombre y número de teléfono.

3.2 What do you think the following phrases mean? Read the dialogue and find out.

a Llamo por el anuncio
b Quería solicitar una entrevista
c Dígame por favor su nombre

el puesto	*post*
la entrevista	*interview*
el anuncio	*advertisement*
me va bien	*it's all right with me*
un momentito (from **momento**)	*just a moment*

How do you say it?

Answering the phone

¿Díga? ¿Dígame?	*Hello?*
Se ha equivocado (de número).	*You've got the wrong number.*

Asking to speak to someone on the phone and responding

¿Está el señor/la señora... ?	*Is señor/señora ... there?*
Quisiera/Quería hablar con ...	*I'd like to speak to ...*
¿Me puede(s) poner con ... ?	*Can you put me through to ... ?*
Soy yo.	*Speaking.*
¿De parte de quién? De parte de ...	*Who's calling? (caller's name)*
En seguida le/te pongo.	*I'll put you through right away.*
Ahora se pone.	*He/she will be with you right away.*

Taking and leaving messages

¿Quiere dejar(le) algún
  recado?

*Do you want to leave
(him/her) a message?*

Por favor, dígale que ...

Please, tell him/her that ...

Making appointments on the phone

Quisiera solicitar una
  entrevista con ... /ver a ... /
  pedir hora con el doctor.

*I'd like to arrange an
interview with ... /see .../
make an appointment
with the doctor.*

Saying what someone is doing

Está hablando por otra línea.

*He/she is speaking on
another line.*

i The following passage gives some instructions on how to make certain types of telephone calls in Spain. Read and find out.

Para llamar por teléfono fuera de España tienes que **marcar**, *dial*, primeramente el 07, que es el número de acceso a la Central internacional. Luego esperas un segundo **tono**, *tone*, y marcas **el prefijo**, *code*, del país al que quieres llamar, el prefijo de la ciudad, y el número de teléfono de la persona con la que quieres hablar. Por ejemplo, para llamar a Londres debes marcar: 07 + 44 (Inglaterra) + 20 + número que deseas. Para hacer **una llamada personal**, *a personal call*, o **una llamada de cobro revertido**, *a transferred charge call*, tienes que llamar a la **operadora** o al **operador**, *operator*, y decir: **"Quiero hacer una llamada ..."**, *'I want to make a ... call'*.

Grammar

1 Está hablando (*He/she is speaking*)

To say what you or someone else is doing at the moment of speaking, use **estar** followed by the Spanish equivalent of -ing, as in 'speaking'. This is formed by *adding* -**ando** *to the stem of* -**ar** verbs, and -**iendo** *to that of* -**er** *and* -**ir** *verbs*:

hablar – hablando   hacer – haciendo   escribir – escribiendo

Está hablando por teléfono.

*He/she is (speaking) on the
telephone.*

¿Qué estás haciendo?

What are you doing?

Estoy escribiendo una carta.

I'm writing a letter.

Note the use of this construction in

Está comunicando.

It's engaged.

2 Poner (*to put through*), ponerse al teléfono (*to come to the phone*)

¿Me puedes poner con María?	*Can you put me through to María?*
En seguida te pongo.	*I'll put you through right away.*

Note also that in the second expression the verb is **ponerse**.

Ahora se pone María.	*María will be with you right away.*

3 Latin American usage on the phone

Here are some common alternative expressions for use on the phone which you may hear when travelling in Latin America.

¿Bueno? (Mexico), ¿Aló? (most countries)	*Hello?*
¿Con quién hablo?	*Who am I speaking to?*
Con él/ella *or* Con él mismo.	*Speaking.*
Está equivocado *or* Equivocado.	*You've got the wrong number.*

4 Por, para

Note the use of **por** and **para** in

Llamo por el anuncio para el puesto de traductor.	*I'm calling about the ad for a translator's post.*
Está hablando por otra línea.	*He/she is speaking on another line.*
Está hablando por teléfono.	*He/she is (speaking) on the telephone.*

Practice

1 Una conversación telefónica

Ricardo phoned his friend Leonor but she wasn't at home. How would you fill the gaps in this conversation between Ricardo and the speaker at the other end of the line?

– ¿Dígame?
– ¿_____?
– No, Leonor está en la universidad. ¿_____?
– De Ricardo.
– ¿_____?

– Sí, por favor. Dígale que me llame al número 580 2133, que necesito hablar urgentemente con ella.
– Muy bien.

▶ **2 ¿Qué está haciendo?**

Listen to Raquel phoning her friend Lorenzo at home.

a   What is Lorenzo doing? Choose the right picture below.
b   What message does Raquel leave for him?

la entrada	*ticket*

▶ **3 ¿Me puede poner con la señora Smith?**

A Spanish-speaking person phones your place of work and asks to speak to one of your colleagues. Follow the guidelines below and fill in your part of the conversation.

– *Say 'Hello?'*
– ¿Me puede poner con la señora Smith, por favor?
– *Say señora Smith is speaking to a client* (un cliente) *at the moment. Ask who's calling.*
– Juan Astaburuaga.
– *Ask him whether he would like to leave a message.*
– Sí, dígale por favor que me llame al 763 21 34.
– *Say that's all right. You'll give her his message.*

▶ **4 Hora con el doctor**

Javier is making an appointment with his doctor. When is his appointment for? Listen and find out.

5 Ahora tú

You have been shortlisted for one of the jobs advertised below and you phone to arrange an interview.

EMPRESA DE PLANTAS ARTIFICIALES JARDINERAS Y MUEBLES DE JARDÍN BUSCA:
V E N D E D O R / A

PARA: MADRID Y ZONA CENTRO

Se requiere:
● Persona dinámica y trabajadora
● Dedicación exclusiva ● Vehículo propio
● Experiencia en el Sector de Floristería, Regalo y Mobiliario de Jardin.
Se ofrece:
● Incorporación a una empresa sólida y estable ● Remuneración a convenir más incentivos.
Interesados enviar C.V. o telefonear a: Sr. YBERN C/. Roger de Llúria 29 1°–B, 08009 BARCELONA, telef. (93) 802 21 88, Ref. M.C./91

CADENA DE TIENDAS DE ENMARCACION precisa para su tienda de Majadahonda

**E N C A R G A D A
D E   T I E N D A**

Se requiere: *Aptitudes para la venta, aunque no es necesaria experiencia en puesto similar.*Buena actitud y predisposición para el trabajo.*Se valorará residencia en zona de Majadahonda. Se ofrece:*Contrato fijo.*Sueldo atractivo con porcentaje en las ventas (Empresa en expansión) Interesados enviar a la mayor brevedad curriculum con fotografía reciente a L.S. CONSULTORES. Clara Rey, 90, 1° F. 28002 Madrid.

**SECRETARIA
BILINGÜE**
Inglés nativo
Técnicas de Secretariado
**PARA DESPACHO
DE ABOGADOS**
C.V.: Castellana, 964
28046 MADRID

Empresa de distribución busca programador que cumpla los siguientes requisitos:
- -
✔ Licenciado o diplomado en Informática o equivalente.
✔ Imprescindible 1 año de experiencia profesional demostrable programando en IFORMIX 4GL y SQL.
✔ Se valorará experiencia en lenguaje "C".
✔ Remuneración bruta 3.000.000 más incentivos.
**Mandar C.V. urgentemente
vía fax al 558 04 19**

a   How would you state the purpose of your call?
b   How would you request to speak to the person in charge (**el encargado/la encargada**)?
c   How would you request an interview?
d   They suggest you come to their offices on Wednesday at 4.30. How would you say that is all right with you?

15

fue un viaje estupendo

it was a great journey

In this unit you will learn
- how to talk about past events
- how to say how long ago
  something took place
- how to talk about the
  weather

▶ 1 Regresé hace una semana

Alicia travelled to Mexico on business and on her return she talks about her journey to her friend Alejandro.

1.1 Listen to the conversation several times, each time focusing attention on a different point:

a What did Alicia think of Mexico? Listen and find out.
b How long did she stay in each city? Listen to your recording again a few times and fill in the table.

Ciudad de México	
Guadalajara	
Guanajuato	

c When did she return? Listen once more.

Alejandro	¿Qué tal tu viaje a México?
Alicia	Fue un viaje estupendo. Me encantó México. Conocí mucha gente y salí muchísimo.
Alejandro	Es un país muy bonito. ¿Estuviste en ciudad de México?
Alicia	Sí, estuve diez días allí y luego viajé a Guadalajara. Allí me quedé cinco días. Y después fui a Guanajuato donde pasé un fin de semana.
Alejandro	¿Cuándo regresaste?
Alicia	Hace una semana.

1.2 Now read the dialogue and find the Spanish for

a Were you in Mexico City?
b I met a lot of people and I went out a lot.
c I went to Guanajuato.

fue	*it was*	**me encantó**	*I loved it*
fui	*I went*	**estuve**	*I was*

▶ 2 No hace calor

Alejandro and Alicia talk about the weather in Mexico.

2.1 Listen to the recording several times and, as you do, try finding the answers to these questions.

a   What is the weather like in Mexico City?
b   Why does Alicia consider herself lucky?
c   What was the weather like in Cancún when Alejandro was there?

Alejandro ¿Qué tal el tiempo en la ciudad de México?

Alicia Es muy agradable. No hace mucho calor, aunque en esta época del año llueve bastante. Pero tuve suerte, sólo llovió una vez.

Alejandro Yo estuve diez días en Cancún el año pasado e hizo muchísimo calor.

estuve diez días en Cancún

2.2 Now read the dialogue and make a note of all the words and expressions related to the weather.

llover	*to rain*	**en esta época**	*at this time*
aunque	*although*	**una vez**	*once*
e	*and* (before **hi** or **i**)		

How do you say it?

Talking about past events

¿Qué tal tu viaje?	*How was your journey?*
Fue un viaje estupendo.	*It was a wonderful journey.*
¿Dónde fuiste/estuviste?	*Where did you go/were you?*
Primero fui a .../estuve en ...,	*First I went to .../was in ...,*
después/luego viajé a ...	*then I travelled to ...*

Saying how long ago you did something

Regresé/Volví hace una semana/	*I came back a week/*
un mes.	*a month ago.*

Talking about the weather

No hace/hizo (mucho) calor/ frío.	*It isn't/wasn't (very) warm/ cold.*
Llueve/Llovió bastante/ mucho.	*It rains/rained quite a lot/ very much.*

Grammar

1 Saying what you did: the preterite tense

To say what you did at some point in the past, as in 'I returned last week', you need the *simple past tense*, which is known as *preterite tense*. There are two sets of endings for this tense, one for -ar verbs and another one for verbs ending in -er and -ir. The first person plural, **nosotros/as**, of -ar and -ir verbs is the same as that of the present tense.

regresar *to come back*	**conocer** *to meet*	**salir** *to go out*
regresé	conocí	salí
regresaste	conociste	saliste
regresó	conoció	salió
regresamos	conocimos	salimos
regresasteis	conocisteis	salisteis
regresaron	conocieron	salieron

Regresé hace dos días.	*I came back two days ago.*
Él la conoció en Mexico.	*He met her in Mexico.*
Salimos a las 3.00.	*We went out at 3.00.*

2 Irregular preterite forms

The number of irregular verbs in the preterite tense is small but some of them are very common, so try to learn them as they come up. Many of them, like **hacer** *to do, to make*, **estar** *to be*, **tener** *to have*, share the same endings so it should be easier to memorize them. **Ser** *to be*, and **ir** *to go*, have exactly the same forms.

hacer	estar	tener	ser/ir
hice	estuve	tuve	fui
hiciste	estuviste	tuviste	fuiste
hizo	estuvo	tuvo	fue
hicimos	estuvimos	tuvimos	fuimos
hicisteis	estuvisteis	tuvisteis	fuisteis
hicieron	estuvieron	tuvieron	fueron

¿Qué hiciste el verano pasado?	*What did you do last summer?*
Estuve en España.	*I was in Spain.*
Tuvimos suerte.	*We were lucky.*
Fue un viaje estupendo.	*It was a wonderful journey.*
Alicia fue a México.	*Alicia went to Mexico.*

3 Time phrases associated with the preterite

There are several words and phrases associated with this tense, the most common of which are

anoche	*last night*
ayer	*yesterday*
antes de ayer/anteayer*	*the day before yesterday*
el lunes/martes pasado	*last Monday/Tuesday*
la semana pasada	*last week*
el mes/año pasado	*last month/year*
en 1985	*in 1985*
hace mucho tiempo	*a long time ago*

* Some Latin American countries, including Mexico, use the expression *antier*.

4 How long ago?

To say how long ago you did something, use **hace** with *a time phrase* and a verb in the *preterite tense*.

¿Cuánto tiempo hace que llegaste?	*How long ago did you arrive?*
Llegué hace un mes *or* Hace un mes que llegué.	*I arrived a month ago.*

Compare this construction with **Hace** + *time phrase* + *verb in the present tense*, which you learned in Unit 10.

Hace poco tiempo que estoy aquí.	*I've been here for a short time.*

5 *Hacer* in weather expressions

To say what the weather is like use **hacer** *to do*, *to make*, in expressions like the following:

Hace frío/calor/sol/viento.	*It is cold/warm/sunny/windy.*
Hace bueno.	*The weather is good.*
Hace buen/mal tiempo.	*The weather is good/bad.*
Hace un grado bajo cero.	*It's one degree below (zero).*

To say what the weather was like at a particular time in the past, use **hizo**.

Ayer hizo mucho calor.	*It was very warm yesterday.*

Note also the use of **llover** (o > ue) *to rain*, in

Llueve (bastante/mucho)	*It rains quite a lot/very much.*
Está lloviendo.	*It's raining.*
Llovió mucho.	*It rained a lot.*

Practice

1 Una carta

Read this extract from a letter sent by Alicia from Mexico to a friend, and change the verbs in brackets into the appropriate form of the preterite tense. Note that **llegar** adds a **-u** in the first person singular of the preterite tense, so that the pronunciation of the **-g** may remain the same as in the infinitive.

Querida Carmen:

Llegué a la ciudad de México hace tres días.
El avión (salir) a la hora y el vuelo (ser) estupendo. El primer día (yo) no (hacer) nada especial, (cenar) temprano y luego (acostarse). Al día siguiente (tener) una reunión con nuestro representante aquí en México y por la tarde (ir) al Museo de Antropología. Me (gustar) mucho. Ayer al mediodía (pasar) un rato en uno de los mercados, que son maravillosos, y por la noche (salir) con unos amigos mexicanos a bailar. ¡Lo pasé estupendamente! ¡Me encantó México!

pasarlo estupendamente	*to have a great time*
un rato	*a while*

2 ¿Qué hizo?

Can you say what Alejandro did when he went on holiday to Cancún? Match the drawings with the verbs and put these in the appropriate form of the preterite tense.

a (salir) a bailar
b (ir) a pescar
c (nadar) muchísimo

d (conocer) a una chica mexicana
e (hacer) vela
f (tomar) el sol

3 Fui a Estados Unidos

A Spanish-speaking friend went on a holiday. What questions would you ask your friend to get the replies below? For some of the questions you'll need interrogative words. Choose from the following: **¿dónde? ¿cuándo? ¿adónde? ¿con quién? ¿cuánto tiempo?** and remember to use the informal form.

a Fui a Estados Unidos.
b Fui solo.
d Estuve en Nueva York y San Francisco.
d En Nueva York pasé una semana. En San Francisco estuve diez días.
e Sí, me gustó mucho. San Francisco es una ciudad preciosa.
f Volví anteayer.

4 De Madrid a Sevilla

Pepe and Sara took the tour advertised below. How would they answer their friend Ignacio's questions about their tour? Look at the itinerary and answer for them. Note that Ignacio is using the informal **vosotros** form of the verb, and that the answers will require the **nosotros** form.

ANDALUCIA – COSTA DEL SOL 3 días

TODO EL AÑO	LUN	MAR	MIE	JUE	VIE	SAB	DOM
ALL YEAR ROUND	MON	TUE	WED	THU	FRI	SAT	SUN

ITINERARIO:

Día 1.° MADRID. – Salida a las 09.00 horas hacia Córdoba. Almuerzo y visita de la ciudad (Mezquita, Sinagoga y Barrio Judío). **Sevilla**. Cena y alojamiento.

Día 2.° SEVILLA. – Media pensión. Por la mañana visita de la ciudad (Catedral, Alcázar, Barrio Sta. Cruz y Parque María Luisa).

Día 3.° SEVILLA. – Desayuno y salida con dirección a **Jerez**. Visita panorámica. Continuación del viaje hasta **Cádiz**. Almuerzo y por Estepona y Marbella llegada a **Torremolinos/Benalmádena**. FIN DEL VIAJE.

NOTA: Las salidas de los Jueves tendrán las siguientes modificaciones: –3ᵉʳ. día. SEVILLA - Desayuno. Salida a Torremolinos. FIN DEL VIAJE.

a ¿A qué hora salisteis de Madrid?
b ¿Dónde almorzasteis el primer día?
c ¿Qué sitios visitasteis ese día?
d ¿Dónde cenasteis?
e ¿Tomasteis la pensión completa en Sevilla?
f ¿Qué hicisteis por la mañana del segundo día?
g Y después de Sevilla, ¿adónde fuisteis?
h ¿Cuántos días duró el viaje?

la mezquita	*mosque*	**el barrio judío**	*the Jewish district*

5 Ahora tú

¿Qué tal tus últimas vacaciones? ¿Dónde las pasaste? ¿Con quién fuiste? ¿En qué viajaste? ¿Cuánto tiempo estuviste allí? ¿Dónde te quedaste? ¿Qué hiciste durante las vacaciones?

6 ¿Hace cuánto tiempo?

How would you ask Verónica how long ago she did each of the following? And how would she reply? The first question and answer have been done for you.

– ¿Cuánto tiempo hace que empezaste a estudiar inglés?
– Empecé a estudiar inglés hace (X) años.

a 1992: empezar a estudiar inglés.
b 1993: viajar a la India.
c 1994: hacer un curso de informática.
d 1995: comenzar a trabajar.
e 1996: mudarse de casa.
f 1997: conocer a Ramón.

---

la informática   *computing*

---

7 Ahora tú

¿Cuánto tiempo hace que empezaste a trabajar/estudiar?
¿Cuánto tiempo hace que empezaste a estudiar español?

8 ¿Qué tal el tiempo?

You'll be travelling through Spain on business, so you want to know what the weather is like in the places you'll visit.

8.1 First, match each weather symbol with an appropriate phrase

a está cubierto
b hay niebla
c hace sol
d está nevando
e hace viento
f está nublado
g hay tormenta
h esta lloviendo

8.2 Can you say what the weather is like in the following cities? Look at the map overleaf.

a Málaga
b Sevilla
c Madrid
d Valladolid
e Bilbao
f Barcelona

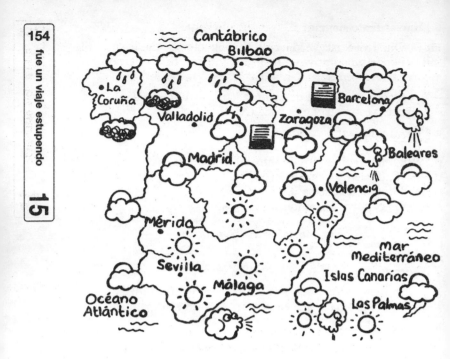

9 ¿Qué temperatura hizo?

Your next assignment will be in the Americas, so here is a chart with yesterday's temperatures in the main cities.

Iberoamérica	M.	m.		M.	m.
Bogotá............	18	7	Miami...............	30	26
Buenos Aires....	22	13	Montevideo	29	16
Caracas...........	29	20	Panamá...........	34	23
Guatemala.......	27	17	Quito...............	20	10
La Habana.......	34	24	R. de Janeiro....	28	16
La Paz	16	2	San Juan	33	24
Lima...............	18	14	Santiago...........	22	7
México.............	24	12	Sto. Domingo ...	32	23

Look at the chart and answer the questions.

a ¿Qué temperatura máxima (M.) hizo en Bogotá?
b ¿Qué temperatura mínima (m.) hizo?
c ¿En qué ciudad hizo más calor?
d ¿En qué ciudades hizo más frío?
e ¿Dónde hizo más calor, en San Juan o Santo Domingo?

▶ 10 El tiempo

Now listen to this weather report from a Chilean radio station and try to get the gist of what it says. As you do so, say whether the statements below are true or false (**verdadero o falso**).

Para hoy, en la región metropolitana, se anunció:

a nublado y precipitaciones débiles
b temperaturas extremas de 5 y 22 grados

Para mañana, se anunció:

c sol
d temperaturas extremas de 7 y 14 grados

las precipitaciones débiles	*light rain*
el grado	*degree*

16

¿dónde naciste?

where were you born?

In this unit you will learn
- how to talk about events in your life
- how to talk about other people's lives
- how to say how long you have been doing something (2)

▶ 1 Nací en San Clemente

In the course of a radio interview, Miguel Montes, a tennis player, talked about his life.

1.1 Listen to the interview several times, each time focusing attention on a different point:

a Where and when was Miguel born?
b What did he do in Cuenca? And in Valencia?
c How long has he been playing tennis?

Entrevistadora	Cuéntanos algo acerca de tu vida, Miguel. ¿Dónde naciste?
Miguel	Nací en San Clemente.
Entrevistadora	¿Cuándo naciste?
Miguel	El 23 de abril de 1968.
Entrevistadora	¿Y dónde hiciste tus estudios?
Miguel	Los hice en Cuenca. Me fui a Cuenca en 1979 para hacer el bachillerato, que terminé en el ochenta y cinco. Al año siguiente, en 1986, me fui a Valencia, donde viví hasta finales del ochenta y siete.
Entrevistadora	¿Qué hiciste en Valencia?
Miguel	Trabajé como administrativo en una empresa.
Entrevistadora	¿Y cuándo llegaste a Madrid?
Miguel	Llegué a principios del ochenta y ocho. Ese mismo año entré en la universidad a estudiar Derecho, pero no terminé los estudios. Dejé la universidad en el noventa y uno y me dediqué completamente al tenis, que es lo que me apasiona.
Entrevistadora	¿Cuánto tiempo llevas jugando al tenis?
Miguel	Diez años.

llevo diez años
jugando al tenis

contar (o > ue)	*to tell*
administrativo	*office clerk*
el bachillerato	*secondary education*
irse	*to go, to leave*

1.2 Now read the interview and fill in the gaps in Miguel's c.v. with the missing verbs. The first one has been filled for you.

1968 **Nací** en San Clemente, Cuenca, el 23 de abril de 1968
1979 _____ a Cuenca para hacer el bachillerato
1985 _____ el bachillerato
1986 _____ a Valencia donde _____ como administrativo
1988 _____ a Madrid y _____ en la universidad
1991 _____ la universidad y _____ al tenis

How do you say it?

Talking about events in your life

¿Dónde/Cuándo naciste/ nació Vd.?	*Where/when were you born?*
Nací en .../el ...	*I was born in .../on ...*
Empecé/Terminé mis estudios en ...	*I started/finished my studies in (date)*
Entré en el colegio/la universidad en ...	*I started school/university in (date)*
Estudié/Hice ...	*I studied/did (career)*
Trabajé como (*position*) en (*place*).	*I worked as ... in ...*

Talking about other people's lives

Nació en España/ Gran Bretaña.	*He/she was born in Spain/ Great Britain.*
Estudió en ...	*He/she studied in (place)*
Trabajó como ... en ...	*He/she worked as (occupation) in (place).*

Saying how long you have been doing something

¿Cuánto tiempo llevas jugando al tenis/estudiando español?	*How long have you been playing tennis/studying Spanish?*
(Llevo) un año (jugando al tenis/estudiando español).	*(I've been playing tennis/ studying Spanish) for a year.*

Grammar

1 Meses y fechas (*months and dates*)

Months, like the days of the week, are not written with capital letters in Spanish.

enero	*January*	mayo	*May*	se(p)tiembre	*September*
febrero	*February*	junio	*June*	octubre	*October*
marzo	*March*	julio	*July*	noviembre	*November*
abril	*April*	agosto	*August*	diciembre	*December*

To say 'in', as 'in January', use **en**:

> ¿En qué mes naciste?   *In which month were you born?*
> Nací en enero.   *I was born in January.*
> En marzo de 1988.   *In March 1988.*

To say 'on', as in 'on the 25th', use **el**:

> El 25 de julio.   *On July 25.*
> El 30 de septiembre de 1991. *On 30 September 1991.*

2 Preterite tense: irregular and spelling-changing verbs

Irse *to leave, to go*, is irregular and is conjugated like **ir** *to go* (see Unit 15).

> Me fui a Cuenca.   *I left for Cuenca.*
> ¿Cuándo se fue?   *When did you/he/she leave (go)?*

Some verbs undergo a spelling change in the first person singular of the preterite tense so that the pronunciation of the stem may remain the same:

• Verbs ending in **-gar** change 'g' to **gu** before 'e', e.g. **llegar** *to arrive*

> Lle**gu**é ayer.   *I arrived yesterday.*

• Verbs ending in **-car** change 'c' to **que** before 'e', e.g. **dedicarse a** *to devote oneself to, to do*

> Me dedi**qu**é al tenis.   *I devoted myself to tennis.*

• Verbs ending in **-zar** change 'z' to **c** before 'e', e.g. **empezar** *to begin*, **realizar** *to do, to carry out*

> Empe**c**é el colegio en 1979.   *I started school in 1979.*

3 ¿Cuánto tiempo llevas ...?
(How long have you been ...?)

To ask and say how long someone has been doing something use the *present tense* of **llevar**, followed by a *time phrase* and the *-ando or -iendo form of the verb*, equivalent to -ing in English (see Unit 14).

| ¿Cuánto tiempo llevas trabajando/viviendo allí? | *How long have you been working/living there?* |
| Llevo dos años (trabajando/ viviendo) allí. | *I've been (working/living) there for two years.* |

Compare this with the alternative expression **hace** + *time phrase* + **que** + *present tense*, which you learned in Unit 10.

Practice

1 La historia de mi vida

Isabel Blanco, a journalist, tells her life-story. Can you match the pictures with the sentences?

a Me casé con Antonio en 1994.

b Entré en la universidad a la edad de 18 años.

c Nací en Aranjuez el 7 de mayo de 1966.

d Terminé la carrera a los 23.

e Empecé el colegio a los 6 años.

f Empecé a trabajar como periodista en enero de 1990.

---

empecé (from **empezar**)   *I started*

2 Con relación a su anuncio …

Sebastián, an unemployed hotel receptionist, wrote the following letter in reply to a job advertisement. Complete the letter by changing the infinitives in brackets into the right form of the preterite tense.

Muy señor mío:

Con relación a su anuncio en el periódico *El Mundo*, estoy interesado en el puesto de jefe de recepción.

Me llamo Sebastián García Robles e hice estudios de hostelería en el Instituto Mediterráneo de Málaga, los que (terminar) en 1987. Entre 1988 y 1994 (trabajar) como recepcionista en el Hotel Andaluz de Marbella. En junio de 1995 (irse) a Alicante e (ingresar) en el grupo hotelero Iberotur. (Desempeñar) el puesto de recepcionista en el Hotel San Jaime, cargo que (ocupar) hasta diciembre de 1996, fecha en que (perder) mi empleo por reducción de plantilla …

la reducción de plantilla	*reduction in the workforce*
desempeñar	*to hold (job)*
ingresar	*to join*

i En cartas formales o comerciales, como la anterior, se utiliza la expresión **Muy señor mío**, *Dear Sir*, para dirigirse a un hombre. Si la carta está dirigida a una mujer puedes utilizar la expresión **Distinguida señora** o **Estimada señora**, *Dear Madam*. La fórmula más común para terminar una carta formal es **Atentamente** o **Muy atentamente**, *Yours sincerely*.

dirigirse	*to address*

3 Estudié empresariales

Read this résumé of Maribel Domínguez's career.

3.1 How would she answer the following questions about her professional background?

a ¿Cuántos años trabajó usted en el departamento de producción?

b ¿En qué año ingresó en Expometal?

c ¿En qué año ascendió a subdirectora comercial?

Me llamo Maribel Domínguez Alvarez y ocupo el cargo de directora comercial. Estudié empresariales en la Universidad de Vizcaya, y luego de terminar mis estudios trabajé durante cuatro años como ayudante de producción en Electrodomésticos Bilbao. Ingresé en Expometal en 1989 como encargada del área de maquinaria industrial, en el departamento de marketing. Al año siguiente ascendí a subdirectora comercial, y dos años más tarde fui nombrada directora.

3.2 Now read the résumé again and say how the following is expressed:

a Soy directora comercial.

b Hice empresariales.

c después de terminar

d dos años después

el cargo	*post*	**el encargado**	*person in charge*
empresariales	*business studies*	**la maquinaria**	*machinery*
el/la ayudante	*assistant*	**ascender**	*to be promoted*

4 Una entrevista

Your company needs a Spanish-speaking person and you've been asked to conduct an interview in Spanish with one of the applicants. What questions would you ask to get these replies? Use the formal form.

a Nací en Costa Rica.

b Nací el 25 de octubre de 1970.

c Hice mis estudios universitarios en San José.

d Estudié traducción e interpretación.

e Terminé mis estudios en junio de 1992.

f Actualmente trabajo como traductor en un organismo internacional.

5 ¿Quién es?

Here's the life story of a famous Spanish actor.

5.1 Read the information and try guessing who he is. You will find the answer in the **Key to the activities**. Note the irregular preterite form **hubo** *there was/were*, from **haber** (see **hay** *there is/are*, in Unit 4).

- Nació en Málaga en 1961.
- Filmó 5 películas con Pedro Almodóvar, que lo hicieron famoso internacionalmente.
- Hollywood lo adoptó como el nuevo 'Latin lover' y le asignó papeles en películas como *Philadelphia*, *La casa de los espíritus*, y *Los reyes del mambo*.
- No siempre tuvo éxito. Hubo algunos fracasos, como *Loco de amor*, *Asesinos*, y *Nunca hables con extraños*.
- Se casó con la actriz Melanie Griffith y en septiembre de 1996 tuvieron su primer hijo.
- El director de cine Alan Parker lo seleccionó para el papel del narrador en *Evita*, película que se estrenó en 1997.

5.2 Now list all the preterite forms in the article with their corresponding infinitive.

▶ **6 Un diseñador industrial**

You have been asked to write about the life and career of Nicolás Rivas, a Mexican industrial designer. Listen to his talk and fill in the gaps with the missing dates and expressions of time:

a Nicolás Rivas nació en Guadalajara, México, el _____ .
b Empezó la carrera de diseño industrial en _____ .
c Terminó sus estudios en _____ .
d Trabajó como diseñador industrial en Metromex desde _____ hasta _____ .
e En _____ de ese mismo año, fue nombrado gerente de diseño en Metalsa.
f _____ conoció a Margarita, su primera mujer.
g Se casaron en Mérida el _____ .
h Tuvieron un hijo en _____ .
i Se divorciaron _____ .

▶ **7 ¿Cuánto tiempo llevas …?**

How would you ask Soledad how long she has been doing each of the following, and how would she reply? First, match the drawings with the phrases on the following page, then ask and answer for her using the construction with **llevar** in the familiar form. Do this before you listen to the recording.

a vivir en Londres: 2 años
b estudiar inglés: 1 año y medio
c hacer atletismo: 3 años
d trabajar como enfermera: 1 año

8 Ahora tú

You are preparing for a job interview in Spanish. Reply to the following questions:

a ¿Cómo se llama Vd.?
b ¿Dónde nació?
c ¿En qué fecha nació?
d ¿Dónde hizo sus estudios secundarios/universitarios?
e ¿Cuándo los empezó/terminó?
f ¿Qué otros estudios tiene?
g ¿A qué se dedica Vd. actualmente?
h ¿Cuánto tiempo lleva estudiando/trabajando allí?
i ¿Dónde estudió/trabajó anteriormente?
j ¿Cuánto tiempo estuvo allí?

17

era muy
pequeña

it was very small

In this unit you will learn
- how to ask and give reasons
- how to say what a place was like
- how to say what someone was like

▶ 1 ¿Por qué?

Gonzalo tells Ana María why he changed jobs. Two key expressions in this dialogue are **¿por qué?** *why?* and **porque** *because.*

1.1 Listen to the dialogue several times and say

a Why Gonzalo changed jobs.
b How he describes his former colleagues.
c How he describes his boss.

Ana María	¿Por qué cambiaste de trabajo?
Gonzalo	Porque la empresa donde estaba era muy pequeña, no había muchas posibilidades de ascenso y el sueldo no era muy bueno.
Ana María	Y el ambiente de trabajo, ¿qué tal era?
Gonzalo	Mis compañeros de trabajo eran muy simpáticos, pero mi jefe tenía un carácter muy difícil. No me sentía a gusto allí.

1.2 Now read the dialogue and find the phrases which mean approximately the following:

a la compañía no era grande
b era difícil ascender
c el salario era malo
d no estaba contento

cambiar de trabajo	*to change jobs*
el ascenso	*promotion*
sentirse a gusto	*to feel at ease*

▶ 2 ¿Por qué os mudasteis de hotel?

Pilar tells Marta about the hotel where she and her family were staying.

2.1 Listen to the conversation and say which of the two hotels below corresponds to the one in which they were staying.

2.2 Why did Pilar and her family move from their hotel? Listen again a few times and complete these sentences with the verbs used by her: **tenía, era, había, estaba.**

El hotel en que estábamos _____ un hotel de dos estrellas, y _____ lejos de la playa. No _____ piscina para los niños y no _____ aparcamiento. Además, _____ un poco caro y la comida no _____ muy buena.

Marta   ¿Por qué os mudasteis de hotel?
Pilar   Porque el hotel en que estábamos era un hotel de dos estrellas y estaba lejos de la playa. No tenía piscina para los niños y no había aparcamiento. Además, era un poco caro y la comida no era muy buena.

2.3 Now read the dialogue several times, then cover Pilar's answer and play her part in the conversation.

How do you say it?

Asking and giving reasons

¿Por qué cambiaste de trabajo/os mudasteis?   *Why did you change jobs/move?*

Porque el sueldo no era muy bueno/estaba muy lejos de la playa.   *Because the salary was not very good/it was very far from the beach.*

Asking what something or someone was like

¿Qué tal/Cómo era?   *What was it/he/she like?*

Saying what a place was like

Era caro y no había piscina. *It was expensive and there was no swimming pool.*

Saying what someone was like

Eran muy simpáticos. *They were very nice.*
Tenía un carácter muy difícil. *He/she had a very difficult character.*

Grammar

1 Past description: the imperfect tense

a Uses

- To describe something or someone you knew in the past you need the *imperfect* tense.

- Unlike the preterite tense (Units 15 and 16), the imperfect cannot be used to indicate a definite and completed action in the past. In descriptive language in general, for instance **La empresa era pequeña**, *The company was small*, there is no concern for time, except to show that a past experience is being referred to.

- Compare this with **¿Por qué cambiaste de trabajo?** *Why did you change jobs?* in which **cambiaste** refers to an action which occurred at some specific point in the past.

- The imperfect often occurs in conjunction with the preterite, as a kind of framework or context for the actions that took place. Note for example:

Sandra tenía (*imperfect*) veinte   *Sandra was twenty years old*
años cuando se casó (*preterite*).   *when she got married.*

b Formation

There are two sets of endings for the imperfect tense, one for **-ar** verbs and another one for **-er** and **-ir** verbs.

estar *to be*	**tener** *to have*	**sentirse** *to feel*
est**aba**	ten**ía**	me sent**ía**
est**abas**	ten**ías**	te sent**ías**
est**aba**	ten**ía**	se sent**ía**
est**ábamos**	ten**íamos**	nos sent**íamos**
est**abais**	ten**íais**	os sent**íais**
est**aban**	ten**ían**	se sent**ían**

Note that the first person singular, e.g. **yo estaba** *I was*, is the same as the third person, **usted/él/ella estaba** *you (formal)/he/she/it was*.

Note also the written accents on **estábamos** and in all forms of -er and -ir verbs, e.g. **tenía**.

Estaba a media hora de allí.	*It was half an hour from there.*
El hotel no tenía sauna.	*The hotel didn't have a sauna.*
¿Cómo te sentías allí?	*How did you feel there?*

2 Irregular verbs

There are only three verbs which are irregular in the imperfect: **ser** *to be*, **ver** *to see*, and **ir** *to go*. The last two will be covered in Unit 18.

ser *to be*	
era	éramos
eras	erais
era	eran

Mi ex marido era muy antipático.	*My former husband was very unpleasant.*
No éramos felices.	*We were not happy.*

3 Time phrases associated with the imperfect tense

The following are the most common expressions of time associated with this tense:

antes	*before*
entonces	*at that time*
en esa/aquella epoca	*at that time*
en esos/aquellos años	*in those years*
de pequeño/joven *or*	
cuando era pequeño/joven	*when I was young*

Note the use of **aquella** *that* (fem.), **aquellos** *those* (masc.), used for reference to a more distant past.

Practice

1 ¿Sabes la razón?

Match each of the following questions with an appropriate answer. Use **por qué** and **porque,** as appropriate.

a ¿ _____ dejaste la empresa?
b ¿ _____ decidiste estudiar español?
c ¿ _____ vendió Vd. su ordenador/computador(a) (L.Am.)?
d ¿ _____ no fueron a Cuba de vacaciones?
e ¿ _____ se mudaron de casa?
f ¿ _____ no viniste en el coche?

1 _____ era muy caro.
2 _____ tenía una avería.
3 _____ el sueldo era muy bajo.
4 _____ la que tenían era muy pequeña.
5 _____ mi novio es colombiano.
6 _____ necesitaba uno con más memoria.

2 El piso de Marta

Here is a plan of the house where Marta used to live. Can you describe it to someone else?

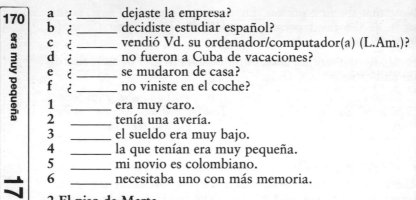

a ¿Cuántas plantas tenía?
b ¿Cuántos dormitorios tenía?
c ¿Cuántos baños había?
d ¿En qué planta estaban el comedor y el baño?
e ¿Dónde estaban la cocina y los dormitorios?

3 Ahora tú

A Spanish-speaking friend asks you about the place where you used to live:

a ¿Dónde estaba tu casa/piso/apartamento?
b ¿Era grande o pequeño/a?
c ¿Cuántos dormitorios tenía?
d ¿Tenía jardín?
e ¿Qué tal eran el barrio y tus vecinos?
f ¿Te gustaba vivir allí?, ¿por qué?

▶ 4 Así era

How would you ask Gonzalo about the company where he used to work? And how would he reply? Fill in the gaps in the questions with an appropriate verb from the list in the imperfect tense, then reply using the information below.

---

tener   haber   llamarse   ser   estar

---

a ¿Cómo _____ la empresa?
b ¿Dónde _____ ?
c ¿Qué número de teléfono _____ ?
d ¿Quién _____ el director gerente?
e ¿Cuántos empleados _____ en la empresa?

Nombre de la empresa:	Computel S.A.
Dirección:	Calle León, 15, 7°, 28003 Madrid
Teléfono:	374 0962
Director gerente:	Alfonso García Méndez
Plantilla:	150

S.A. (Sociedad Anónima)	*public limited company*
la plantilla	*staff*

5 Ahora tú

In the course of a job interview you are asked to describe a place where you used to work or study. Use the questions below to prepare a brief talk and add other information if you wish:

a ¿Cómo se llamaba el lugar donde trabajabas/estudiabas?
b ¿Dónde estaba?
c ¿Cómo era?
d ¿Cómo te sentías allí?

6 Palabra por palabra

6.1 Can you find the opposites of the words listed on the next page? They are all words used for describing people's character and personality. You can refer to the **Vocabulary** list at the back of the book and check the answers in the **Key to the activities**.

a divertido	f cortés	k trabajador
b triste	g optimista	l irresponsable
c audaz	h simpático	m inmaduro
d tonto	i fuerte	n inseguro
e modesto	j desagradable	

6.2 Can you spot the opposites in this word square? One of them has been marked for you. The completed word square is at the end of the unit.

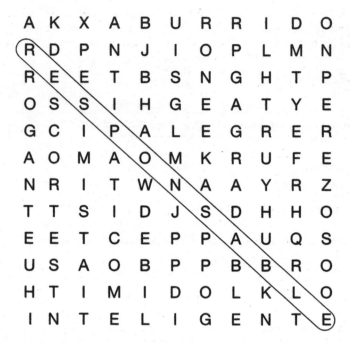

▶ **7 ¿Qué tal tu jefe?**

Carmen, a secretary, describes her former and her present boss to her friend José. Listen to the conversation several times and complete the sentences below with the character description of each person.

a Mi jefe actual es _____ y tiene _____
b Mi jefe anterior era _____ y tenía _____

---

guapo *good-looking*   **feo** *ugly*

8 Ahora tú

How would you describe the character of people you knew? Try using some of the words from Activity 6.

a un/a profesor/a o un/a jefe/a
b compañeros/as de clase/trabajo
c otra/s persona/s (un/a amigo/a, pariente/a, vecino/a)

9 La población española

The following extract looks at Spanish population figures since the end of the civil war (1936–39), and makes some interesting predictions for the twenty-first century. Read the text and, as you do so, answer the following questions:

a What was the Spanish population in 1940?
b What trend can you see if you compare population figures for 1984 and 1991?
c What prediction is made with regard to certain sectors of the population in the twenty-first century?

En 1940, al terminar la guerra civil española, que causó medio millón de muertos y medio millón de exiliados, los españoles eran 26.188.000. En 1984, la población de España ascendía a 39.294.000, y en 1991 había 38.872.000.

Se estima que, al comenzar el siglo XXI, habrá menos niños y niñas y más viejos, lo que puede constituir un serio problema para el sistema del bienestar social.

muertos	*dead*	**exiliados**	*exiled*
habrá	*there will be*	**el bienestar social**	*social welfare*

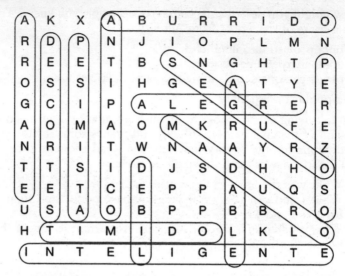

Answer to Activity 6

A	K	X	A	B	U	R	R	I	D	O
R	D	P	N	J	I	O	P	L	M	N
R	E	E	T	B	S	N	G	H	T	P
O	S	S	I	H	G	E	A	T	Y	E
G	C	I	P	A	L	E	G	R	E	R
A	O	M	A	O	M	K	R	U	F	E
N	R	I	T	W	N	A	A	Y	R	Z
T	T	S	I	D	J	S	D	H	H	O
E	E	T	C	E	P	P	A	U	Q	S
U	S	A	O	B	P	P	B	B	R	O
H	T	I	M	I	D	O	L	K	L	O
I	N	T	E	L	I	G	E	N	T	E

18

¿qué hacías allí?

what were you doing there?

In this unit you will learn
- how to say where you used to live
- how to say what work you used to do
- how to say how you used to spend your time

▶ 1 ¿Dónde vivías antes?

Rodolfo asks Elena about her life before arriving in Barcelona.

1.1 Listen to the conversation several times, each time focusing attention on a different point.

a Where did Elena live before arriving in Barcelona?
b Why did she like living there?
c What did Elena and her friends use to do in the evenings? And at weekends?
d What did she do there?

Rodolfo	¿Dónde vivías antes de llegar a Barcelona?
Elena	Vivía en Almería. Estuve allí varios años.
Rodolfo	¿Te gustaba?
Elena	Sí, me encantaba. Tenía un buen trabajo y conocía muchísima gente. Tenía un grupo de amigos a los que veía prácticamente todos los días. Nos reuníamos en algún café por la noche, a veces salíamos a cenar, los fines de semana íbamos al cine o a bailar. Lo pasábamos muy bien. Los echo mucho de menos.
Rodolfo	¿Qué hacías allí?
Elena	Era profesora. Trabajaba en un instituto.

los fines de semana
iba a bailar

1.2 Now read the dialogue and list all forms of the imperfect tense with the corresponding infinitive, e.g. **íbamos: ir**.

reunirse	*to get together*
pasarlo bien	*to have a good time*
echar de menos	*to miss*
el instituto	*secondary school (Spain)*

How do you say it?

Asking people where they used to live, and responding

¿Dónde vivías?   *Where did you live?*
Vivía en …   *I used to live in …*

Asking people what work they used to do, and responding

¿Qué hacías? ¿A qué te
dedicabas?
What (work) did you do?

Era profesora.
I was a teacher.

Trabajaba en ...
I used to work in ...

Saying how you and others used to spend the time

Salía/Salíamos a cenar, iba/
íbamos al cine.
*I/We used to go out for
dinner/go to the cinema.*

Grammar

1 Saying what you used to do or were doing: Imperfect tense

To refer to a state or action in progress over an unspecified period in the past, you need the *imperfect* tense (see Unit 17):

En aquel tiempo ella vivía en
España.
*At that time she lived/used
to live/was living in Spain.*

(Yo) tenía un buen trabajo.
I had a good job.

Los fines de semana íbamos
a bailar.
*At weekends we used to go
dancing.*

If a definite period of time is mentioned, even when the action took place over a long period, you need the *preterite* tense (see Units 15 and 16) and not the imperfect:

Estuve allí varios años.
I was there for several years.

El fin de semana pasado
fuimos a un partido de
fútbol.
*Last weekend we went to a
football match.*

2 Irregular verbs

Other than **ser** (see Unit 17), only **ir** *to go*, and **ver** *to see*, are irregular in the imperfect tense. Note that the endings for **ver** are the same as those of regular -er and -ir verbs.

ir	iba	ibas	iba	íbamos	ibais	iban
ver	veía	veías	veía	veíamos	veíais	veían

Sara iba a España todos los
veranos.
*Sara used to go to Spain every
summer.*

Por la tarde veíamos la
televisión.
*In the evenings we used to
watch television.*

3 Preposition + infinitive

Note that in the phrase **antes de llegar** *before arriving*, Spanish uses the infinitive, whereas English uses the -ing form.

Here are two more examples:

después de salir	*after going out*
luego de cenar	*after having dinner*

Practice

1 ¿Qué hacía Pablo?

Pablo remembers his childhood years. How would he tell someone what he used to do? Match the drawings with the phrases below, and put the verbs in the right form of the imperfect tense.

a	(dormir) la siesta	**d**	(hacer) los deberes
b	(jugar) con mi pelota	**e**	(levantarse) a las 8.00
c	(ir) a la escuela	**f**	(comer) con mi madre

▶ **2 Cuando tenía 18 años …**

Elvira, from Jaén, tells a friend about her life when she was eighteen. Put the infinitives in the right form of the imperfect tense.

Cuando (yo) tenía dieciocho años ...

(Vivir) con mis padres en Jaén.
(Trabajar) como dependienta en un supermercado.
(Ir) al trabajo en bicicleta.
(Empezar) a las 9.00 y (salir) a las 7.00.
(Ganar) 40.000 pesetas mensuales.
(Estar) soltera.
(Tener) un novio que (llamarse) Manuel.
Manuel y yo (verse) por la tarde, (dar) largos paseos y (hablar) de amor.

| **verse** *to meet* | **el amor** *love* |

3 El rey cuenta su vida

King Juan Carlos of Spain was born in Rome and brought up in Switzerland. In an interview given to a Spanish magazine, he remembers his childhood, when he was only five and lived in Switzerland. Read the text and answer the following questions:

a What did he use to do on Thursdays?
b Who did he meet from time to time?
c Where did they use to meet sometimes?
d How did he feel about the place where they used to meet?

El rey cuenta su vida

En Suiza iba los jueves a ver a mi abuela a Lausanne y me reunía de vez en cuando con mis primos. A veces nos encontrábamos en el hotel Royal. Este hotel era un poco como mi casa, y ahora todavía sigue teniendo para mi un encanto especial, con aquellos salones de lujo anticuado y aquellos camareros que conocimos cuando éramos pequeños.

| **encontrarse** *to meet* | **como** *like* |
| **el encanto** *charm* | **el lujo** *luxury* |

4 Recuerdos de la infancia

Ángeles Mastretta, a Mexican writer and author of *Mal de amores*, among other novels, tells about her childhood and her parents.

4.1 Read the interview and say whether the statements which follow are true or false (**verdadero o falso**).

a Los padres de Ángeles Mastretta eran muy modernos.
b Angeles tiene buenos recuerdos de su infancia.
c En Italia, el padre de Ángeles se dedicaba a vender coches.

– ¿Cómo eran tus padres?
– Ahora diría que conservadores. Recuerdo una infancia feliz. Mis padres permitían cosas que otros padres no permitían. Con naturalidad dormíamos en el campo, paseábamos en bicicleta. Como Josefa y Diego en *Mal de amores*, ellos consideraban que la humanidad era buena. Creo que se equivocaban, pero crecí con esa certeza.
– ¿A qué se dedicaba tu padre?
– Luego de estudiar ingeniería textil en Italia, mi padre volvió a Puebla (México) y, al no conseguir trabajo en eso, vendía autos. Era muy mal comerciante.

4.2 Read the interview again and find the expressions which mean the following:

a tradicionales   c montábamos
b niñez   d no tenían razón

equivocarse	*to be wrong*	**la certeza**	*certainly*
crecer	*to grow up*	**el/la comerciante**	*dealer*
diría	*I would say*	**el auto**	*car* (L.Am.)

5 Ahora tú

¿Dónde vivías cuando eras pequeño/a? ¿Qué hacía tu padre? ¿Y tu madre? ¿Quién te llevaba a la escuela? ¿Te gustaba ir a la escuela? ¿Dónde pasabas tus vacaciones? ¿Qué hacías allí?

¿quién?	*who*	**la escuela**	*school*

▶ 6 ¿A qué se dedicaban?

Begoña and Esteban, from Spain, and Víctor, from Mexico, talk about their previous and present jobs. Can you say what they used to do and what they do now? Listen and fill in the gaps with the appropriate names and change the verbs into the right tense, the present or the imperfect.

_____ a   (Ser) intérprete. (Trabajar) por su cuenta.
_____ b   (Ser) azafata. (Trabajar) en una línea aérea.
_____ c   (Trabajar) en un restaurante. (Ser) camarero.
_____ d   (Estar) sin trabajo.
_____ e   (Ser) estudiante. (Estudiar) idiomas.
_____ f   (Ser) programador. (Trabajar) en una compañía especializada en programación.

por mi/su cuenta	*freelance*
la línea aérea	*airline*
la programación	*programming*

7 ¿Qué hacían Delia y Pepe?

Delia and Pepe had similar duties in the company where they both worked. Can you say what they were? Choose from the phrases in the box below and write an appropriate sentence under each drawing indicating what they used to do, e.g. **asistir a reuniones – Asistían a reuniones.**

> mandar faxes, servir café a los clientes,
> contestar el teléfono, trabajar en el ordenador,
> leer la correspondencia, atender al público

8 Asistíamos a reuniones

How would Delia and Pepe tell someone else what they used to do? Begin like this: **Asistíamos a reuniones …**

9 Una entrevista

You are taking part in an interview with a Spanish-speaking person. How would you ask him/her the following?

a what work he/she did before
b where he/she used to work
c how much he/she earned
d how many weeks holiday a year he/she had

10 Ahora tú

a ¿A qué te dedicabas antes?, ¿estudiabas o trabajabas?
b ¿Dónde estudiabas/trabajabas?
c ¿A qué te dedicas ahora?
d ¿Dónde estudias/trabajas?

19

ha sido una equivocación

In this unit you will learn
- how to pass on a message
- how to make complaints
- how to claim lost property
- how to say what you have done

▶ 1 Ha llamado dos veces

Ricardo passes on some messages to Marta, his boss.

1.1 Listen to the conversation and, as you do so, try completing these sentences. Note these new verb forms: **ha llamado** *she/he has called*, **ha hecho** *he/she has made*, **han reservado** *they have booked*.

a   Isabel ha llamado dos veces para _____ .
b   Ha hecho una reserva para _____ .
c   El hotel Cuernavaca ha reservado una habitación para _____ .

Marta	¿Hay algún recado para mí, Ricardo?
Ricardo	Sí, Isabel, de Ibertour, la ha llamado dos veces para confirmar el vuelo a México. Ha hecho una reserva para el sábado 2 de septiembre.
Marta	Estupendo.
Ricardo	También me ha dicho que ha recibido un fax del hotel Cuernavaca y que le han reservado una habitación para el día 3.

1.2 Now read the dialogue and say what expressions have been used to say the following:

a She has told me.   b She has received a fax.

---

dos veces *twice*

▶ 2 He pedido una habitación exterior

Marta complains to the hotel receptionist in Mexico City about the room she's been given.

2.1 Listen to the dialogue and say whether the statements below are true or false (**verdadero o falso**). Note the expression **dar a** *to look out on*.

a   La habitación doscientos veinte da a la calle.
b   La habitación trescientos cincuenta es interior.
c   El aire acondicionado de la habitación no funciona.

Marta	Buenos días.
Recepcionista	Buenos días, señora.
Marta	Mire, yo he pedido una habitación exterior y ustedes me han dado una interior. Además, el aire acondicionado no funciona.

Recepcionista	Perdone, pero ha sido una equivocación. ¿Qué número de habitación tiene usted?
Marta	Estoy en la habitación doscientos veinte.
Recepcionista	Puedo darle la trescientos cincuenta, que está libre. Ésa da a la calle.
Marta	Muy bien, gracias.

2.2 Now read the dialogue and find the right form of the verb for the infinitives in brackets:

a He (pedir) _____   **c** Ha (ser) _____
b Me han (dar) _____

pedir	*to ask for*	**dar**	*to give*

i Complaining about services in a foreign country may not be an easy task for someone who does not know the language well, and understanding the bureaucratic procedures for asserting your rights as a consumer may be even more daunting. In Spain, there are certain established procedures for filing complaints, which are meant to help consumers. What are these? Read the text and find out.

Tus derechos

En España, si no estás conforme con el servicio que has recibido en un hotel, restaurante u otro establecimiento comercial, tienes tres alternativas: a) Puedes presentar tu **queja** *complaint*, directamente a la persona encargada, por ejemplo, el gerente del hotel. b) Puedes pedir una **hoja de reclamación** *a complaints form (see below)*, y expresar tu queja **por escrito** *in writing*. Todos los establecimientos que prestan servicios al público tienen la obligación de tenerla y deben responder a tu queja en un plazo de 10 días. c) Si no lo hacen o no estás conforme con la respuesta, puedes ir a la Oficina Municipal de Información al Consumidor (OMIC), que se ocupará de tu caso.

los derechos	*rights*	**el consumidor**	*consumer*
estar conforme	*to be happy*	**se ocupará de**	*it will see to*
encargado/a	*in charge*		

2.3 Now look at the complaints form on the next page. What is this person complaining about?

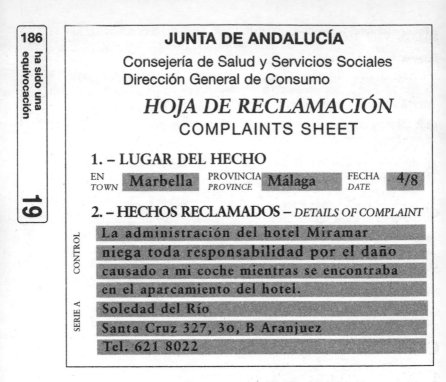

JUNTA DE ANDALUCÍA

Consejería de Salud y Servicios Sociales
Dirección General de Consumo

HOJA DE RECLAMACIÓN
COMPLAINTS SHEET

1. – LUGAR DEL HECHO

EN *TOWN* **Marbella**   PROVINCIA *PROVINCE* **Málaga**   FECHA *DATE* **4/8**

2. – HECHOS RECLAMADOS – *DETAILS OF COMPLAINT*

CONTROL

La administración del hotel Miramar
niega toda responsabilidad por el daño
causado a mi coche mientras se encontraba
en el aparcamiento del hotel.

SERIE A

Soledad del Río

Santa Cruz 327, 3o, B Aranjuez

Tel. 621 8022

▶ 3 He olvidado mi paraguas

Marta has left her umbrella in a restaurant and she goes back to claim it.

3.1 Listen and find out how she describes her umbrella.

Marta	Perdone, esta tarde he comido aquí con unos amigos y he olvidado mi paraguas. Es un paraguas azul, de cuadros.
Camarero	¿Es éste?
Marta	Sí, es ése. Muchísimas gracias.
Camarero	De nada, señora.

3.2 Now read the dialogue and say how the following is expressed

a I had lunch here.   **b** I forgot my umbrella.

---

olvidar   *to forget*

How do you say it?

Passing on a message

¿Hay algún recado para mí?
Isabel ha llamado/hecho la
  reserva/recibido un fax.

Is there a message for me?
Isabel has called/made the
  reservation/received a fax.

Making complaints

Yo he pedido …
  y Vds. me han dado …
El aire acondicionado/la
  calefacción no funciona.

I have asked for …
  and you have given me …
The air conditioning/
  heating doesn't work.

Claiming lost property

He olvidado/dejado mi
  paraguas/una chaqueta.

I forgot/left my umbrella/
  a jacket.

Saying what you have done

He comido/estado aquí.

I have eaten/been here.

Grammar

1 Talking about the recent past

a The perfect tense

To ask and answer questions about the recent past, e.g. 'Has he phoned?' and to talk about past events which have taken place over a period of time that has not yet ended, e.g. 'He has not phoned yet', you need the *perfect* tense.

b Formation

The perfect tense is formed with the *present tense* of **haber** *to have*, and a *past participle*, which is that part of the verb which in English usually ends in '-ed'. In Spanish, the endings are

- **-ado** for **-ar** verbs, e.g. **llamar**, llam**ado**: *called*
- **-ido** for **-er** and **-ir** verbs, e.g. **recibir**, recib**ido**: *received*

In Spanish, as in English, there are some irregular forms, e.g. **hecho**, *done*. A list of the most common ones is given in 2 below.

llamar *to call*		ser *to be*		recibir *to receive*	
he	llamado	he	sido	he	recibido
has	llamado	has	sido	has	recibido
ha	llamado	ha	sido	ha	recibido
hemos	llamado	hemos	sido	hemos	recibido
habéis	llamado	habéis	sido	habéis	recibido
han	llamado	han	sido	han	recibido

c Notes on usage

Note that when reference is to the *recent* past, British English normally uses the preterite tense instead of the perfect tense.

Carlos ha llamado hoy.	*Carlos phoned today.*
Esta mañana he recibido un fax de Antonio.	*I received a fax from Antonio this morning.*

In this context, Latin Americans tend to use the preterite (see Units 15 and 16) instead of the perfect tense.

If reference is to past events which have taken place over a period of time which has not yet ended, both Spanish and English use the perfect tense:

Isabel ha llamado dos veces.	*Isabel has phoned twice (and she may phone again).*
He recibido dos cartas esta semana.	*I have received two letters this week.*

Latin American usage in this context varies, with some countries still showing preference for the preterite tense.

2 Irregular past participles

The most common irregular past participles are:

abrir	abierto (*open*)	**poner**	puesto (*put*)
decir	dicho (*said*)	**romper**	roto (*broken*)
escribir	escrito (*written*)	**ver**	visto (*seen*)
hacer	hecho (*done, made*)	**volver**	vuelto (*come back*)

¿Qué ha dicho?	*What did he/she say?*
Todavía no lo hemos hecho.	*We haven't done it yet.*

3 Time phrases associated with the perfect tense

hoy	*today*
esta mañana	*this morning*
esta semana/este mes/año	*this week/month/year*
alguna vez	*ever*
nunca	*never*
ya	*already*
todavía/aún	*yet*

¿Has estado alguna vez allí?   *Have you ever been there?*
No he visitado nunca ese sitio. *I've never visited that place.*
Ya he visto esa película.   *I've already seen that film.*
Todavía/aún no han llegado. *They haven't arrived yet.*

Practice

▶ 1 Un recado

Your boss does business with Spain. On your answerphone this morning you find a message for him in Spanish. Listen, and make a note of it in English and pass it on.

encontrar	*to find*	**aplazar**	*to put off*

2 Una queja

An angry customer wrote a letter of complaint to the manager of an airline that lost his luggage. Complete the letter by changing the infinitives in brackets into the appropriate form of the perfect tense. One of them has been done for you.

Muy señor mío:

Por razones de trabajo viajo regularmente entre Madrid y Canarias. En el último viaje que realicé, el 24 de abril, la línea aérea que usted representa perdió mi equipaje. Hice el reclamo inmediatamente en el aeropuerto, pero han pasado tres semanas y mi maleta no (aparecer). (Yo) (escribir) dos cartas y (llamar) en varias oportunidades a la persona

encargada, pero no (tener) ninguna respuesta
satisfactoria. Tampoco (recibir) ninguna indemnización. Este
hecho me (causar) serios problemas, ya que la maleta
contenía material indispensable para mi trabajo …

| **la indemnización** *compensation* | **el hecho** *fact* |

▶ **3 ¿De qué se quejan?**

Laura and her husband had booked a hotel room through
an agency, but on arrival they were greatly disappointed and
complained to the hotel manager. Something went wrong.

3.1 Listen to the conversation several times, and say which of the
two ads below fits in their expectations.

7 HOTEL EXCELSIOR *
Vara del Rey, 17, San Antonio,
Tel.: 34 01 85

Situado en pleno centro de San
Antonio a escasos minutos de la
playa, hotel de ambiente y
explotación familiar, todas sus
habitaciones cuentan con baño
o ducha. Asimismo dispone de
salón social y de televisión, al
igual que de bar y restaurante.

35 HOTEL CONDES **
Zona Comercial Carabela, Puerto
de Alcudia, Tel.: 54 54 92

Situado a 100 mt. de la orilla del mar,
en un lugar perfecto donde podrá
practicar toda clase de deportes
acuáticos. Dispone de una gran piscina
y solarium, salón de T.V y vídeo, bares
en el interior y en la terraza y zona
especial para niños entre los jardines.
Las habitaciones disponen todas de
baño completo y terraza con vistas
al mar.

3.2 Listen again a few times and say whether the following
statements are true or false (**verdadero o falso**).

a   El recepcionista les ha dado una habitación con vistas a un
    aparcamiento.
b   Laura y su marido han estado dos veces en esa ciudad.
c   Es la segunda vez que les pasa algo así.

| **¡Es el colmo!** | *This is the last straw!* |
| **¡Esto es increíble!** | *This is incredible!* |

---

4 Palabra por palabra

Here are some of the things that might go wrong in your hotel room. How many of them can you guess? Look up the words you don't know.

a La calefacción, el aire acondicionado, la televisión, el grifo del agua caliente/fría … no funciona.

b El váter, el lavabo, la bañera … está atascado/a.

c Falta jabón, champú, papel higiénico.

d No hay suficientes toallas.

| **faltar** | *to be lacking, not to be enough* |
| **atascado/a** | *blocked* |

5 Ahora tú

It's your first day in your hotel room and you call reception to complain about some of the facilities in the room. How would you say the following?

a The heating doesn't work.

b The washbasin is blocked.

c There is no soap in the bathroom.

d I need more blankets on my bed.

| **la manta** | *blanket* (Spain) | **la cama** | *bed* |

6 Una carta a un periódico

Sonia wrote to a newspaper editor to complain about something quite different. What is her problem? Read and find out.

No encuentro trabajo por ser mujer

■ Querría hacer constar mi protesta: soy delineante de edificios y obras, sobradamente preparada y con 21 años; cansada de pedir trabajo inútilmente, he llegado a la conclusión de que por el hecho de ser mujer, cosa que implica llevar nueve meses una criatura dentro, he de presentar aparte del currículum vitae un certificado médico en el que verifique que soy estéril. Quizás así me darían trabajo.

SONIA CAL REY
Cardedeu

querría	*I would like*
hacer constar	*to make known*
el/la delineante	*draughtsman/woman*
sobradamente	*very well*
he de	*I have to*
me darían	*they would give me*

▶ 7 Objetos perdidos

Margarita left something behind in señor Palma's office. What did she leave and how does she describe it? Read the dialogue or listen to the recording and find out.

Margarita   Perdone, he estado en el despacho del señor Palma esta mañana y he dejado una cartera con unos documentos. Es una cartera negra, de piel. ¿Puede decirme si la han encontrado? Es muy importante.

Recepcionista   Sí, señora. Su cartera está aquí en la recepción.

8 Ahora tú

You were in a bar with a friend at midday, and after leaving the place you realized that you had left something behind. Choose from the following and tell the waiter what you have lost, and ask whether he has found it.

9 ¿Ha llamado usted al director del banco?

You have a busy day at the office today and your Spanish boss is checking your progress. Here is a list of the things you needed to do, with a tick for those you have already done. How would your boss ask whether you have done each of the following? And how would you reply? Follow the examples.

Ejemplos:

- ¿Ha llamado Vd. al director del banco?
- No, *todavía no lo he llamado.*
- ¿Ha contestado Vd. la carta de Angela Salas?
- *Sí, ya la he contestado.*

a	*Llamar al director del banco*	✗
b	*Contestar la carta de Ángela Salas*	✓
c	*Pedir hora con el doctor Prado*	✓
d	*Escribir a los distribuidores en Nueva York*	✓
e	*Hacer el pedido de material de oficina*	✗
f	*Ver a la señora Martínez*	✓
g	*Abrir la caja con las mercancías*	✗

10 Un visitante extranjero

You have been asked to look after a Spanish-speaking visitor. How would you ask him/her the following?

a whether he/she has been to your country before
b what places he/she has seen already
c what he/she has done today
d whether he/she has had lunch already

20

iremos a la playa
we'll go to the beach

In this unit you will learn
- how to say what you will do
- how to express supposition and certainty
- how to express conditions

▶ 1 Hasta el viernes

Ángel, who lives in New York, phones his friend Isabel to confirm his travel arrangements.

1.1 Listen to the dialogue several times and try answering these questions.

a ¿Adónde viaja Ángel?
b ¿Cuándo sale Ángel de Nueva York?
c ¿Cuándo y a qué hora llega a España?

1.2 Listen again and find out why Isabel is not taking her own car to the airport, and whose car she's borrowing. Note the use of ¡**hombre!** (literally *man*), used commonly in Spain for emphasis or to convey different types of emotions. In this context it translates into English as *well!*

Isabel	¿Dígame?
Ángel	Hola, Isabel. Soy Ángel.
Isabel	Hola, Ángel, ¿cómo estás?
Ángel	Bien, gracias. Mira, Isabel, mi vuelo está confirmado. Salgo de Nueva York mañana por la noche y llego a Barcelona el viernes a las siete y media de la mañana. ¿Vendrás a recogerme al aeropuerto?
Isabel	¡Hombre, por supuesto! Supongo que traerás mucho equipaje.
Ángel	Sí, bastante.
Isabel	Bueno, le pediré el coche a Rafael. El mío es demasiado pequeño.
Ángel	Vale, muchas gracias. Hasta el viernes, entonces.
Isabel	Adiós, Ángel. Que tengas buen viaje. Un beso.

Le pediré el coche a Rafael. El mío es demasiado pequeño.

1.3 Now check the meaning of the following infinitives and try matching them with the forms used in the conversation, e.g. **llegar – llego.**

a   salir   c   suponer   e   pedir
b   venir   c   traer   f   tener

recoger	to pick up
por supuesto	of course
¡que tengas buen viaje!	have a good journey!
el equipaje	luggage
pedir	to ask for
un beso	a kiss

▶ 2 Me imagino que querrás descansar

Ángel tells Isabel about his journey and they make some plans.

2.1 Listen to the conversation several times, each time focusing attention on different information.

a   How was Ángel's flight?
b   What is Isabel's immediate plan for Ángel?
c   What does she suggest they do that evening?

2.2 Listen again a few times and try completing these sentences.

a   Si _____, saldremos a cenar.
b   Si _____, iremos a la playa.

Isabel	¿Qué tal el viaje?
Ángel	Ha habido mucha turbulencia y no he dormido en toda la noche.
Isabel	Estarás muy cansado, ¿no?
Ángel	Sí, muchísimo.
Isabel	Me imagino que querrás descansar. Te llevaré a casa y podrás dormir un rato. Y esta noche, si estás bien saldremos a cenar. ¿Qué te parece?
Ángel	Estupendo. Y mañana, si hace bueno iremos a la playa. ¿Vale?
Isabel	De acuerdo. El tiempo ha estado buenísimo y seguro que mañana hará calor.

2.3 Now read the dialogue and find the sentences which mean the following:

a He pasado toda la noche sin dormir.
b Probablemente estás muy cansado.
c Supongo que quieres descansar.
d Seguramente mañana hará calor.

cansado/a	*tired*
descansar	*to rest*
imaginarse	*to imagine, to suppose*

How do you say it?

Saying what you will do

Salgo de …/Llego a … a las …	*I leave … /arrive in … at …*
Le pediré el coche …	*I will borrow his/her car.*

Expressing supposition and certainty

Estarás muy cansado, ¿no?	*You must be very tired.*
Supongo/me imagino que querrás descansar.	*I suppose/imagine you'll want to rest.*
Seguro que mañana hará calor.	*I'm sure it'll be warm tomorrow.*

Expressing conditions

Si estás bien/hace bueno, iremos a la playa.	*If you are all right/the weather is good, we'll go to the beach.*

Grammar

1 Present tense with future meaning

The present tense is often used to refer to the immediate future, especially with verbs of movement, for example **salir** to *leave*, **llegar** to *arrive*, **ir** to *go*.

Sale mañana por la noche.	*He/she is leaving tomorrow night.*
Llega pasado mañana.	*He/she arrives the day after tomorrow.*
Mañana vamos al campo.	*Tomorrow we are going to the country.*

2 The future tense

In Unit 13 you learned to talk about future plans and intentions by using expressions like **ir a** + *infinitive*, e.g. **Voy a viajar a España,** *I am going to travel to Spain,* and **pensar** + *infinitive,* e.g. **Pienso volver la próxima semana,** *I am thinking of coming back next week.* Expressions like these are far more common in Spanish than the future tense, which has other more specific uses, as you will see below.

a Formation

The future tense is formed with the *whole of the infinitive,* to which the endings are added. These are the same for **-ar, -er,** and **-ir** verbs.

llevar *to take*	**traer** *to bring*	**ir** *to go*
llevaré	traeré	iré
llevarás	traerás	irás
llevará	traerá	irá
llevaremos	traeremos	iremos
llevaréis	traeréis	iréis
llevarán	traerán	irán

Note that all forms except the first person plural have an accent.

b Uses

- To refer to actions which have not been pre-arranged:

Te enseñaré las fotos de nuestro viaje.	*I will show you the photographs of our trip.*

- To convey determination or a promise:

Te prometo que no te dejaré   *I promise I will not leave you*
  solo.   *alone.*

- To express supposition:

Supposition is normally expressed with the verbs **suponer** *to suppose*, and **imaginarse** *to imagine*, followed by **que** and the *future tense*:

Supongo que nos escribirás.   *I suppose you will write to us.*

- To express certainty:

Certainty is expressed with expressions such as **seguro que** ... and **seguramente** *surely, for sure*, **estar seguro/a de que** ..., *to be sure that* ...

Estoy seguro/a de que te   *I am sure you will like it.*
  gustará.

- To make predictions:

Estará despejado.   *It will be clear.*

- Generally, in writing, especially in a formal style, to refer to future actions and events:

Escribo para informarle que   *I am writing to inform you*
  llegaremos a Madrid a las   *that we will arrive in Madrid*
  14.00 horas.   *at 2.00 p.m.*

3 Irregular future forms

Some verbs have an irregular stem in the future tense, but the endings are the same as those of regular verbs. Here is a list of the most common.

decir	*to say*	diré ...	saber	*to know*	sabré ...
hacer	*to do, make*	haré ...	salir	*to go out*	saldré ...
poder	*can, be able to*	podré ...	tener	*to have*	tendré ...
poner	*to put*	pondré ...	venir	*to come*	vendré ...
querer	*to want*	querré ...			

Note also the impersonal form **habrá** (**hay**, in the present tense): *there will be.*

4 Si ... (If ...)

To express ideas such as 'If it's fine we'll go to the beach', use the construction **si** + *present tense* + *future tense*:

Si tengo dinero **saldré** de vacaciones.	*If I have money I will go on holiday.*
Si veo a Alberto le **diré** que estás aquí.	*If I see Alberto I will tell him that you are here.*

5 Mío, tuyo ... (mine, yours ...)

To say 'mine, yours', etc., use the following set of words, which agree in *gender* (masc. or fem.) and *number* (sing. or pl.) with the noun referred to (not with the owner):

mío/a(s)	*mine*	**nuestro/a(s)**	*ours*
tuyo/a(s)	*yours* (inf.)	**vuestro/a(s)**	*yours* (inf.)
suyo/a(s)	*yours* (formal), *his, hers, its*	**suyo/a(s)**	*yours* (formal), *theirs*

In sentences like the following, these words are preceded by **el**, **la**, **los** or **las**:

Mi equipaje es éste. El **tuyo** es ése.	*My luggage is this one. Yours is that one.*
Su casa está muy lejos. La **mía** está más cerca.	*His/her house is very far. Mine is nearer.*

El, **la**, **los** or **las** are not needed after the verb **ser**, and in sentences which translate into English as 'of mine, of yours', etc.

Ese dinero es suyo.	*That money is yours.*
Son amigos míos.	*They are friends of mine.*

Practice

1 Un viaje de negocios

Álvaro García is travelling to South America on business. A few days before his departure he sent a fax to one of his hosts, giving details of his journey. Fill in the gaps in the text with a verb from the list, using the future tense.

quedarse	llevar	llamar	llegar	salir

Para:	Sra. Sonia Álvarez, directora de Farmasur S.A.
De:	Álvaro García
Fecha:	25 de abril de 2002
Páginas:	1

Estimada Sra. Álvarez:

Con relación a mi próxima visita a Santiago, me es muy grato comunicarle que _____ de Madrid en el vuelo AB 145, el martes 28 de abril a las 10.45 de la noche y que _____ a Santiago el miércoles 29 a las 11.00 de la mañana.

_____ en el hotel Carrera, en la calle Teatinos, y la _____ por teléfono esa misma tarde para confirmar nuestra reunión. _____ toda la documentación que Vd. me ha solicitado.

---

me es muy grato   *I have pleasure in*

---

i **Estimado/a** … (masc./fem.), *Dear* …, es más personal que **Muy señor mío**, *Dear sir*, o **Distinguida señora**, *Dear madam*. Se utiliza frecuentemente en correspondencia comercial, por ejemplo **Estimada señora**, *Dear madam*, **Estimado señor Reyes**, *Dear Mr Reyes*. También se utiliza con el nombre de pila, *first name*, para dirigirse a personas a las que no se conoce bien, por ejemplo **Estimada Victoria**, *Dear Victoria*.

▶ 2 Las noticias

You are spending some time in Spain and, to keep up with the latest news, you listen to a news broadcast on Spanish radio. Listen to each news item several times, trying to get the gist of what it says. As you do so, consider each of the statements below and say whether they are true or false (**verdadero o falso**):

a La reina Sofía inaugurará una exposición de esculturas y pinturas del artista colombiano Fernando Botero.
b El presidente del gobierno español saldrá el lunes en visita oficial a la República Argentina.
c Entre los planes de Airbus está la construcción de un avión que podrá llevar hasta 555 pasajeros.
d Un tren de alta velocidad permitirá viajar entre París y Bruselas en menos de una hora y media.
e En Madrid, mañana estará nublado y posiblemente lloverá.

| la escultura | *sculpture* | de alta velocidad | *high-speed* |
| la pintura | *painting* | | |

3 Si …

Paco is speculating about his future at work. Form conditional sentences by matching the phrases on the left with those on the right.

a	Si tengo que trabajar horas extras	1	trabajaré como programador
b	Si no me aumentan el sueldo	2	podré irme a Estados Unidos
c	Si hago un curso de informática	3	me apuntaré para cobrar el paro
d	Si aprendo inglés	4	pediré un aumento de sueldo
e	Si no encuentro trabajo	5	buscaré otro trabajo

apuntarse para cobrar el paro	*to go on the dole*

4 Seguro que te las pedirán

Your friend Ángela is uncertain about getting the job she applied for, but you try to reassure her. Look at the first sentence, which has been done for you, and reply to each of Ángela's statements in a similar way.

a Si me *piden* referencias tendré que dar tu nombre.
Seguro que te las pedirán.
b Si me *entrevistan* tendré que prepararme muy bien.
Estoy seguro/a de que …
c Si me *ofrecen* el puesto lo aceptaré.
Seguramente …
d Si el sueldo no *es* muy bueno pediré más dinero.
Estoy seguro/a de que …
e Si me *dan* un coche de la empresa elegiré un Mercedes.
Seguro que…

5 Supongo …

While doing a Spanish course in Salamanca, Peter will be staying with a Spanish family. Everyone in the family is speculating about Peter. Rephrase their questions, using the expressions given to you. The first sentence has been done for you.

a	¿Conoce Salamanca?	Supongo que conocerá Salamanca.
b	¿Viene solo?	Me imagino que ...
c	¿Tiene nuestra dirección?	Supongo que ...
d	¿Sabe cómo llegar aquí?	Me imagino que ...
e	¿Entiende algo de español?	Supongo que ...

6 Está mal aparcado

Fill in the gaps with a possessive, using either short forms like **mi, tu, su,** or long forms such as **mío, tuyo, suyo,** as appropriate. Use **el, la, los** or **las** where necessary.

a   b

7 ¿Cómo serán las ciudades en el año 2025?

The following article looks at the growth of cities in the first quarter of the twenty-first century. What changes might you expect to take place?

7.1 As you read the text, decide whether the statements which follow are true or false (**verdaderos o falsos**).

a Three-quarters of the world population will be city-dwellers by 2025.

b By the year 2025 the world population will be double in relation to 1995.

c The number of cities with a million people or more will be 300.

d The increase in population will be greater in developed countries.

e The gap between the rich and the poor will be greater than what it is now.

En el año 2025, alrededor de 5 mil millones de personas, es decir, dos tercios de la población mundial, vivirán en ciudades. La población del mundo pasará de los 2.100 millones que había en 1995 a 5 mil millones dentro de 25 años.

Según datos de 'Urban XXI', en un plazo de 25 años existirán ciudades con más de 30 millones de habitantes, habrá 100 ciudades con más de cinco millones de personas y serán 300 las urbes con más de un millón de residentes.

La mayor parte de este crecimiento se producirá en los países en desarrollo, especialmente en África, Asia y América Latina y el Caribe, que en conjunto duplicarán su población urbana. El incremento será mayor en África, que duplicará su población urbana en sólo 30 años.

El siglo XXI traerá una gran división en las ciudades. La diferencia entre ricos y pobres crecerá aún más.

7.2 Read the text again and find other words and expressions meaning the following:

a las dos terceras partes	**d** residentes
b dentro de	**e** aumento
c las urbes	**f** países no industrializados

la población mundial	*world population*
según	*according to*
en conjunto	*altogether, combined*
crecer	*to grow*

21

me encantaría

I'd love to...

In this unit you will learn

- how to make suggestions
- how to invite people and accept and decline an invitation
- how to arrange to meet someone
- how to say what you would do and would like to do

▶ 1 ¿Qué te apetece ver?

Margarita suggests to Santiago going out in the evening.

1.1 Listen to the conversation several times, each time focusing attention on different information. Note the use of **gustar** in **Me gustaría** *I would like to.*

a ¿Qué quiere hacer Margarita esta noche?
b ¿Qué película quiere ver?
c ¿Por qué no va a ir en el coche?
d ¿A qué hora empieza la película?

Margarita	¿Qué te parece si vamos al cine esta noche?
Santiago	Vale. ¿Qué te apetece ver?
Margarita	Me gustaría ver *La flor de mi secreto.* ¿La has visto?
Santiago	No, pero me gustaría verla. ¿Dónde la ponen?
Margarita	En La Vaguada.
Santiago	¿Vas a ir en el coche?
Margarita	No, allí es muy difícil aparcar, si no iría en coche. La película empieza a las nueve. Podríamos quedar delante del cine sobre las nueve menos cuarto. ¿Qué te parece?
Santiago	Sí, me parece bien.
Margarita	Vale. Hasta luego.
Santiago	Hasta luego.

1.2 Now read the dialogue and find the expressions which mean the following:

a ¿Qué tal si …?   c Quisiera verla.
b ¿Qué quieres ver?

apetecer	*to feel like, fancy*	**quedar**	*to meet*
poner	*to show (film)*	**si no**	*if not, otherwise*

▶ 2 ¿Queréis venir a cenar a casa?

Manuel invites his new colleagues Maite and Simón to his house. Simón is Mexican.

2.1 Listen to the conversation several times and, as you do so, answer the following questions. The key expressions here are **Me encantaría** *I'd love to*, and **tener un compromiso** *to have an engagement*.

a ¿Adónde invita Manuel a sus colegas?
b ¿A qué otra persona ha invitado?
c ¿Por qué no puede aceptar la invitación Simón?

Manuel ¿Queréis venir a cenar conmigo el próximo viernes? He invitado a Julio también.
Maite Yo, encantada, gracias.
Simón A mí me encantaría, pero no puedo. Tengo un compromiso. ¿Otro día quizás?
Manuel Sí, sí, otro día.

2.2 Now read the dialogue and say what expressions are used to say:

a That's fine by me.   c Another day perhaps?
b I'd love to, but I can't.

conmigo	*with me*

How do you say it?

Making suggestions

¿Qué te parece si vamos a …/   *What about going to …/*
  vemos …   *seeing …*

Inviting people and accepting and declining an invitation

¿Queréis venir a cenar/tomar una copa conmigo/ con nosotros?	*Would you like to come and have dinner/a drink with me/us?*
(Yo) Encantado/a.	*That's fine by me.*
(A mí) me encantaría, pero no puedo.	*I'd love to but I can't.*

Arranging to meet someone

Podríamos quedar en .../ delante de ... a las ...	*We could meet in .../in front of ... at (time).*
¿De acuerdo?/¿Qué te parece?/ ¿Te parece bien?	*All right?/What do you think?/ Is it all right with you?*
Vale./De acuerdo./(Me parece) bien.	*O.K./All right/Fine.*

Saying what you would do

Iría/viajaría en ... a ...	*I would go/travel by ... to ...*

Asking people what they would like to do, and responding

¿Qué te gustaría/apetece hacer?	*What would you like to do/ do you feel like doing?*
Me gustaría/apetece ir a ...	*I would like to go/feel like going to ...*

Grammar

1 Saying what you would do: the conditional tense

To say what you *would* do, you need the *conditional* tense. The conditional, like the future (see Unit 20), is formed with the whole infinitive, e.g. **viajar** *to travel*, to which the endings are added. -ar, -er, and -ir verbs share the same endings.

viajar *to travel*	**ser** *to be*	**ir** *to go*
viajaría	sería	iría
viajarías	serías	irías
viajaría	sería	iría
viajaríamos	seríamos	iríamos
viajaríais	seríais	iríais
viajarían	serían	irían

¿Viajarías en tren?	*Would you travel by train?*
Sería mejor.	*It would be better.*
Iríamos a un concierto.	*We would go to a concert.*

Note that the first person singular, e.g. **yo sería** *I would be*, is the same as the third person, **usted/él/ella sería** *you (formal)/he/she would be.*

2 Irregular conditional forms

Irregular conditional forms are the same as those for the future tense, their endings being no different from those of regular verbs.

decir	*to say*	diría ...	saber	*to know*	sabría ...
hacer	*to do*	haría ...	salir	*to go out*	saldría ...
poder	*can,*	podría ...	tener	*to have*	tendría ...
	be able to				
poner	*to put*	pondría ...	venir	*to come*	vendría ...
querer	*to want*	querría ...			

Note also the impersonal form **habría** *there would be.*

Podríamos quedar a las 3.00.	*We could meet at 3.00.*
Yo no sabría qué hacer.	*I wouldn't know what to do.*
Vendrían en el coche.	*They would come in the car.*

3 Parecer (*to seem*), apetecer (*to feel like, to fancy*)

Parecer and apetecer function in the same way as **gustar** (see Unit 12), that is, with the verb in the third person singular or plural, preceded by one of the following pronouns: **me, te, le, nos, os, les.**

Me parece una buena idea.	*It seems a good idea (to me).*
Nos parecen interesantes.	*They seem interesting (to us).*
¿Qué te apetece hacer hoy?	*What do you feel like doing today?*
Me apetece ver televisión.	*I feel like watching television.*

Apetecer is common in Spain but rarely used in Latin America. An alternative to this is the conditional form of **gustar**, which is common in all countries, including Spain:

¿Qué te gustaría hacer?	*What would you like to do?*
Me gustaría ir a la piscina.	*I'd like to go to the swimming pool.*

4 Conmigo (*with me*)

To say 'with me', use the word **conmigo**, and to say 'with you' (informal, singular) use **contigo**. With all other persons use **con** followed by **usted, él, ella,** etc.

¿Quieres venir conmigo?	*Do you want to come with me?*
Voy a ir contigo.	*I will come with you.*
¿Te gustaría salir con ella?	*Would you like to go out with her?*

5 Personal 'a'

Note the use of the preposition '**a**' before a name or a word referring to a person in sentences like the following. This is a feature of Spanish which has no equivalent in English:

He invitado a Julio.	*I have invited Julio.*
Hoy veré a unos amigos.	*I'll see some friends today.*

Practice

1 ¿Qué haría Maite?

Maite is busy at the office today and she is dreaming about the things she would do if she did not have to work. Change the infinitives into the appropriate form of the conditional tense.

Yo
a (Hacer) la compra.
b (Lavar) la ropa.
c (Escribir) algunas cartas.
d (Llamar) a mi novio.

Mi novio y yo
e (Salir) en el coche.
f (Ver) alguna exposición.
g (Tener) tiempo para ir a nadar.
h (Poder) ir a bailar.

2 Pensaba quedarme en casa

It's Saturday and you are making plans for the evening, so you phone a Spanish friend and make arrangements to see a film or a play. Fill in your part of the conversation by following the guidelines below.

Tu amigo/a	¿Dígame?
Tú	*Identify yourself and ask if he/she has any plans for the evening.*
Tu amigo/a	No, ninguno. Pensaba quedarme en casa. ¿Por qué?
Tú	*Suggest going to the cinema or theatre together.*
Tu amigo/a	¿Qué te apetece ver?
Tú	*Choose from the films on page 206 or one of the plays below and say which one you would like to see. Ask whether he/she has seen it.*
Tu amigo/a	No, no la he visto, pero me encantaría verla.
Tú	*Say it's on at the Olimpia and that it starts at 7.00. Suggest meeting in the café opposite the cinema/ theatre at 6.30. Ask if that's all right with him/her.*
Tu amigo/a	Sí, me parece bien.

LAS ESTRELLAS DE LA GUIA DEL OCIO

	Alberto de la Hera	Eduardo Haro Tecglen	Enrique Centeno	Lorenzo L. Sancho
✓ Novedad	Guía del Ocio	El País	Diario 16	ABC
OBRAS EN CARTEL				
1. Mi pobre Marat ✓	★★★★	—	—	★★★★★
2. La evitable ascensión ✓	★★★★	—	★★★★	★★★
3. La zapatera prodigiosa ✓	★★★	★★★★	★★★★	
4. Terror y miseria ...	★★★	★★★	★★★★	★★★★★
5. Los padres terribles ✓	★★★★	★★★	—	★★★★
6. Amor, coraje y compasión	★★★	★★	★★★★	★★

★★★★★ *Excepcional*   ★★★★ *Muy buena*   ★★★ *Buena*   ★★ *Regular*   ★ *Mala*

3 ¿Te interesaría ver esta película?

Read this review of a Spanish film.

Bwana

España. Color. Director Imanol Uribe. Con Andrés Pajares, María Barranco, Alejandro Martínez y Emilio Buale. COMEDIA.

Una familia corriente y moliente (padre taxista, madre ama de casa y dos críos) pasan una tarde no menos corriente en una playa donde, sin embargo, un hecho singular cambiará sus ordinarias vidas y su manera de ver y entender el problema del racismo: encuentran a un africano que acaba de llegar al país en una patera. Basada en la novela *La mirada del hombre oscuro*, de Ignacio del Moral. (13).

3.1 Which word in the text tells you what the main theme is?

3.2 Which of these sentences best summarizes the storyline?

a Es la historia de una familia africana que acaba de llegar al país.

b Es la historia de una familia española y su relación con un inmigrante africano ilegal.

c Es la historia de un taxista africano y su encuentro con una familia española.

corriente y moliente	*ordinary* (fam.)
la patera	*small boat*
los críos	*children*

▶ 4 Unas invitaciones

Lucía and señor Flores, from Spain, and Mario, from Mexico, each have an invitation. Where are they being invited? Which of them accepts the invitation, and what excuse is given by those who decline it? Listen and fill in the box below.

Nombre	Invitación	¿Acepta o no?	Excusa
Lucía			
Sr. Flores			
Mario			

conmigo	with me	tomar una copa	to have a drink
el cóctel	cocktail party	el cumpleaños	birthday

5 Una invitación informal

On your desk this afternoon you find the following note from a Spanish colleague. Where is he inviting you, and where and at what time does he suggest you meet?

> ¡Hola!
>
> Tengo dos entradas para ver a Joaquín Cortés. ¿Quieres venir conmigo? La función es a las 8.00 y podríamos quedar en el bar que está al lado del teatro a las 7.30.
> ¿Qué te parece? Llámame.
>
> Rafael

6 Ahora tú

Write a note to your Spanish friend inviting him/her to one of the following and suggest a place and time when you can meet.

el ballet	un concierto (de rock/jazz)	el fútbol
la ópera	una obra de teatro	el tenis

7 Una invitación formal

On a visit to a Spanish-speaking country you and your travelling companion receive a formal invitation. Your colleague does not understand Spanish, so he asks you to translate it for him.

> La Cámara de Comercio de Santa Cruz tiene el agrado de invitar a usted a la ceremonia de inauguración de nuestras nuevas oficinas.
>
> El acto de apertura, que contará con la asistencia de las autoridades locales, se realizará en la Avenida del Libertador el martes 25 de mayo a las 19.30.

i Read this passage dealing with invitations and punctuality among Spanish and Latin American people, and find out how their customs differ from those in your country.

En España y en Latinoamérica, en invitaciones y citas de tipo formal, cuando no hay una relación íntima o de amistad con los anfitriones, la gente es más o menos puntual. Pero, si el que invita es un amigo o pariente, la puntualidad no suele ser la norma. ¿Un amigo te ha invitado a una fiesta para las 9.00 o las 10.00? Pues, si llegas a la hora tu amigo seguramente se sorprenderá, y quizás él mismo no estará preparado para recibirte a esa hora. Media hora o incluso una hora de retraso se considera normal. En algunos países de habla española se utiliza la expresión **hora inglesa** cuando se espera puntualidad, por ejemplo **Quedamos a las seis, pero a las seis hora inglesa, ¿eh?** *So, six o'clock it is, but six o'clock sharp, OK?*

la amistad	*friendship*	**el/la pariente**	*relative*
los anfitriones	*hosts*	**sorprenderse**	*to be surprised*

22

¿le sirvo un poco más?

shall I give you some more?

In this unit you will learn
- how to talk about what you had done
- how to express compliments
- how to express gratitude and pleasure

▶ 1 ¿Y qué le parece la ciudad?

On a visit to Guanajuato in Mexico, Laura Sánchez, from Spain, is invited for dinner by señor Rojas and his wife.

1.1 Listen to the conversation a few times and find out:

a Whether Laura had been to Guanajuato before.
b What she thinks of the city.

Sr. Rojas ¿Había estado aquí antes?
Laura Había estado en San Miguel de Allende, pero nunca había venido a Guanajuato.
Sr. Rojas ¿Y qué le parece la ciudad?
Laura Me encanta. Es una ciudad preciosa.

1.2 Now read the dialogue and find the expressions which mean the following:

a Had you been here before?
b I had never been to Guanajuato.
c What do you think of the city?

---

precioso/a *beautiful*

▶ 2 Este pescado está buenísimo

Laura compliments her hosts on the meal.

2.1 Listen to the conversation a few times, each time focusing attention on different information.

a ¿Qué lleva el plato principal: carne, pollo, o pescado?
b ¿Qué otra expresión se utiliza en el diálogo para decir *¿Le sirvo un poco más?*?
c ¿Qué significan estas expresiones: ¿De verdad?, De verdad, gracias?

Laura Este pescado está buenísimo.
Sr. Rojas Es una especialidad mexicana. ¿No lo había comido nunca antes?
Laura No, nunca. Está delicioso.
Sra. Rojas ¿Le sirvo un poco más?
Laura No, gracias.
Sra. Rojas ¿De verdad?
Laura De verdad, gracias.
Sr. Rojas ¿Quiere un poco más de vino?
Laura Gracias, pero sólo un poco.

2.2 Now read the dialogue and find the expressions which mean the following:

a Está muy bueno.
b Está exquisito.

c Es un plato mexicano.

¿no lo había comido nunca?	Had you never eaten it?

▶ 3 ¡Qué tarde es!

Laura thanks her hosts for the invitation. In the dialogue you'll hear several standard phrases used by people on formal occasions. Complete the sentences in the bubbles with one of the alternatives given below, then listen to the conversation to see whether you were right.

a tenerla en nuestra casa
b de haberla conocido

c la invitación
d muy amables

1

Laura	¡Uy, qué tarde es! Debo irme. Muchas gracias por la invitación. Han sido ustedes muy amables.
Sr. Rojas	Ha sido un placer tenerla en nuestra casa. Me alegro mucho de haberla conocido.
Sra. Rojas	Yo también. ¡Que tenga un buen viaje!
Laura	Gracias.

amable	kind	alegrarse	to be glad
el placer	pleasure		

ℹ En España cuando se quiere invitar a una persona, especialmente a una persona a la que no se conoce bien, generalmente se la invita a un restaurante u otro sitio similar. La mayor parte de la vida social en España y en la mayoría de los países latinoamericanos tiene lugar en sitios públicos, tales como restaurantes, bares o cafés. La invitación a comer o cenar en casa generalmente está reservada para amigos más íntimos o parientes, y en ocasiones más especiales. En algunos países de Latinoamérica, sin embargo, la gente acostumbra invitar a sus amigos y conocidos a casa con más frecuencia.

Si la invitación es para comer o cenar en casa de un amigo, no es obligación llevar algo, pero si quieres hacerlo, puedes llevar una botella de vino o el postre. Pero, si la relación es formal, tendrás que llevar algo, por ejemplo champán o flores o bombones (*chocolates*) para la señora de la casa.

How do you say it?

Talking about what you had done

¿Había estado/venido aquí antes?	*Had you been/come here before?*
Nunca había estado/venido a Guanajuato.	*I had never been/come to Guanajuato.*

Expressing compliments

Este pescado/Esta carne está buenísimo/a/delicioso/a.	*This fish/meat is very good/delicious.*

Expressing gratitude and pleasure

Muchas gracias por la invitación.	*Thank you very much for the invitation.*
Ha/n sido usted/ustedes muy amable/s.	*You have been very kind.*
Es/Ha sido un placer conocerlo/a.	*It is/has been a pleasure to meet you.*
Me alegro mucho de haberte/lo/la conocido.	*I'm glad to have met you.*

Grammar

1 Saying what you had done: the pluperfect tense

To express ideas such as 'Had you never eaten this before?', 'I had never been here', you need the *pluperfect* tense. This is formed with the *imperfect* of **haber** (see Unit 17) and a *past participle* (see Unit 19), which is invariable.

estar *to be*	comer *to eat*	vivir *to live*
había estado	había comido	había vivido
habías estado	habías comido	habías vivido
había estado	había comido	había vivido
habíamos estado	habíamos comido	habíamos vivido
habíais estado	habíais comido	habíais vivido
habían estado	habían comido	habían vivido

Habíamos estado allí muchas veces antes de casarnos. — *We had been there many times before we got married.*

¿Nunca habías comido esto antes? — *Had you never eaten this before?*

Habían vivido muchos años en el sur de España. — *They had lived in southern Spain for many years.*

2 Bueno, buenísimo (*good, very good*)

To intensify the meaning of words such as **bueno, malo**, remove the final vowel and add **-ísimo** (masc.) or **-ísima** (fem.):

Esto está buenísimo. — *This is very good.*
La comida está malísima. — *The food is very bad.*

Words ending in **-co**, e.g. **rico**, change their spelling:

La paella está riquísima. — *The paella tastes very good.*

3 Shall I ...?

To offer someone something, as in 'Shall I give you some more?' Spanish uses the *present tense*, preceded by **le** or **les** (*you*, formal, sing./pl.) or **te** or **os** (*you*, informal, sing./pl.):

¿Le sirvo más vino? (from **servir** *to serve*). — *Shall I give you some more wine?*
¿Te traigo una gaseosa? — *Shall I bring you a soft drink?*

4 Exclamations

To say *how*, as in 'How late it is!' 'How kind you are!' use **qué**:

¡Qué tarde es! — *How late it is!*
¡Qué amable es usted! — *How kind you are!*

Practice

1 Lo que había hecho Francisco

Here are some of the things Francisco had done before he got married. Match the drawings with the phrases below, then use the verbs in brackets to say what he had done.

a (escribir) un libro de poemas
b (terminar) la carrera de medicina
c (viajar) por el mundo
d (aprender) a conducir
e (hacer) el servicio militar
f (estudiar) guitarra clásica

2 ¿Qué había hecho?

You have been asked to look after a Spanish-speaking person who is visiting your town. How would you ask him/her the following?

a Had you been here before?
b Had you never visited this company?
c You had stayed in this hotel before, hadn't you?
d You hadn't eaten this before, had you?

▶ 3 Una invitación formal

You are visiting a Spanish-speaking country and during your stay you are invited for lunch. Follow the guidelines and fill in your part of the conversation.

Mujer ¿Había estado aquí antes?
Tú *Say you had never been here before. Add that it is a very nice country.*
Mujer Gracias.
Tú *(The main course consists of* mariscos, *seafood.) Tell your hosts that the* mariscos *are very good.*
Marido Es un plato típico de aquí.
Tú *Say they are delicious.*
Mujer ¿Le sirvo un poco más?
Tú *Say yes, but just a little.*
Marido ¿Le pongo un poco más de vino?
Tú *Say no, thank you.*
Marido ¿De verdad?
Tú *Say yes, sure, thank you, you can't drink any more because you have to drive* (conducir).

4 Ahora tú

You are having a formal dinner party with people you don't know well. How would you offer your guests more of the following? Try varying the expressions you use.

5 ¿Qué dirías tú?

Each of these sentences contains one mistake. Can you spot it?

a Muchas gracias para tu regalo. Es precioso.
b Gracias, señora. Has sido usted muy amable.
c Me alegro mucho haberte conocido, Antonio.
d Ha sido un placer conocerlo, señora.

| **el regalo** | *present* |

6 Una carta de agradecimiento (*a thank-you letter*)

On her return to Spain, Laura sent a thank-you letter to her host in Mexico. Can you fill in the gaps in her letter with one of these words?

| placer | visita | mujer | poder | agradecer | estancia |

Estimado señor Rojas:

Quisiera _____ a usted y a su _____ las muchas atenciones que tuvieron conmigo durante mi _____ en México.

Fue realmente un _____ haberlos conocido y espero _____ corresponder de igual forma durante su próxima _____ a España.

Lo saluda atentamente

Laura Sánchez

| **de igual forma** | *in the same way* |

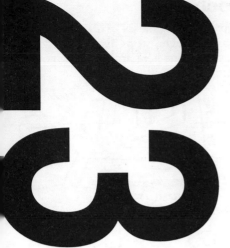

23

siga todo recto

go straight on

In this unit you will learn
- how to ask and give directions
- how to give instructions

▶ 1 Gire a la derecha

Outside the Telefónica on avenida Tejada (N° 16 on the map) Agustín, who is visiting a Spanish town, stops his car to ask for directions. Key words and expressions here are **seguir** *to go on*, **girar** *to turn*, **todo recto** *straight on*.

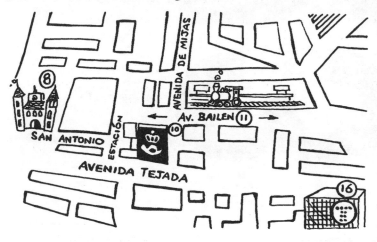

1.1 Listen to the dialogue several times while you follow directions on the map and, as you do so, answer these questions:

a What place is Agustín looking for?
b What does he have to do when he reaches Avenida de Mijas?
c How would you complete the following expressions?

   la segunda _____, la cuarta _____

Listen again.

Agustín   Oiga, por favor, ¿podría decirme dónde está Correos?
Señora   Mire, siga todo recto por esta calle, y al llegar a la avenida de Mijas gire a la derecha. Correos está en la calle de Bailén, la segunda a la izquierda.
Agustín   ¿Hay que tomar la avenida de Mijas, me ha dicho?
Señora   Sí, tome la cuarta a la derecha.
Agustín   Muchas gracias.
Señora   De nada.

1.2 Now read the dialogue and say what expressions are used by Agustín to ask:

a where the post office is
b whether he has to take Avenida de Mijas

| **hay que** | *you have/one has to* |

▶ 2 Suba usted por esa escalera

Back at his hotel, Agustín asks the hotel receptionist how to get to the restaurant.

2.1 Listen to the conversation a few times and say whether the following statements are true or false (**verdadero o falso**).

a   Para ir al restaurante hay que bajar al primer piso.
b   El restaurante está en el pasillo de la izquierda.
c   Está enfrente del bar.

Agustín   Perdone, ¿dónde está el restaurante, por favor?
Recepcionista Suba usted por esa escalera hasta el primer piso y tome el pasillo de la izquierda. El restaurante está pasado el bar.
Agustín   Gracias.

2.2 Now complete the following sentence without looking at the dialogue; then read this and check if you were right:

Suba usted _____ esa escalera _____ el primer piso y tome el pasillo _____ la izquierda.

la escalera *stairs*		**el pasillo** *corridor*

▶ 3 Hágalo después de la señal

Agustín phoned a doctor's surgery to make an appointment, but he got a recorded message.

3.1 Listen to the recorded message several times, each time focusing attention on a different point.

a   ¿Cuál es el horario de atención al público del doctor García?
b   ¿A qué número hay que llamar para urgencias?
c   ¿Qué número hay que marcar para anular una cita?

Contestador: Esta es la consulta del doctor Ignacio García. Lamentamos no poder atender a su llamada en este momento. Nuestro horario de atención es de 9.00 a 11.30 de la mañana y por la tarde de 4.00 a 6.00. Para urgencias, llame al 642 21 09. Para anular una cita, marque el 759 55 32. Para pedir hora con el doctor, indíquenos su nombre y número de teléfono y le confirmaremos su cita. Hágalo después de la señal. Gracias.

3.2 Formal instructions can also be given with the infinitive, for example **dejar** instead of **deje** su número de teléfono, *leave your telephone number*. Now read the dialogue and try to identify the verb forms corresponding to these infinitives, and study the way in which they have been used:

a marcar   e indicar
b llamar   d hacer

> **la consulta** *surgery*
> **lamentar** *to regret*
> **la señal** *signal*
> **pedir hora** *to ask for an appointment (with a doctor)*

How do you say it?

Asking for directions

¿Podría decirme dónde está correos/el museo? *Could you tell me where the post office/museum is?*
¿Sabe usted dónde está el hotel Real/la catedral? *Do you know where the Hotel Real/cathedral is?*

Giving directions formally

Siga todo recto/de frente/ derecho (L.Am.) *Go straight on.*
Gire a la derecha/izquierda. *Turn right/left.*
Tome/Coja (Spain) la primera/ segunda a la izquierda. *Take the first/second (turning) on the left.*
Suba/Baje por esa escalera. *Go up/down those stairs.*
Está pasada la recepción/ pasado el bar. *It is past the reception/bar.*

Giving instructions formally

Llame al/Marque el 642 21 09. *Call/dial 642 21 09.*
Hágalo después de la señal. *Do it after the signal.*

Grammar

1 Giving directions and instructions: the imperative form

a Uses

Unit 23 takes you a step further from units 4 and 6 in which you learned to ask and give directions with the present tense, e.g. **Usted toma el autobús número 12**, *You take bus number 12.*

This unit introduces the *imperative* or *command* form, which is used not only for directions but also for instructions and requests, for example:

Tome el autobús número 12. *Take bus number 12.*
Llame al 654 23 12. *Call 654 23 12.*
Páseme el azúcar, por favor. *Pass the sugar, please.*

In fact, you are already familiar with some imperative forms, for example

mire *look* (from **mirar** *to look*)
oiga *excuse me* (from **oír** *to hear, listen*)
deme *give me* (from **dar** *to give*)
¿diga? *hello?, Can I help you?* (from **decir** *to say, tell*)

In the context of directions, the imperative is just as common as the present tense, so you need at least to be able to understand it. But if you find yourself in the position of having to give someone directions, you can choose between the present or the imperative, as both will sound perfectly natural to a native speaker.

b Formation

In this unit you will learn the *formal* imperative, corresponding to **usted** (*you*, sing.) and **ustedes** (*you*, pl.), which is formed with the *stem* of the *1st person singular* of the *present tense*, e.g. **tom**, from **tomo** *I take*, to which the *endings* are added: **-e** for **-ar** verbs and **-a** for **-er** and **-ir** verbs.

Infinitive	Present tense	Imperative
tomar *to take*	(yo) tomo	tome
coger *to take*	(yo) cojo	coja
subir *to go up*	(yo) subo	suba

For the plural **ustedes** add **-n**: tomen, cojan, suban.

Remember that **coger**, though very common in Spain, is a taboo word in some Latin American countries. **Tomar** will be acceptable in all places.

Tome/Coja la carretera nacional. *Take the national highway.*
Suba hasta el segundo piso. *Go up to the second floor.*

2 Irregular imperative forms

Verbs which are irregular in the first person singular of the present tense are also irregular in the imperative. This rule also applies to radical-changing verbs, e.g. **volver**, in which the **o** of the stem changes into **ue**. Examples:

Infinitive	Present tense	Imperative
decir *to say*	(yo) digo	diga
hacer *to do*	(yo) hago	haga
oír *to hear, listen*	(yo) oigo	oiga
seguir *to go on*	(yo) sigo	siga
volver *to come back*	(yo) vuelvo	vuelva

The imperative form of **ir** *to go*, is **vaya** *go*.

Siga hasta el semáforo.	*Go on as far as the traffic lights.*
Vuelva mañana.	*Come back tomorrow.*
Vaya en autobús.	*Go by bus.*

3 Position of pronouns with imperatives

Pronouns like **me** *me*, **te** *you* (informal), **lo** *him*, *it*, are attached to the end of positive imperatives but precede negative imperatives:

Positive	Negative
Llámeme (*call me*).	No **me** llame (*don't call me*).
Hágalo (*do it*).	No **lo** haga (*don't do it*).

A written accent is usually necessary to show that the stress remains in the same position when the pronoun is added, e.g. **llame** *call*, **llámeme** *call me*.

Note that the formal imperative of verbs ending in **-car**, like **indicar** *to indicate*, *to tell*, ends in **-que**, so that pronunciation may remain consistent. Verbs ending in **-ger**, e.g. **coger** *to take*, *to catch*, change **-g** to **-j**.

Indíquenos su nombre.	*Tell us your name.*
Coja la primera a la izquierda.	*Take the first turning on the left.*

4 Hay que (*you have to*)

Hay que is an impersonal form meaning 'one has to, you have to':

Hay que tomar la avenida de Mijas.	*You have to take avenida de Mijas.*
Hay que llamar al 542 89 12.	*You have to call 542 89 12.*

5 Por, para

Note the following uses of these two words:

Siga todo recto por esta calle. *Go straight on along this road.*
Suba usted por esa escalera. *Go up those stairs.*
Para urgencias llame al ... *For emergencies call ...*

Practice

1 Señales de tráfico

Can you match the following traffic signs with their meanings below?

a Gire a la derecha.
b No toque la bocina.
c Ceda el paso.
d Cruce de peatones. Conduzca con cuidado.

e Zona de escuela. Disminuya la velocidad.
f Cruce ferroviario. Pare, mire y escuche
g No adelantar.
h No entrar.

▶ 2 Está una calle más arriba

Look at this map showing some hotels in Cuzco, Peru. In which hotel is this tourist now and which one is he looking for? Listen and follow the directions on the map.

---

más arriba *further up*

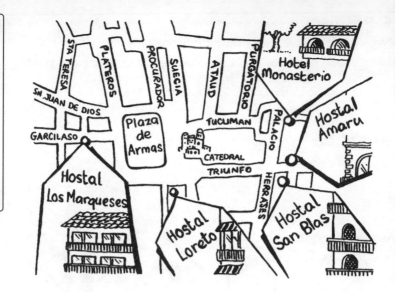

3 Hay una desviación

Read this note with directions sent to Antonia by someone she is visiting, and fill in the gaps with the appropriate formal imperative forms of these verbs: **tomar, subir, seguir, preguntar, girar.**

_____ usted de frente por la avenida de Suel y al llegar a la carretera nacional 340 _____ usted a la izquierda en dirección al aeropuerto. Antes de llegar al aeropuerto hay una desviación hacia Santa Clara. _____ usted esa desviación y _____ todo recto hasta llegar a una estación de servicio. Nuestra fábrica está pasada la estación de servicio. _____ usted hasta nuestras oficinas, que están en el tercer piso, y _____ por mí en recepción.

la desviación	_diversion_

4 ¿Sabe usted dónde hay un banco?

A Spanish-speaker asks you for directions in your own town. Use the guidelines below to complete your part of the conversation.

– Perdone, ¿sabe usted dónde hay un banco?
– *Say yes and tell him/her to go straight on and take the third turning on the left, then take the first turning on the right and go straight on as far as the end of the road. The bank is opposite the station.*

5 Ahora tú

You are at the reception of the hotel on calle San Antonio, N° 8 on the map on page 224, when a Spanish person asks you the way to the railway station (N° 11 on the map). What directions would you give him/her?

6 Tráigamela, por favor

Study this brief exchange between Mario and his boss.

Mario ¿Le traigo la correspondencia de hoy?
Jefe Sí, tráigamela, por favor.

Can you instruct Mario to do what he is offering? Don't forget to use written accents where appropriate. Follow the example above.

a ¿Envío el fax ahora?	d ¿Le traigo las carpetas?
b ¿Llamo a la secretaria?	e ¿Mando estas cartas hoy?
c ¿Hago el pedido?	f ¿Le enseño el informe?

---

la carpeta *file*   **enseñar** *to show*

24

me duele la cabeza
cabeza
I have a headache

In this unit you will learn
- how to say how you feel
- how to explain what is wrong with you
- how to make requests
- how to give advice

▶ 1 Un dolor de cabeza

Marta is feeling unwell and she describes her symptoms to her friend Luis.

1.1 Listen to the conversation a few times and, without looking at the text below, try completing these sentences:

a _____ tráeme una aspirina y un vaso _____
b _____ muchísima sed
c Sí, espera _____

Luis ¿Qué te pasa?
Marta Tengo un dolor de cabeza horrible.
Luis ¿Quieres tomar algo?
Marta Sí, por favor tráeme una aspirina y un vaso de agua. Tengo muchísima sed.
Luis Sí, espera un momento. Vuelvo en seguida.

1.2 Now read the text and find the phrases which mean the following:

a What's wrong with you?
b I'll be right back

la cabeza	*head*
el vaso	*glass*
tener sed	*to be thirsty*

▶ 2 Tengo mucho calor

Luis comes back to Marta after some time.

2.1 Listen to the conversation and, as you do, try answering these questions:

a How do you think Marta is feeling now? Listen and find out.
b Why does she ask Luis to open the window? Listen again.
c What does Luis suggest she does?

Luis ¿Te sientes mejor?
Marta No, no me encuentro bien. Me duele la cabeza todavía y tengo mucho calor. Por favor abre la ventana un poco.
Luis Vale. Mira, ¿por qué no descansas un rato? Trata de dormir. Te hará bien.
Marta Sí, ¿podrías apagar la luz, por favor?
Luis Muy bien.

2.2 Now read the dialogue and find phrases which are similar in meaning to the following:

a No estoy bien. c ¿Puedes abrir la ventana?
b Tengo dolor de cabeza. d Tienes que descansar.

encontrarse (o > ue)	*to feel*
apagar la luz	*to turn off the light*
tratar de	*to try to*
descansar	*to rest*

How do you say it?

Saying how you feel

Tengo sed/calor.   *I'm thirsty/hot.*
No me encuentro/siento bien.   *I don't feel well.*

Explaining what is wrong with you

Me duele (un poco/mucho)   *I have a (slight/bad) headache*
  la cabeza/el estómago.   *stomach ache.*
Tengo dolor de garganta/   *I have a sore throat/toothache.*
  muelas.
Tengo (un poco de) fiebre.   *I am (a little) feverish.*

Making requests

Tráeme una aspirina/   *Bring me an aspirin/a*
  un vaso de agua.   *glass of water.*

Abre/Cierra la ventana.	*Open/close the window.*
¿Podrías apagar/encender la luz?	*Could you turn off/on the light?*

Giving advice

¿Por qué no descansas/ duermes un rato?	*Why don't you rest/sleep for a while?*
Trata de dormir/descansar.	*Try to sleep/rest.*

Grammar

1 Making informal requests and giving advice: the informal imperative

In Unit 23 you learned to use the formal imperative for giving directions and instructions. But if you are addressing people in an informal way you need to use the informal imperative. In this unit you will learn to use this to make requests and give advice.

a Formation

The informal imperative has different positive and negative forms. Here you will learn and practise positive forms only. The **tú** form is like the *present tense* **tú** form of the verb, but *without the* -s. For the **vosotros** form, *replace the* -r *of the infinitive with a* -d.

Infinitive	Present tense	Imperative (tú/vosotros)
esperar	(tú) esperas	espera/esperad
traer	(tú) traes	trae/traed
abrir	(tú) abres	abre/abrid

Espera un momento.	*Wait a moment.*
Por favor, tráeme una taza de té.	*Please, bring me a cup of tea.*
Abrid la puerta, por favor.	*Open the door, please.*

b Making requests

Note that the expression **por favor** is often added to requests made with the imperative, in order to make this less commanding, e.g. **Ayúdame, por favor.** *Help me, please.*

Care must also be taken with intonation. A rising intonation towards the end of the sentence will show the listener that what he is hearing is a request rather than a command.

You may, of course, make requests with the *present tense* (see Unit 5, **Grammar**, 2) or with **poder** *can*.

¿Me da algo para el dolor de cabeza, por favor?	*Will you give me something for a headache, please?*
¿Puedes traerme algo de la farmacia?	*Can you bring me something from the chemist's?*
¿Podrías encender la luz?	*Could you turn on the light?*

c Giving advice

The imperative, as in **trata de dormir** *try to sleep*, is only one of a range of expressions used for giving advice. For other alternatives see the **How do you say it?** section.

2 Irregular imperative forms

A few verbs have irregular positive familiar forms:

decir	to say	di	salir	to go out	sal
hacer	to do, make	haz	ser	to be	sé
ir	to go	ve	tener	to have	ten
poner	to put	pon	venir	to come	ven

3 It hurts!

To say that you have a pain, you can use either of the two expressions below:

a Doler (o > ue), literally *to hurt*, which has only two forms in the present tense: **duele**, for *singular*, and **duelen**, for *plural*:

me duele/n	nos duele/n
te duele/n	os duele/n
le duele/n	les duele/n

Me duele el tobillo.	*I have a pain in my ankle.*
Me duelen los pies.	*My feet ache.*
Le duelen los oídos.	*He/She has an earache.*

b Tener dolor (de ...), *to have a pain (in ...)*

Tengo un dolor de espalda horrible.	*I have a terrible backache.*
Tengo un dolor aquí.	*I have a pain here.*
Tiene dolor de muelas.	*He/she has a toothache.*

4 'Tener' for 'to be'

Ideas like *to be thirsty*, *to be hungry*, *to be cold* or *to be warm*, are expressed in Spanish with **tener** *to have*.

Tengo sed.	*I'm thirsty.*
¿Tienes hambre?	*Are you hungry?*
¿No tienes frío?	*Aren't you cold?*
Tengo mucho calor.	*I'm very hot.*

Practice

1 Las dolencias más comunes

Which do you think are the most common ailments in your country? Would you expect these to be the same or different in Spain and other European countries? Why? Look at the chart below which lists the most common complaints in different European countries, including Spain, and compare the figures. How many words can you guess? Look up the ones you don't know in the vocabulary list at the back of the book.

Las dolencias más comunes en Europa							
%	España	Bélgica	Alemania	Italia	Países Bajos	Francia	Reino Unido
Fiebre/resfriado	70	69	51	65	51	64	81
Dolor de cabeza	48	43	35	46	35	49	63
Fatiga	31	40	14	29	14	47	45
Reumatismo	33	34	32	49	32	43	38
Ansiedad/insomnio	41	42	25	37	25	41	39
Problemas digestivos	27	32	22	33	22	34	28

Fuente: Secodip.

Which countries seem the most healthy, according to the chart?

▶ 2 Una visita al doctor

You will hear two conversations between a patient and a Spanish doctor. Listen to the dialogues and, as you do, try answering these questions. The first patient is from Spain, the second is from Mexico.

a Which of the complaints in the chart do you associate with the patients' symptoms?
b What does each doctor advise the patient to do or what does he or she prescribe?

| **intranquilo** | *anxious* | **recetar** | *to prescribe* |
| **estresado** | *under stress* | **la pastilla** | *tablet* |

3 Describe los síntomas

On a visit to a Spanish-speaking country you go to the doctor because you are feeling unwell. Describe your symptoms by filling in the gaps with one of these verbs:

| tener | tener dolor | sentirse/encontrarse | doler |

a No _____ bien.
b _____ la cabeza.
c _____ de estómago.
d _____ un poco de fiebre.
e _____ todo el cuerpo.
f _____ muy cansado/a.

| **el cuerpo** | *body* |

▶ 4 Un día de mucho calor

The heat seems to have affected you during your stay in a Spanish-speaking country, so you ask a friend for help. Follow the guidelines below and fill in your part of the conversation. Alternatively, listen to the recording and do this orally.

Amigo/a	¿Qué te pasa?
Tú	*Tell your friend that you are not feeling well.*
Amigo/a	¿Qué tienes?
Tú	*Say that you have a terrible headache and you are feverish.*
Amigo/a	¿Quieres tomar algo?
Tú	*Ask your friend to bring you a glass of mineral water. Say you are very thirsty.*
Amigo/a	Muy bien. ¿Quieres algo más?
Tú	*Ask your friend to open the door. Say you are very hot.*
Amigo/a	¿Quieres comer algo?
Tú	*Say no, thank you, you are not hungry.*

239 me duele la cabeza 24

5 Consulta abierta

Two readers of a health magazine wrote to the editor seeking help with their problems.

5.1 What are their problems? Read the letters and find out.

✉

CONSEJOS PARA MANTENER EL PESO IDEAL

UNA MUJER DE MEDIANA EDAD CONSULTA POR UN PROBLEMA DE PESO.

Tengo 32 años y un problema común a muchas mujeres: subo y bajo de peso constantemente. Esto no sucede de un día para el otro, pero sí en el lapso de unos meses. Por ejemplo: hace dos meses yo pesaba 53 kilos (mido 1,60) y ahora peso 56 y sé que si me pongo a hacer dieta voy a bajar, pero lo que en realidad necesito es una solución definitiva para terminar con este problema.

Rosa

✉

DOLORES DE CABEZA CRÓNICOS

UN JOVEN QUE SUFRE PERIÓDICAMENTE ESTOS TRASTORNOS DESEA SABER CÓMO EVITARLOS.

Trabajo ocho horas diarias en un banco y, al final del día, suele atacarme un dolor de cabeza devastador que se localiza en el costado superior izquierdo y que me incapacita para todo. Después siento náuseas, que por lo general concluyen en vómitos. Quisiera poner fin a este calvario, pero hasta ahora no tuve éxito. ¿Pueden ayudarme?

Nelson

5.2 Read the first letter again and find words and expressions which mean the same as the following ones.

a	continuamente	**c**	seguir un régimen
b	pasa	**d**	de verdad

5.3 Now read the second letter and find words and expressions which are similar in meaning to the following.

a	al día	**c**	generalmente
b	terrible	**d**	terminan con

el peso	*weight*	**el costado**	*side*
pesar	*to weigh*	**el calvario**	*suffering*
suceder	*to happen*	**tener éxito**	*to succeed*

6 ¿Qué consejos les darías?

Consider these words of advice. Which would be suitable for Rosa and which for Nelson? Classify them accordingly.

a No trabajes demasiado.
b No debes comer en exceso.
c No consumas demasiadas grasas.
d Trata de relajarte.
e ¿Por qué no cambias de actividad?
f Ten cuidado con lo que comes.

tener cuidado	*to be careful*

i Los españoles y latinoamericanos hablan con relativa frecuencia de sus **dolencias y enfermedades**, *complaints and illnesses*. Las afecciones más comunes, como puede ser **una gripe**, *flu*, son a menudo tema de conversación entre quienes las padecen, especialmente entre la gente mayor. Y la visita al médico no siempre es necesaria.

La automedicación, *medication without prescription*, constituye un verdadero problema en muchos países de habla hispana. La lista de **medicamentos**, *medicines*, que pueden obtenerse directamente en la farmacia, sin una **receta médica**, *prescription*, es amplia, aunque cada vez hay más restricciones.

En España, la mayoría de la gente recibe atención médica a través de **la Seguridad Social**, *social security*. Otros utilizan **la sanidad privada**, *private health services*. Los visitantes de otros países de la Unión Europea pueden recibir atención médica a través de la Seguridad Social. En caso de accidente u otra emergencia se puede recibir atención rápida en una Casa de Socorro o en **un Puesto de Socorro**, *first-aid post*.

la afección	*complaint*	**la gente mayor**	*the elderly*
padecer	*to suffer*		

25

¿qué tipo de persona buscas?

what kind of person are you

In this unit you will learn
- how to say what sort of place or person you are looking for
- how to express hope with regard to others
- how to express doubt

▶ 1 ¿Qué tipo de piso busca?

Paloma would like to rent a flat and she makes enquiries at an accommodation agency.

1.1 Listen to the conversation a few times, each time focusing attention on a different point.

a ¿Dónde prefiere vivir Paloma?
b ¿Cuántos dormitorios quiere?
c ¿Cuánto quiere pagar?
d ¿Quiere un piso amueblado o sin muebles?

Paloma	Buenos días.
Empleado	Buenos días. ¿Dígame?
Paloma	Quisiera alquilar un piso. ¿Tienen ustedes alguno en este momento?
Empleado	¿Qué tipo de piso busca usted?
Paloma	Bueno, busco algo que esté cerca del centro, que tenga tres o cuatro dormitorios, y que no sea muy caro. No quiero pagar más de seiscientos euros mensuales. Y lo prefiero amueblado.
Empleado	Un momento, por favor. Voy a ver lo que tenemos.

1.2 Now read the dialogue, then look at the advertisement below and say which of the flats listed in it might suit Paloma.

INMOBILIARIA SEGURA
Compra-Venta, Alquiler, Pisos, Locales

• **En urb, cerca Vendrell.** Torre de una planta en alquiler de 2 dorm, por todo el año, alquiler mensual 480 €
• **Piso alq. Cornellá.** 3 dorm., 520 €
• **Piso alquiler.** Amuebl. 3 dorm., en San Ildefonso, 580 €

• **San Ildefonso.** Planta baja en alquiler 660 €, 2 dormitorios.
• **Piso,** 2 dorm., en venta en San Ildefonso. precio de 54.000 €.
• **Parcela en Vallirana.** Urb. Can Prunera 1300 m², 18.000 €.

C/. Desmayo, 1 Bjos. • T. 375 55 52 • CORNELLA

---

la urbanización	*housing development*
la torre	*villa*
la planta	*storey*
amueblado	*furnished*
la planta baja	*ground floor*
la parcela	*plot*

▶ 2 Espero que encuentres a alguien

Paloma has rented a flat and now she would like to share it. She tells her friend Germán about it.

2.1 Listen to the conversation several times and say whether the statements below are true or false (**verdadero o falso**).

a Paloma busca una persona que tenga su misma edad.
b Quiere una persona que trabaje en casa.
c Prefiere una persona que no fume y que sea vegetariana.
d Quiere alguien que no tenga gatos.

Paloma	Estoy buscando una persona para compartir mi piso. Si sabes de alguien, dímelo.
Germán	Vale. ¿Qué tipo de persona buscas?
Paloma	Pues, quiero una persona de mi edad, que trabaje fuera de casa, que no fume, que sea vegetariana, y que le gusten los gatos, como a mí.
Germán	Espero que encuentres a alguien, pero no creo que sea fácil.

2.2 Now read the dialogue and find the expressions which mean the following:

a I hope you'll find someone.
b I don't think it'll be easy.

compartir	*to share*	**el gato**	*cat*
alguien	*someone*		

i En España, es común que muchos jóvenes de veinte, veinticinco o incluso treinta años vivan con sus padres. La imposibilidad de encontrar un empleo limita su independencia. La vivienda es cara en las grandes ciudades como Madrid y Barcelona, y aquéllos que trabajan a menudo prefieren compartir un apartamento con amigos, al menos en los primeros años.

En Latinoamérica, por tradición, es normal que los jóvenes, tanto hombres como mujeres, vivan con sus padres hasta el momento de casarse. Los jóvenes latinoamericanos, en general, son menos independientes que los españoles, y los padres ejercen más control sobre sus hijos.

un empleo	*job*	**al menos**	*at least*
la vivienda	*housing*	**ejercer**	*to exert*

How do you say it?

Asking people what sort of place or person they are looking for

¿Qué tipo de piso/persona busca/prefiere/quiere Vd.?	*What kind of flat/person are you looking for/do you prefer/ want?*

Saying what sort of place or person you are looking for

Busco un piso que esté cerca del centro/que tenga dos dormitorios.	*I'm looking for a flat which is near the centre/with two bedrooms.*
Quiero/Prefiero una persona que no fume/que sea vegetariana.	*I want/prefer a person who doesn't smoke/is a vegetarian.*

Expressing hope with regard to others

Espero que encuentres a alguien.	*I hope you find someone.*

Expressing doubt

No creo que sea fácil.	*I don't think it will be easy.*

Grammar

1 Expressing requirements: the subjunctive

To express requirements with regard to a place or a person you want or are looking for, as in 'I am looking for someone who doesn't smoke', you need a special form of the verb which is known as *subjunctive*. A general function of this verb form is to indicate that the action or state that it refers to is not a reality. Consider for example:

Estoy buscando una persona que no fume.	*I'm looking for a person who doesn't smoke.*
Busco un piso que no sea caro.	*I'm looking for a flat which is not too expensive.*

The non-smoker and the flat mentioned here are not yet a reality, and so the action and the state referred to must be expressed with the subjunctive.

The subjunctive is normally dependent on another verb, for example **buscar** *to look for*, **querer** *to want*, **preferir** *to prefer*, **necesitar** *to need*. In the sentences above, it is dependent on **buscar**, the main verb, with the subjunctive acting as secondary verb, preceded by the word **que** *that*.

a The present subjective

If the *main verb* verb is in the *present*, for example **busco** *I'm looking for*, the *secondary verb* must be in the *present subjunctive*. It is this form, very common in all forms of spoken and written Spanish, which you will learn in this course. For other forms and uses of the subjunctive you will need to refer to a more advanced course such as *Teach Yourself Spanish Extra!*, or to a reference grammar.

b The forms of the present subjunctive

The present subjunctive, just like the formal imperative which you learned in Unit 23, is formed by removing the -o of the first person of the present tense, e.g. **trabaj-**, from **trabajo** *I work*, to which the following endings are added:

-ar verbs:	-e, -es, -e, -emos, -éis, -en
-er *and* **-ir verbs:**	-a, -as, -a, -amos, -áis, -an

Busco una secretaria que hable español. — *I'm looking for a secretary who speaks Spanish.*

Necesitamos un conserje que viva aquí. — *We need a porter who can live here.*

c Irregular forms

Common irregular verbs in the present subjunctive are:

dar *to give*	dé,	des,	dé,	demos,	deis,	den
estar *to be*	esté,	estés,	esté,	estemos,	estéis,	estén
ir *to go*	vaya,	vayas,	vaya,	vayamos,	vayáis,	vayan
saber *to know*	sepa,	sepas,	sepa,	sepamos,	sepáis,	sepan
ser *to be*	sea,	seas,	sea,	seamos,	seáis,	sean

The present subjunctive for **hay** *there is/are*, is **haya**.

Prefiero un piso que no esté muy lejos de la oficina. — *I prefer a flat which is not too far from the office.*

Quiero una persona que sea vegetariana. — *I want a vegetarian person.*

2 Expressing hope with regard to others

Hope with regard to others is expressed with the construction **esperar que** + *subjunctive*.

Espero que encuentres un inquilino. — *I hope you find a tenant.*

Esperamos que ella sepa
español.

*We hope she knows
Spanish.*

But note:

Espero encontrar un inquilino.   *I hope to find a tenant.*

3 Expressing doubt

A phrase such as **No creo que ...**, *I don't think that ...*, must be
followed by a verb in the subjunctive.

No creo que sea fácil.   *I don't think it will be easy.*

But

Creo que es fácil.   *I think it is easy.*

Practice

1 Buscando un lugar donde vivir

Look at the advertisements below placed by people looking for
a flat or room to rent or let, or someone to share.

1.1 Can you give the contact
name or telephone number for
each of the following?

a   an English teacher wanting to
share a flat
b   someone offering a room to a
vegetarian and non-smoker
c   a student of French looking for
accommodation with a
French family
d   someone offering a large,
sunny room to a female
e   someone looking for a two-
bedroom flat to rent
f   someone looking for free
accommodation for a weekend

1.2 One of the advertisements is
in Catalan. Can you spot it? Give
the contact number.

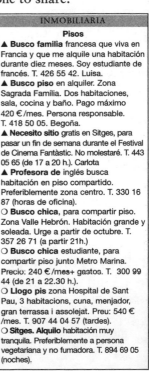

INMOBILIARIA

Pisos

▲ **Busco familia** francesa que viva en
Francia y que me alquile una habitación
durante diez meses. Soy estudiante de
francés. T. 426 55 42. Luisa.

▲ **Busco piso** en alquiler. Zona
Sagrada Família. Dos habitaciones,
sala, cocina y baño. Pago máximo
420 € /mes. Persona responsable.
T. 418 50 05. Begoña.

▲ **Necesito sitio** gratis en Sitges, para
pasar un fin de semana durante el Festival
de Cinema Fantàstic. No molestaré. T. 443
05 65 (de 17 a 20 h.). Carlota

▲ **Profesora de** inglés busca
habitación en piso compartido.
Preferiblemente zona centro. T. 330 16
87 (horas de oficina).

○ **Busco chica,** para compartir piso.
Zona Valle Hebrón. Habitación grande y
soleada. Urge a partir de octubre. T.
357 26 71 (a partir 21h.)

○ **Busco chica** estudiante, para
compartir piso junto Metro Marina.
Precio: 240 € /mes+ gastos. T. 300 99
44 (de 21 a 22.30 h.).

○ **Llogo pis** zona Hospital de Sant
Pau, 3 habitacions, cuna, menjador,
gran terrassa i assolejat. Preu: 540 €
/mes. T. 907 44 04 57 (tardes).

○ **Sitges. Alquilo** habitación muy
tranquila. Preferiblemente a persona
vegetariana y no fumadora. T. 894 69 05
(noches).

2 Estudiante busca familia española

One of your friends is travelling to Salamanca to do a Spanish course and would like to stay with a family. His/her Spanish is not very good, and he/she needs help to compose the following advertisement. Try making sense of what he/she wants by changing the verbs in brackets into the appropriate form of the present subjunctive.

> *Estudiante busca habitación con familia española*
>
> Estudiante de habla inglesa de 20 años busca familia española que (vivir) en Salamanca y que me (alquilar) una habitación durante el mes de agosto. Prefiero una familia en la que (hay) otras personas de mi edad que (poder) ayudarme con mi español. Preferiblemente un sitio que (estar) cerca de la universidad. T. +44 (0)20 7741 3462.

3 Ahora tú

You will be spending some time in a Spanish-speaking country in order to improve your Spanish, and would like to share a flat with someone. Write an advertisement like those in Activity 1, or a note like the one above, saying what you are looking for.

4 No creo que..., espero que...

Raúl and his flatmates are trying to choose another person to share their flat. His friend Juan hopes the person they are discussing will be the right one, but Carmen is rather pessimistic. Follow the example and answer for Juan and Carmen.

Raúl   ¿Pagará puntualmente?
Juan   Espero que pague puntualmente.
Carmen   No creo que pague puntualmente.

a   ¿Será sociable?
b   ¿Estará dispuesto a hacer la limpieza?
c   ¿Sabrá guisar?
d   ¿Tendrá sentido del humor?
e   ¿Le gustarán los animales domésticos?
f   ¿Se llevará bien con nosotros?

¿le gustarán los animales domésticos?

dispuesto a	*willing to*
los animales domésticos	*pets*
hacer la limpieza	*to clean (up)*
llevarse bien con	*to get on well with*

5 Los requisitos más importantes

Here is a list of requirements people sometimes demand from job applicants.

5.1 Give the English for each of the following:

a saber idiomas
b saber conducir
c saber relacionarse
d ser creativo
e ser dinámico
f tener experiencia
g tener buena presencia
h tener estudios superiores
i tener conocimientos de informática
j tener vehículo propio
k estar dispuesto a viajar
l estar disponible de inmediato

5.2 Which requirements do you fulfil?

| **disponible** | *available* |

5.3 Would you add other requirements to the list? Which ones?

6 Se busca

6.1 Which of the requirements above can be found in the advertisements below?

6.2 Which are new?

EMPRESA COMERCIAL requiere:
SECRETARIA EJECUTIVA BILINGÜE
Area Comercial

- Dominio idioma Inglés
- Manejo Word
- Buena presencia.
- Aptitud para coordinar servicios menores.
- Experiencia en cargo similar a lo menos 2 años.

Enviar curriculum vitae con foto y pretensiones de renta a:
Casilla 13-D, Santiago.

IMPORTANTE
EMPRESA REQUIERE
CONTRATAR
PROGRAMADOR/A
Título profesional universitario.
Experiencia mínima 3 años.
Conocimiento lenguajes.
QBasic. Visual Basic.
Experiencia Red Novell 3.12
Disponibilidad inmediata.
Enviar antecedentes con pretensiones de sueldo líquido y fotografía reciente a:
CASILLA 13–28
SANTIAGO

▶ 7 ¿Qué tipo de persona buscan?

Alfonso's place of work is expanding and they need a public relations employee. What sort of person do you think they might be looking for?

7.1 Listen to this conversation between Alfonso and his colleague Isabel, and say which of the requirements in Activity 5 they are asking for.

7.2 You've been asked to draft some information which is to be sent to job applicants. Can you complete the passage below? Listen again.

Buscamos una persona que _____ bien con la gente, y que _____ dos o tres años _____ como mínimo, que _____ y, preferiblemente, algo de _____, que _____ conocimientos de _____ y que _____ conducir.

| **trabajar en equipo** | *to work in a team* |

8 Una historia personal

In Spain, as in other industrialized countries, the people most affected by *unemployment*, **el desempleo**, are the young. A *university degree*, **un título universitario**, is not enough, and companies are looking for people with experience and who are *highly qualified*, **muy bien cualificados**. The following extract from a Spanish magazine tells about Jaime's experience with job-hunting. Read the text and find out how the situation in Spain compares with that in your country. First, look at these questions and try to find the answer to them as you read.

a ¿Qué estudios tiene Jaime?
b ¿Qué idiomas sabe?
c ¿Cómo es su carácter?
d ¿Tiene experiencia?
e ¿Qué exigen los empleadores (*employers*)?
f ¿Cómo se siente Jaime?

> Jaime M. tiene veintiocho años, la carrera de empresariales, un máster de una universidad británica, habla y escribe perfectamente inglés, habla y escribe menos perfectamente francés. Extrovertido, simpático … Nunca ha conseguido un empleo. No sabe lo que es trabajar en una oficina, en un despacho, tener un jefe o

un compañero … No encuentra un empleo, aunque ha ido docenas de veces al INEM (Instituto Nacional del Empleo), ha enviado su currículum cien veces, se sabe de memoria los anuncios de los periódicos … En unos sitios le exigen experiencia; en otros, creen que con sus títulos merece más de lo que le pueden ofrecer, y Jaime M. está desesperado. Total y absolutamente desesperado … Jaime M. no es una excepción …

conseguir	*to get*
el despacho	*office*
docenas de veces	*a dozen times*
el anuncio	*advertisement*
saber de memoria	*to know by heart*
merecer	*to deserve*

9 Ahora tú

a ¿Cómo es la situación en tu país? ¿Es difícil encontrar empleo?

b ¿Quiénes tienen más dificultad para encontrar empleo: los hombres, las mujeres, los jóvenes en general?

c ¿Qué tipo de persona buscan normalmente las empresas?

Congratulations on completing *Teach Yourself Spanish*!

We hope you have enjoyed working your way through the course. We are always keen to receive feedback from people who have used our course, so why not contact us and let us know your reactions? We'll be particularly pleased to receive your praise, but we should also like to know if things could be improved. We always welcome comments and suggestions, and we do our best to incorporate constructive suggestions into later editions.

> You can contact us through the publishers at:
> Teach Yourself Books, Hodder Headline Ltd,
> 338 Euston Road, London NW1 3BH, UK

We hope you will want to build on your knowledge of Spanish and have made a few suggestions to help you do this in the section entitled **Taking it further**, on page 262.

¡Buena suerte!
Juan Kattán-Ibarra

Units 1–5

1 Fill in the gaps in this dialogue with an appropriate question word.

a '¿ _____ se llama usted?' 'Maricarmen García.'
b '¿ _____ está?' 'Muy bien, gracias, ¿y usted?'
c '¿De _____ es usted?' 'De Bilbao.'
d '¿ _____ número de teléfono tiene?' 'El 209 1520.'
e 'Y el teléfono de su oficina, ¿ _____ es?' 'El 312 2104.'
f '¿ _____ vive?' 'En la calle de San Pablo.'
g '¿ _____ va a tomar?' 'Quiero pescado con patatas fritas.'

(Units 1, 2, 3, 4, 5)

2 Fill in the gaps in this dialogue with the correct form of **ser** and **estar**.

Jaime   Hola, ¿cómo _____ (tú)?
Eloísa   (Yo) _____ muy bien, gracias.
Jaime   Ésta _____ Mónica, una amiga.
Eloísa   Hola, ¿qué tal? (Tú) no _____ española, ¿verdad?
Mónica   No, _____ argentina. _____ de Salta.
Eloísa   ¿Dónde _____ Salta?
Mónica   _____ en el norte de Argentina.

(Units 1, 2, 4)

3 You'll be meeting a group of Spanish speakers, so be prepared to exchange greetings and some personal information.

a Say 'good afternoon', and give your name and nationality.
b Spell your name and surname.
c Say what languages you speak.
d Tell someone you are pleased to meet him/her. (Give two alternatives.)

e Introduce Sarah Johnson, a colleague, to someone you don't know well.

f Say where you live and what your telephone number is.

(Antes de empezar, Units 3, 4)

4 You arrive in a hotel in a Spanish-speaking country. Use the guidelines below to fill in your part of the conversation with the hotel receptionist.

– ¿Dígame?
– *Say good evening, and that you want a single room with a bathroom for three nights.*
– De acuerdo.
– *Ask where the restaurant is.*
– En el primer piso.
– *Ask whether you can have dinner now.*
– Sí, el restaurante está abierto.
– *Ask if there is a bank nearby. You want to change money.*
– *The receptionist is speaking too fast. Ask him/her to speak more slowly.*

(Antes de empezar, Units 3, 4)

5 Which place or street in the map below does each of the following sentences refer to? You are at the corner of Defensa and México, looking towards calle San Juan.

a Hay uno al final de la calle Defensa, a la derecha.
b Está enfrente del banco.
c Está a la izquierda, al lado del supermercado.
d Está en la esquina de Defensa a Estados Unidos.
e Está en la calle Defensa, casi esquina a Independencia, a la izquierda.
f Es la tercera calle.
g Es la segunda calle.

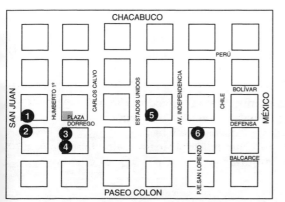

1 banco
2 iglesia
3 museo
4 supermercado
5 Hotel Nacional
6 correos

(Unit 4)

6 Change the verbs in italics into the appropriate form of the present tense.

a (Nosotros) *querer* el menú del día.
b (Yo) *querer* pescado a la plancha con patatas fritas.
c ¿Qué *querer* tú?
d (Yo) *preferir* pollo con puré.
e ¿Qué *tener* (usted) de postre?
f (Nosotros) *tener* flan, helados y melón.
g Por favor, ¿me *traer* (usted) un helado de fresa?

(Units 2, 3, 5)

Units 6–10

1 Answer the questions below with **Es la ...**, **Son las ...**, **A la/las ...**, as appropriate. Use the times in brackets.

a Por favor, ¿qué hora es? (1.15)
b ¿Qué hora es? (2.40)
c ¿A qué hora sale el próximo tren para Salamanca? (5.45)
d ¿Y a qué hora llega? (6.30)
e ¿Tienes hora? (4.10)
f ¿A qué hora cierra la tienda? (1.00)

(Unit 6)

2 Study this exchange between a customer and a shop assistant, then write similar dialogues using the words below.

– ¿Cuánto cuestan esos pantalones?
– ¿Éstos?
– Sí, ésos.

a (las) gafas
b (el) perfume
c (la) crema para el sol
d (los) zapatos

(Unit 7)

3 Fill in the gaps in these sentences with one or more of these words: **me, le, les, lo, los, la, las, nos**. Add an accent where appropriate.

a Perdone, estas camisetas, ¿en qué color _____ tiene?
b Esta chaqueta es muy bonita. ¿Puedo probar _____?
c ¿Cómo _____ quedan esos zapatos, señor?
d Estos zapatos _____ quedan muy bien. _____ _____ llevo.
e Por favor, de _____ un billete de ida y vuelta para Málaga.
f Quisiéramos alquilar un coche. ¿Qué coche _____ recomienda?

g ¿Quieren ustedes un coche económico? Pues, _____ recomiendo éste.

(Units 7, 8)

4 Rita and Ramón are planning a holiday and they are comparing two possible hotels, rating these from 1 to 5, with 5 being the highest mark and 1 the lowest. Look at the chart below and write comparative sentences with the following words, using expressions like **más ... que, mejor, tan ... como**, as appropriate.

a cerca	**d** barato
b vista	**e** grande
c tranquilo	**f** cómodo

(Unit 9)

	Hotel Costa Azul	Hotel Playa Blanca
precio	5	3
comodidad	4	2
cercanía a la playa	1	4
tranquilidad	3	3
tamaño de las habitaciones	4	4
vista	3	4

5 Rosa wrote to someone about herself and her family. Change the infinitives in brackets into the right form of the present tense.

Me llamo Rosa, (tener) 28 años, (estar) casada y (tener) un hijo de dos años. (Ser) enfermera y (trabajar) en un hospital. Mi marido se llama Antonio, (tener) 30 años, (ser) contable y (trabajar) en un banco. Antonio y yo (estar) casados desde hace cuatro años y (vivir) en Toledo desde hace tres años y medio.

(Units 9, 10)

6 While staying at a hotel in a Spanish-speaking country you meet someone. How would you ask the following? Use the informal form.

a how long he/she has been there
b whether he/she is there with his/her family
c what he/she does for a living
d how long he/she has been working there
e how many weeks holidays a year he/she has

(Unit 10)

Units 11–15

1 Fill in the missing verbs in this chart with the appropriate form of the present tense.

yo	tú	él/ella	nosotros/as
me levanto	——	——	nos levantamos
——	sales	——	——
——	——	va	——
——	——	——	empezamos
——	vuelves	——	——
——	——	come	——
——	——	——	nos acostamos

(Unit 11)

2 Antonio wrote to a friend describing his daily routine. Fill in the gaps with a verb from the list, using the appropriate form of the present tense. Do not repeat any.

> almorza   desayunar   leer   levantarse   trabajar   ver
> volver   ducharse   llegar   salir

Normalmente _____ a las siete de la mañana, luego _____
Después de ducharme, _____, normalmente un café y unas
tostadas. A las ocho y media _____ para el trabajo y _____ allí
sobre las nueve. Al mediodía _____ con unos colegas en un
restaurante cerca de la oficina. Por la tarde _____ desde las tres
hasta las siete. A las siete _____ a casa, _____ el periódico o
_____ la televisión un rato.

(Unit 11)

3 In a letter to a friend, Carmen wrote about the things she and her family like to do in their spare time. Rewrite the following passage, using the right form of the infinitives in brackets.

A mí (encantar) los deportes. El tenis, especialmente, (gustar) mucho. Pero a Javier, mi marido, no (gustar) nada los deportes. Él (preferir) leer y ver la televisión. A mis hijos (fascinar) la televisión también. A nosotros (encantar) salir fuera de la ciudad los fines de semana. Y a ti, ¿qué (gustar) hacer en tu tiempo libre?

(Unit 12)

4 Everyone has an assignment at the office today. How would you ask the following people what they are going to do, and how

would they reply? Look at the information below and write out the questions and answers, using the appropriate form of **ir a +** *infinitive*, e.g. **¿Qué va a hacer? Va a trabajar,** *What is he/she going to do? He/she is going to work.*

Use the familiar form:

a Paco escribir un informe
b María y Pepe contestar unas cartas

Use the formal form:

c Sra. Martínez recibir a un cliente
d Sr. Díaz y Srta. Pérez realizar unas entrevistas

(Unit 13)

5 You are left in charge of the phone at Anglohispania, a company which does trade with Spain and Latin America, and you need to make some calls yourself. How would you express the following in Spanish?

a Hello?
b You've got the wrong number.
c Who's calling?
d I'll put you through right away.
e He'll be with you right away.
f Do you want to leave a message?
g I'd like to speak to señor Julián.
h Can you put me through to señora Lira?
i I'd like to arrange an interview with the manager.
j Please tell him/her that I phoned.

(Unit 14)

6 After his return from a holiday in Cuba, Emilio wrote a letter to a friend, describing it. Change the infinitives in brackets into the proper form of the preterite tense.

Querida Marta:

Hace sólo una semana que (regresar) de Cuba y no te imaginas lo bien que lo (pasar). (Estar) una semana en La Habana. Es una ciudad preciosa. Me (encantar). También (ir) a Varadero. Allí (quedarse) en casa de Alejandro, un amigo cubano. Alejandro y yo (visitar) Trinidad, una ciudad colonial y luego (volver) juntos a La Habana, donde (yo) (tomar) el avión para regresar a España. (Llegar) a Madrid el sábado por la tarde y el lunes pasado (empezar) a trabajar ...

(Unit 15)

7 How would you tell someone about Emilio's holiday? Begin like this:

Emilio regresó de Cuba hace una semana y lo pasó muy bien ...

(Unit 15)

Units 16–20

1 Use the verbs in brackets to complete this biography of King Juan Carlos I of Spain. You'll need to use the preterite tense.

Juan Carlos de Borbón y Borbón, rey de España, (nacer) en Roma en el año 1938. Su abuelo (ser) el rey Alfonso XIII, quien (abdicar) en el año 1931. Juan Carlos (educarse) en Suiza y a la edad de 16 años (ingresar) en la Academia Militar de Zaragoza. Más tarde (realizar) estudios de económicas, política y derecho en la Universidad de Madrid. En el año 1962 (casarse) con la Princesa Sofía de Grecia. En 1969 (ser) designado futuro rey, en lugar de su padre, y en 1975, dos días después de la muerte de Franco, (empezar) su reinado como Juan Carlos I.

(Units 15, 16)

2 Víctor remembers the time he met Elisa. Complete his account by choosing the right verb, the preterite or the imperfect tense.

(Yo) (conocí/conocía) a Elisa en el año 1951, cuando (yo) (tuve/tenía) sólo veinte años. En aquel tiempo (yo) (estuve/estaba) en la universidad. Elisa (fue/era) mi nueva vecina, (tuvo/tenía) diecisiete años, y (vivió/vivía) con su madre, que (trabajó/trabajaba) en Correos. Recuerdo el primer día que la (vi/veía). (Yo) (fui/iba) a la universidad y ella (volvió/volvía) de la compra. La (saludé/saludaba) al pasar, pero no me (respondió/respondía). Días más tarde la (vi/veía) otra vez y le (hablé/hablaba). Ése (fue/era) nuestro primer encuentro ...

(Units 15, 16, 17, 18)

3 Julio and his colleagues Rafael and Silvia are talking about what they have done at the office today. Choose an appropriate verb from the list to complete the sentences below. The first sentence in each column has been done for you.

> hablar   entrevistar   hacer   ir   enviar
> volver   escribir   asistir

Julio

a   He llegado a la oficina
    a las 8.30.
b   _____ muchas llamadas
    telefónicas.
c   _____ varios faxes.
d   _____ con varios clientes.
e   _____ a dos reuniones.

Rafael y Silvia

f   Hemos despachado varios
    pedidos.
g   _____ muchísimas cartas.
h   _____ a tres personas
    para un nuevo puesto.
i   _____ al aeropuerto.
j   _____ a casa muy cansados.

(Unit 19)

4 How would you tell someone else what Julio and his colleagues Rafael and Silvia have done? Change the verbs above into the right form.

(Unit 19)

5 Ana is planning a holiday, and she tells a friend what she will do. Fill in the gaps in the following sentences with an appropriate verb from the box, using the future tense.

> hacer   quedarse   ir   llegar   viajar   volver   salir

a   Este año _____ de vacaciones a Buenos Aires.
b   _____ de Madrid el día 23.
c   _____ en Iberia.
d   El avión _____ escala en San Pablo.
e   _____ a Buenos Aires al día siguiente.
f   _____ en casa de unos amigos argentinos.
g   _____ a Madrid el 7 de agosto.

(Unit 20)

6 How would you tell someone what Ana will do? Change the verbs into the appropriate form.

(Unit 20)

Units 21–5

1 José and his friends Raquel and Pablo are talking about the things they would do if they won a big prize in the lottery. Speak for them by changing the infinitives in brackets into the appropriate form of the conditional tense (Unit 21).

José

a No (trabajar) más.
b (Hacer) un viaje alrededor del mundo.
c (Comprar) una casa para mí y otra para mis padres.
d (Poner) el dinero en un banco y (vivir) de los intereses.

Raquel y Pablo

e (Poder) pagar todas nuestras deudas.
f (Enviar) a nuestros hijos a los mejores colegios.
g (Ayudar) a nuestras familias.
h (Irse) a vivir al mejor barrio de la ciudad.

(Unit 21)

2 A Spanish-speaking person is visiting your place of work and you are having lunch with them. How would you express the following in Spanish? The relationship is formal.

a Had you been to (*your own country or town*) before?
b What do you think of the city?
c Shall I give you some more?
d Would you like some more wine?
e I'll take you to your hotel in my car.
f I'm very glad to have met you.

(Unit 22)

3 You are staying in a hotel at the corner of Antonio Varas and Diagonal Oriente and you need to visit a place at number 1436 on Eduardo de la Barra. A note with directions has been left for you at reception, but these are wrong. Look at the map and correct them.

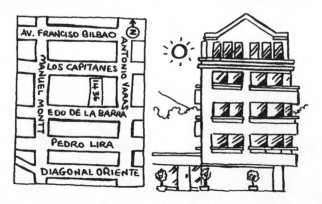

Siga todo recto por Antonio Varas y al llegar a Eduardo de la Barra gire a la derecha. El número 1436 está a la izquierda, entre Antonio Varas y Los Capitanes.

Some Spanish-speaking people are visiting your place of work and they are asking for directions. How would you express the following? Use the formal form.

a Go straight on and then take the third turning on the left. The bank is at the end of that street.

b Go up those stairs to the first floor. The toilets are on the right, past the telephones.

(Unit 23)

5 Match each statement on the left with the most appropriate request or advice on the right.

a	Tengo sed	1	Abre la ventana, por favor.
b	Tengo hambre	2	Ve al dentista.
c	Tengo frío	3	Tráeme algo para beber.
d	Tengo calor	4	Por favor, dame una aspirina.
e	Tengo dolor de cabeza	5	Ponte un jersey.
f	Me duelen las muelas	6	Come algo.

(Unit 24)

6 Merche and Nicolás are each looking for the ideal partner. What sort of person does each want? Complete the sentences below with the appropriate form of each of the verbs in brackets, making other changes where necessary.

a Merche busca un novio que (ser) inteligente, (tener) sentido del humor, no (fumar) y la (querer) de verdad.

b Nicolás quiere una novia que (ser) guapa, (saber) varios idiomas, (llevarse) bien con él y (estar) dispuesta a casarse.

(Unit 25)

261

testing yourself

taking it further

Sources of authentic Spanish

Spanish newspapers

El País (http://www.elpais.es)
El Mundo (http://www.el-mundo.es/)
La Vanguardia (http://www.lavanguardia.es)
ABC (http://www.abc.es)
El Periódico (http://www.elperiodico.es/)

Spanish magazines

For general information, including Spanish current affairs and world news, try the following:

Cambio 16, Tiempo, Tribuna, etc.

For light reading and entertainment you might like to look at the following magazines:

Hola, Quo, Mía, Pronto, Lecturas, Semana, etc.

These are by far the most popular amongst Spaniards and, as a beginner, you may find some of the articles easier to follow.

Latin American newspapers and magazines

Latin American newspapers and magazines will be more difficult to find outside each country, but if you have internet facilities you will be able to access their websites, although they may be special net versions.

Argentina

La Nación (http://lanacion.com.ar)
Clarín (http://www.clarin.com.ar)

Chile

El Mercurio (http://www.elmercurio.cl)

Colombia

El Espectador (http://www.elespectador.com)

Cuba

Granma (http://www.granma.cubaweb.cu)

México

El Universal (http://www.el-universal.com.mx)

Perú

El Comercio (http://www.elcomercioperu.com.pe)
Correo (http://www.correoperu.com.pe)

Radio and television

An excellent way to improve your understanding of spoken Spanish is to listen to radio and watch television. On medium wave after dark and via satellite you will be able to gain access to Radio Nacional de España, Televisión Española (TVE) and other stations. And for spoken Latin American Spanish, you may like to tune in to the BBC Spanish Latin American Service, which can be heard on short wave.

Travelling in Spain and Latin America

Travelling in a Spanish-speaking country is probably the best way to practise what you have learnt and improve your command of the spoken language. If you are planning to do this, there are a number of good guidebooks which will help you to plan your journey. The well-known *Lonely Planet* guides cover not just specific countries, but also the main regions and cities, including Spain and Latin America. For the latter, the *Mexico and Central American Handbook* and the *South American Handbook* have a long tradition amongst travellers in the region. *Time Out, Michelin, Fodor's,* among several others, have also become well established in the travelling market.

For travellers in Spain, the following websites may prove useful, with information such as tourist attractions, accommodation, travel, restaurants, etc.:

Travelling to Spain: http://www.SiSpain.org/english/travelli

Spain Today (local section of the *Europe Today* travel guide): http://www.wtg-online.com/data/esp/esp.asp

All about Spain: http://www.red2000.com

Páginas amarillas del viajero (yellow pages for travellers): http://www.spaindata.com/data/1index.shtm/.

For the Spanish National Tourist Office try:
http://www.tourspain.co.uk
http://www.spaintour.com/offices.htm

Travellers in Latin America will find useful information in
Travel Latin America: http://www.travellatinamerica.com/es/
Latin America – travel notes:
http://www.travelnotes.org/LatinAmerica/index.htm
Travel Latin America: http://travellatinamerica.com

Culture and history

If you are interested in the culture and history of the Spanish-speaking countries, there are a number of publications in English which deal with such matters, some in less detail than others. Publications in Spanish usually require a much higher level of language than you may have at present, but some are geared towards students of Hispanic studies and may be easier to follow. The best thing is to seek advice from a specialist bookseller of foreign-language books.

Internet users interested in Spain may like to try the following sites:

Historia – Sí Spain: http://www.sispain.org/spanish/history;

About.com – Spanish culture: http://spanisculture.about.com/;

Secretaría de Estado y Cultura de España (for a virtual visit to El Prado Museum) http://museoprado.mcu.es

Users searching other information and websites in the Spanish net may find what they need in *Sí – Spain*:
http://www.sispain.org/english/otherweb.html

For Latin America go to:
Internet resources for Latin America:
http://lib.nmsu.edu/subject/bord/index.html

Latin American Network Information Center:
http://lanic.utexas.edu/las.html

Spanish language courses

The Instituto Cervantes, a worldwide organization, offers courses in Spanish and promotes Spanish culture in general; the Hispanic Council, in the United Kingdom, based in London, may be able to help you with enquiries about Spanish language courses and aspects of life in Spain. For information on Latin American Spanish you can contact the Hispanic Council or the embassy of the country you are interested in.

Information on Spanish language courses in Spain can also be found in a number of websites, several of which relate to specific language schools. For more general information and listings of schools you might like to look up:

Instituto Cervantes, http://www.cervantes.es/

Language schools – learning vacations: http://www.learningvacations.com

For Latin American Spanish, go to

Spanish language schools: http://www.ibw.com.ni/~nssmga/

Worldwide classroom – Mexico schools: http://www.worldwide.edu/ci/mexico

adjectives Adjectives are used to provide more information about nouns, e.g. That school is very *good*. **Ese colegio es muy bueno**. The *new* hotel is *excellent*. **El *nuevo* hotel es *excelente***.

adverbs Adverbs tend to provide more information about verbs. He left *quietly*. **Salió *silenciosamente***. But adverbs can also provide more information on adjectives: It was *totally* unnecessary. **Era *totalmente* innecesario**. In English, adverbs often (but not always) end in **-ly**. The equivalent of this in Spanish is **-mente**.

articles There are two types of articles, *definite* and *indefinite*. In English, the definite article is *the* – **el/la/los/las** in Spanish. **A, un/una**, are the indefinite articles.

comparative When we make comparisons we need the comparative form of the adjective. In English this usually means adding *-er* to the adjective or putting *more* in front of it. This shirt is *cheaper than* that one. **Esta camisa es *más* barata *que* ésa**. This blouse is *more* expensive *than* that one. **Esta blusa es *más* cara *que* ésa**. See also **superlative**.

demonstratives Words like *this éste*, *that ése*, *these éstos*, *those ésos* are called **demonstratives**.

gender In English, gender is usually linked to male and female persons or animals, so, for example, we refer to a man as *he* and to a woman as *she*. Objects and beings of an indeterminate sex are referred to as having *neuter* gender. So, for instance, we refer to a table as *it*. In Spanish, nouns referring to female persons are feminine and those referring to male people are masculine. But all nouns are either masculine or feminine in Spanish and this has nothing to do with sex. **La mesa** *table*, **la mano** *hand*, are feminine, while **el mes** *month*, **el día** *day*, are masculine. While there are some rules to help you, you have to accept that the gender of every noun has to be learned.

imperative The imperative is the form of the verb used to give directions, instructions, orders or commands: *Turn* right at the corner. *Gire* a la derecha en la esquina. First *dial* 020. Primero *marque* el 020.

infinitive The infinitive is the basic form of the verb. This is the form that you will find entered in the dictionary. In Spanish, infinitives end in -ar, -er, and -ir, e.g. habl**ar** *to speak*, com**er** *to eat*, viv**ir** *to live*.

irregular verbs Life would be considerably easier if all verbs behaved in a regular fashion. Unfortunately, Spanish, like other European languages, has verbs which do not behave according to a set pattern and which are therefore commonly referred to as irregular verbs.

nouns Nouns are words like *house* casa, *bread* pan and *wealth* riqueza. They are often called 'naming words'.

number The term is used to indicate whether something is *singular* or *plural*. See **singular**.

object The term *object* expresses the 'receiving end' relationship between a noun and a verb. So, for instance, the thief is said to be at the receiving end of the arrest in the sentence 'The policeman arrested *the thief*'. El policía arrestó *al ladrón*. The thief is therefore said to be the *object* of the sentence.

In sentences such as 'My mother gave *the driver some money*', the phrase '*some money*' is said to be the *direct object*, because the money is actually what the mother gave. The phrase '*the driver*' is said to be the *indirect object* because the driver was the recipient of the giving.

plural See **singular**.

personal pronouns As their name suggests, personal pronouns refer to persons, e.g. *I* yo, *you* tú, usted, *he* él, *she* ella, etc. See **pronouns**.

possessives Words like *my* mi, *your* tu, su, *our* nuestro are called possessives. So are words such as *mine* mío, *yours* tuyo, suyo, etc.

pronouns Pronouns fulfil a similar function to nouns and often stand in the place of nouns which have already been mentioned, e.g. My *girlfriend* (noun) is twenty-five years old. *She* (pronoun) is very pretty. Mi *novia* tiene veinticinco años. *Ella* es muy guapa.

prepositions Words like *in* en, *for* por, para, *between* entre, are called prepositions. Prepositions often tell us about the position of something. They are normally followed by a noun or a pronoun, e.g. The bank is *between* the school and the church. El banco está *entre* el colegio y la iglesia. This present is *for* you. Este regalo es *para* ti.

reflexive pronouns Words such as *myself* me, *yourself* te, se, *ourselves* nos, are called reflexive pronouns.

reflexive verbs When the subject and the object of a verb are one and the same, the verb is said to be reflexive, e.g. *I washed myself* before going out. **Me lavé antes de salir.** We enjoyed *ourselves* very much. **Nos divertimos** mucho.

singular The terms *singular* and *plural* are used to make the contrast between 'one' and 'more than one', e.g. *book/books* libro/libros, *city/cities* ciudad/ciudades.

subject The term *subject* expresses a relationship between a noun and a verb. So, for instance, in the sentence 'My mother gave the driver some money', because it is the mother who does the giving, the mother is said to be the subject of the verb *to give*, dar.

subjunctive mood The so-called subjunctive mood is used very rarely in modern English, but there are remnants of it in such sentences as If I *were* you. **Yo en tu lugar.** I insist that he *come*. **Insisto en que venga.** Spanish uses the subjunctive much more frequently than English.

superlative The superlative is used for the most extreme version of a comparison. This shirt is the *cheapest* of all. **Esta camisa es la más barata** de todas. This blouse is the most expensive of all. **Esta blusa es la más cara** de todas. See also **comparative**.

tense Most languages use changes in the verb to indicate an aspect of time. These changes in the verb are traditionally referred to as tense, and the tenses may be *present*, *past* or *future*, e.g., They *went* out. **Salieron** (*past*). She *is* at home. **Está en casa** (*present*). We *will* go to the cinema **Iremos** al cine (*future*).

verbs Verbs often communicate actions, e.g., *to play* jugar, states, e.g. *to exist* existir, and sensations, e.g. *to see* ver. A verb may also be defined by its role in the sentence, and usually has a subject, e.g. My head (*subject*) aches (*verb*). **Me duele la cabeza.**

1 Definite and indefinite articles (Unit 2)

a   The word for *the* for singular nouns is **el** for masculine and **la** for feminine, e.g. **el hotel, la habitación**. The plural forms are **los, las**, e.g. **los hoteles, las habitaciones**.
b   The word for *a/an* is **un** for masculine and **una** for feminine, e.g. **un señor, una señora**.
c   A + **el** becomes **al**, e.g. Voy **al** cine, and **de** + **el** becomes **del**, e.g. Vengo **del** supermercado (Unit 2).

2 Nouns

2.1 Masculine and feminine (Unit 2)

a   In Spanish, all nouns are either masculine or feminine. Nouns ending in -o are usually masculine, while those ending in -a are usually feminine, e.g. **el desayuno, la cena**.
b   Words referring to males and females, such as occupations, must change. To form the feminine, change -o to -a or add a to the consonant, e.g. **el doctor, la doctora**.
c   Nouns ending in -ista and many of those ending in -nte are invariable, e.g. **el/la artista, el/la estudiante**.
d   Some nouns have different forms for male and female, e.g. **el padre, la madre**.

2.2 Singular and plural (Units 3 and 9)

a   Nouns ending in a vowel form the plural by adding -s, e.g. **el libro, los libros**.
b   Nouns ending in a consonant add -es, e.g. **la ciudad, las ciudades**.

c   The masculine plural of some nouns may be used to refer to members of both sexes, e.g. **el padre, la madre, los padres**.

3 Adjectives (Units 1 and 7)

3.1 Number and gender agreement

Adjectives must agree in gender and number with the noun they describe.

a   Adjectives ending in -o change -o to -a with feminine nouns, e.g. **un hotel pequeño, una habitación pequeña**.

b   As a general rule, adjectives ending in a letter other than -o or -a do not change for masculine and feminine, e.g. **el vestido azul, la camisa azul**.

c   Adjectives indicating nationality form the feminine by adding -a to the consonant or changing -o into -a, e.g. **un amigo español, una amiga española**.

d   To form the plural of adjectives follow the same rules as for nouns.

3.2 Position of adjectives

a   The great majority of adjectives come after the noun, e.g. **una persona inteligente**.

b   Adjectives are sometimes used before nouns for emphasis or to convey some kind of emotion, e.g. **un excelente profesor**.

c   Certain adjectives, among them **grande, pequeño, bueno, malo**, usually precede the adjective, e.g. **un pequeño problema**.

d   **Grande** normally follows the noun when its meaning is 'big' or 'large', but it goes before it when it means 'great'. *Before* the noun, **grande** becomes **gran**, e.g. **una persona grande, una gran persona**.

e   **Bueno** and **malo** become **buen** and **mal** before masculine singular nouns, e.g. **un buen/mal momento**.

3.3 Comparative forms of adjectives (Unit 9)

Comparisons such as **más ... que, tan ... como** and **el/la/los/las más ...**, are explained in Unit 9.

4 Adverbs

a To form an adverb from an adjective, add **-mente** to the singular form of the adjective, e.g. **amable, amablemente**.
b If the adjective ends in **-o**, change the **-o to -a** and then add **-mente**, e.g. **rápido, rápidamente**.
c Many adverbs are not derived from adjectives, e.g. **ahora, mañana, aquí, bien**.

5 Pronouns

5.1 Subject pronouns (Units 1 and 3)

a These are **yo, tú** (*informal, sing.*), **usted** (*formal, sing.*), **él, ella, nosotros/as, vosotros/as** (*informal, pl.*), **ustedes** (*formal, pl.*), **ellos, ellas**.
b Subject pronouns are usually omitted in Spanish, unless you want to show emphasis or to avoid ambiguity.
c **Vosotros** and all forms that go with it are not used in Latin America, where **ustedes** is used in formal and informal address.

5.2 Direct and indirect object pronouns (Units 5, 7, 8)

Object pronouns can be direct, e.g. *La* **invité**, *I invited her*, or indirect, as in *Le* **dije**, *I said to her/him/you* (*formal*).

First and second person
In the first and second person singular and plural there is no distinction between direct and indirect object pronouns, e.g. *Me* **invitó**, *He/she invited me*, *Me* **dijo**, *He/she said to me*.

singular		plural	
me	*me, to me*	**nos**	*us, to us*
te	*you, to you (informal)*	**os**	*you, to you (informal)*

Third person
In the third person, direct and indirect object pronouns differ, e.g. **Lo** *or* **Le invité**, *I invited him*, **Le dije**, *I said to him/her*.

Direct object pronouns				
	singular		*plural*	
masc.	lo/le	you (formal)/him/it	los/les	you (formal)/them
fem.	la	you (formal)/her/it	las	you (formal)/them

i **Le/s,** as a direct object, is used by most people in central and northern Spain when talking about human males, e.g. **Le llamé,** *I called him*, with **lo/s** referring to masculine objects, e.g. **Lo compré,** *I bought it*. In other parts of Spain and in Latin America as a whole most people use **lo/s** for both human males and masculine objects, e.g. **Lo llamé, Lo compré**. In the feminine there are generally no regional differences. The 'lo' form may be easier for you to remember.

Indirect object pronouns	
singular	*plural*
le (to) you (formal)/him/her/it	les (to) you (formal)/them

Le and **les** become **se** before **lo, la, los, las: Se lo daré,** *I'll give it to you (formal)/him/her/it.*

5.3 Position of object pronouns (Unit 8)

a   Object pronouns normally precede the verb: **¿Me trae un café?**

b   In sentences with two object pronouns, the indirect one comes first: **Te las daré,** *I'll give them to you.*

c   With imperatives, they follow positive forms but come before negative ones, e.g. **Dígale, no le diga.**

d   In constructions with a main verb followed by an infinitive (e.g. **llevar**) or a gerund (e.g. **haciendo**), the object pronoun can either precede the main verb or be attached to the infinitive or gerund, e.g. **Voy a llevarlo,** or **Lo voy a llevar** *I'm going to take it*; **Estoy escribiéndola** or **La estoy escribiendo** *I'm writing it.*

5.4 Pronouns with prepositions (Unit 12)

a   With prepositions, use **mí, ti,** for the first and second person singular, and subject pronouns, **él, ella,** etc., for the remaining persons, e.g. **Un café para mí/él.**

b Note the use of this construction in **A mí me gusta.** See Unit 12.

c Note the special use of **con** in **conmigo,** *with me,* **contigo,** *with you (informal).* But **con él/ella/usted,** etc.

5.5 Reflexive pronouns (Unit 11)

These are **me, te, se, nos, os, se,** and they accompany reflexive verbs such as **levantarse,** e.g. **me levanto,** *I get up.* You will find more extensive notes on this in Unit 11.

6 Demonstratives (Unit 7)

See Unit 7.

7 Possessives (Units 5 and 20)

Short forms, e.g. **mi/s** *my,* **tu/s** *your (informal),* etc. are treated in Units 2 and 3, while long forms, e.g. **mío/a, míos/as,** *mine,* etc., are discussed in Unit 20.

8 Prepositions (Units 5, 6, 14, 18, 21 and 23)

Only the most common prepositions and meanings are given here.

- **a**
  at: a las cuatro
  on: a la derecha/izquierda
  per: una vez a la semana
  personal **a:** used before the direct object when this is a person, e.g. **Invité a Manuel.**

- **con**
  with: café con leche

- **de**
  from: Julio es de Granada.
  made of: de lana
  in: la ciudad más grande de México

- **desde**
  from: desde las 2.00 de la tarde
  for: desde hace cinco años

- **en**
  in: viven en Salamanca
  on: las llaves están en la cama
  at: trabaja en la Universidad de Madrid

- **hasta**
  until: hasta las 5.00
  as far as: hasta el semáforo

- **para**
  for: (direction): el tren para Málaga
  for: (with pronouns): para mí, un té
  for/by: (with time phrases): para el lunes
  in order to: iré a Cuenca para ver a María

- **por**
  in: por la tarde
  at: por la noche
  by: por avión
  along: por esa calle
  around: por aquí
  per: por ciento

9 Types of verbs

a According to the ending of the infinitive, Spanish verbs may be grouped into three main categories: **-ar**, e.g. **hablar** *to speak*, **-er**, e.g. **comer** *to eat*, and **-ir**, e.g. **vivir** *to live* (Unit 1).
b Most Spanish verbs are regular, that is, they follow a fixed pattern in their conjugation, but some very common verbs are irregular. A list of these will be found on pages 280–3.
c Radical-changing verbs: see 10.1.
d Reflexive verbs: see 5.5 on reflexive pronouns.

10 Present tense (Units 1–6, 10 and 11)

10.1 Regular verbs (Units 1, 2, 11)

	hablar	comer	vivir
yo	hablo	como	vivo
tú	hablas	comes	vives
Vd./él/ella	habla	come	vive
nosotros/as	hablamos	comemos	vivimos
vosotros/as	habláis	coméis	vivís
Vds./ellos/ellas	hablan	comen	viven

10.2 Radical-changing verbs (Units 3 and 11)

Some verbs undergo a vowel change in the stem in all persons but **nosotros/as** and **vosotros/as**, but their endings remain the same as for regular verbs. The main types of changes are:

a From e to ie, e.g. **empezar, entender, pensar, preferir**, e.g. Yo **empiezo**, *I start.*
b From o to ue, e.g. **acostarse, poder, volver**, e.g. ¿**Puedes** hacerlo? *Can you do it?*
c From e to i, e.g. **pedir, seguir, servir**, e.g. ¿Le **sirvo** un poco más? *Shall I give (serve) you some more?*

11 Preterite tense (Units 15 and 16)

To form the preterite, *add the following endings to the stem.* Verbs in **-er** and **-ir** share the same endings.

stem	*singular*	*plural*
habl-	-é, aste, -ó	-amos, -asteis, -aron
viv-	-í, -iste, -ió	-imos, -isteis, -ieron

The preterite is used for talking about events that took place at a specific point in the past or which lasted over a definite period and ended in the past:

Ayer hablé con él.	*I spoke to him yesterday.*
Viví dos años allí.	*I lived there for two years.*

12 Imperfect tense (Units 17 and 18)

To form the imperfect *add the following endings to the stem.*
Verbs in -er and -ir share the same endings.

stem	singular	plural
trabaj- ten-	-aba, -abas, -aba -ía, -ías, -ía	-ábamos, -abais, -aban -íamos, íais, -ían

The imperfect tense is used for describing people, places and
people known in the past, and to say what one used to do.

La casa tenía dos dormitorios.   *The house had two bedrooms.*
Trabajaban en Buenos Aires.   *They used to work in*
   Buenos Aires.

13 Perfect tense (Unit 19)

The perfect tense is formed with the *present* tense of **haber**
followed by a *past participle*. This ends in -**ado** for -**ar** verbs and
-**ido** for -**er** and -**ir** verbs.

Present of haber   *Past participles*
he, has, ha, hemos, habéis, han llamado, venido

The perfect tense is used for talking about recent events, as well
as actions which have taken place over a period of time which
has not yet ended.

Hoy te ha llamado Alfonso.   *Alfonso has called you today.*
La he visto dos veces.   *I have seen her twice.*

14 Pluperfect tense (Unit 22)

The pluperfect tense is formed with the *imperfect* of **haber** and
a *past participle*.

Imperfect of haber   *Past participles*
había, habías, había,   estado, podido
habíamos, habíais, habían

The pluperfect tense is used to say what one had done:

Gloria había estado aquí antes.   *Gloria had been here before.*

15 Future tense (Unit 20)

To form the future *add the following endings to the infinitive*. The same endings apply to -**ar**, -**er** and -**ir** verbs.

infinitive	singular	plural
Ir	-é, -ás, -á	-emos, -éis, -án

Esta noche iré al cine.   *I'll go to the cinema tonight.*

16 Conditional tense (Unit 21)

To form the conditional *add the following endings to the infinitive*. The same endings apply to -**ar**, -**er** and -**ir** verbs.

infinitive	singular	plural
Ir	-ía, -ías, -ía	-íamos, -íais, -ían

Iría contigo, pero no puedo.   *I would go with you, but I can't.*

17 Present subjunctive (Unit 25)

To form the present subjunctive, *remove the -**o** of the first person of the ordinary present tense*, known as present indicative, *and add the following endings*, one set for -**ar** verbs, another for verbs in -**er** and -**ir**.

present indicative	present subjunctive	
(1st person)	*singular*	*plural*
llamo	-e, -es, -e	-emos, -éis, -en
tengo	-a, -as, -a	-amos, -áis, -an

The present subjunctive has several uses, but only three have been discussed in this book:

- to express requirements with regard to something or someone
- to express hope with regard to others
- to express doubt

Buscan una persona que hable español.   *They are looking for a Spanish-speaking person.*

| Espero que ella me llame. | *I hope she calls me.* |
| No creo que tengan tiempo. | *I don't think they'll have time.* |

Note that all of them occur in a construction with a *main verb*, e.g. **espero**, *followed by* **que** *and the present subjunctive*.

18 Imperative (Units 23 and 24)

Their forms will be found in Units 23 and 24.

19 The gerund (Units 14 and 16)

Gerunds are forms like **trabajando** *working*, **comiendo** *eating*, which are used with **estar** to refer to actions in progress at the moment of speaking: **Estoy trabajando**, *I'm working*. See Unit 14.

20 'Ser' and 'estar' (Units 1, 2, 4, 8, 9 and 14)

20.1 'Ser' is used:

a   to give personal information such as who you are, nationality, where you are from, occupation, marital status (L.Am.), e.g. **Plácido Domingo es español.**

b   to describe people, places and things, e.g. **Barcelona es una ciudad preciosa.**

c   with the time and certain time phrases, e.g. **Mañana es domingo.**

d   to refer to the material something is made of, e.g. **Esta camisa es de algodón.**

e   to denote possession, e.g. **Este libro es mío.**

f   to ask and say how much something is, e.g. **¿Cuánto es?**

g   to indicate where an event will take place, e.g. **La fiesta es en casa de Isabel.**

20.2 'Estar' is used:

a   to ask and say where something is, e.g. **La catedral está en la plaza.**

b   to express marital status (Spain), e.g. **Paco está soltero.**

c   to ask people how they are and respond, e.g. **¿Cómo estás? Estoy bien.**

d to denote a temporary state or condition, e.g. **Gloria está muy guapa hoy.**

e to refer to cost when prices fluctuate, e.g. **¿A cuánto está (el cambio de) la libra?**

f with past participles, to denote a condition resulting from an action, e.g. **El restaurante está abierto.**

g with gerunds, to talk about actions in progress, e.g. **Está hablando por teléfono.**

21 Using 'se' (Unit 3)

Se is used with the third person of the verb:

a to form impersonal sentences, e.g. **¿Cómo se va al aeropuerto desde aquí?**

b to convey the idea that something 'is done', e.g. **Aquí se habla español.**

c with reflexive verbs, e.g. levantarse, e.g. **Se levantaron a las 6.00.**

22 Stress and accentuation

a Words which end in a vowel, **n** or **s** stress the last syllable but one, e.g. **n**a**da, **toman, **h**i**jos.**

b Words which end in a consonant other than **n** or **s** stress the last syllable, e.g. **Madr**i**d, español.**

c Words which do not follow the above rules carry a written accent over the vowel of the stressed syllable, e.g. **allí, autobús, invitación.**

d Differences in meaning between words which are spelt in the same way are shown through the use of an accent, e.g. sí *yes*, si *if*; él *he*, el *the*; sé *I know*, se (reflexive pronoun).

e Question words carry an accent, e.g. **¿dónde? ¿cuándo?**

23 A note on 'ch' and 'll'

'Ch', called 'che' and 'll', called 'elle' ('ll' pronounced like 'y' in 'yes' by the majority of speakers), were traditionally considered separate letters of the Spanish alphabet and had separate entries in all dictionaries. This is no longer the case, and most dictionaries now treat 'ch' within the letter 'c' and 'll' within 'l'.

irregular verbs

The following list includes only the most common irregular verbs. Only irregular forms are given (verbs marked with an asterisk are also radical-changing).

abrir *to open*
past participle: abierto

andar *to walk*
preterite: anduve, anduviste, anduvo, anduvimos, anduvisteis, anduvieron

conducir *to drive*
present indicative: (yo) conduzco
present subjunctive: conduzca, conduzcas, conduzca, conduzcamos, conduzcáis, conduzcan
preterite: conduje, condujiste, condujo, condujimos, condujisteis, condujeron

dar *to give*
present indicative: (yo) doy
preterite: di, diste, dio, dimos, disteis, dieron
present subjunctive: dé, des, dé, demos, deis, den

decir* to say
present indicative: (yo) digo
present subjunctive: diga, digas, diga, digamos, digáis, digan
preterite: dije, dijiste, dijo, dijimos, dijisteis, dijeron
future: diré, dirás, dirá, diremos, diréis, dirán
conditional: diría, dirías, diría, diríamos, diríais, dirían
imperative (familiar, singular): di
gerund: diciendo
past participle: dicho

escribir *to write*
past participle: escrito

estar *to be*
present indicative: estoy, estás, está, estamos, estáis, están
present subjunctive: esté, estés, esté, estemos, estéis, estén
preterite: estuve, estuviste, estuvo, estuvimos, estuvisteis, estuvieron
imperative (familiar, singular): está

hacer *to do, make*
present indicative: (yo) hago
present subjunctive: haga, hagas, haga, hagamos, hagáis, hagan
preterite: hice, hiciste, hizo, hicimos, hicisteis, hicieron
future: haré, harás, hará, haremos, haréis, harán
conditional: haría, harías, haría, haríamos, haríais, harían
imperative: (Vd.) haga, (tú) haz
past participle: hecho

ir *to go*
present indicative: voy, vas, va, vamos, vais, van
present subjunctive: vaya, vayas, vaya, vayamos, vayáis, vayan
imperfect: iba, ibas, iba, íbamos, ibais, iban
preterite: fui, fuiste, fue, fuimos, fuisteis, fueron
imperative: (Vd.) vaya, (tú) ve

leer *to read*
preterite: (él, ella, Vd.) leyó, (ellos, ellas, Vds.) leyeron
gerund: leyendo

oír *to hear*
present indicative: oigo, oyes, oye, oímos, oís, oyen
present subjunctive: oiga, oigas, oiga, oigamos, oigáis, oigan
preterite: (él, ella, Vd.) oyó, (ellos, ellas, Vds.) oyeron
imperative: (Vd.) oiga, (tú) oye
gerund: oyendo

poder* *to be able to, can*
preterite: pude, pudiste, pudo, pudimos, pudisteis, pudieron
future: podré, podrás, podrá, podremos, podréis, podrán
conditional: podría, podrías, podría, podríamos, podríais, podrían

poner *to put*
present indicative: (yo) pongo
present subjunctive: ponga, pongas, ponga, pongamos, pongáis, pongan

preterite: puse, pusiste, puso, pusimos, pusisteis, pusieron
future: pondré, pondrás, pondrá, pondremos, pondréis,
pondrán
conditional: pondría, pondrías, pondría, pondríamos,
pondríais, pondrían
imperative: (Vd.) ponga, (tú) pon
past participle: puesto

querer* *to want*
preterite: quise, quisiste, quiso, quisimos, quisisteis, quisieron
future: querré, querrás, querrá, querremos, querréis, querrán
conditional: querría, querrías, querría, querríamos, querríais,
querrían

saber *to know*
present indicative: (yo) sé
present subjunctive: sepa, sepas, sepa, sepamos, sepáis, sepan
preterite: supe, supiste, supe, supimos, supisteis, supieron
future: sabré, sabrás, sabrá, sabremos, sabréis, sabrán
conditional: sabría, sabrías, sabría, sabríamos, sabríais, sabrían
imperative: (Vd.) sepa

salir *to go out*
present indicative: (yo) salgo
present subjunctive: salga, salgas, salga, salgamos, salgáis, salgan
future: saldré, saldrás, saldrá, saldremos, saldréis, saldrán
conditional: saldría, saldrías, saldría, saldríamos, saldríais,
saldrían
imperative: (Vd.) salga, (tú) sal

ser *to be*
present indicative: soy, eres, es, somos, sois, son
present subjunctive: sea, seas, sea, seamos, seáis, sean
preterite: fui, fuiste, fue, fuimos, fuisteis, fueron
imperfect indicative: era, eras, era, éramos, erais, eran
imperative: (Vd.) sea, (tú) sé

tener* *to have*
present indicative: (yo) tengo
present subjunctive: tenga, tengas, tenga, tengamos, tengáis,
tengan
preterite: tuve, tuviste, tuvo, tuvimos, tuvisteis, tuvieron
future: tendré, tendrás, tendrá, tendremos, tendréis, tendrán
conditional: tendría, tendrías, tendría, tendríamos, tendríais,
tendrían
imperative: (Vd.) tenga, (tú) ten

traer *to bring*
present indicative: (yo) traigo
present subjunctive: traiga, traigas, traiga, traigamos, traigáis,
   traigan
preterite: traje, trajiste, trajo, trajimos, trajisteis, trajeron
imperative: (Vd.) traiga
gerund: trayendo

venir* *to come*
present indicative: (yo) vengo
present subjunctive: venga, vengas, venga, vengamos, vengáis,
   vengan
preterite: vine, viniste, vino, vinimos, vinisteis, vinieron
future: vendré, vendrás, vendrá, vendremos, vendréis, vendrán
conditional: vendría, vendrías, vendría, vendríamos, vendríais,
   vendrían
imperative: (Vd.) venga, (tú) ven
gerund: viniendo

ver *to see*
present indicative: (yo) veo
present subjunctive: vea, veas, vea, veamos, veáis, vean
imperfect indicative: veía, veías, veía, veíamos, veíais, veían
imperative: (Vd.) vea
past participle: visto

volver* *to come back*
past participle: vuelto

Introductory unit

– Buenas tardes.
– Buenas tardes.

—

– Buenas noches.
– Hola, buenas noches.

Unit 1

Activity 2

a Me llamo Silvia, soy española. Soy de Barcelona. Hablo español y catalán.
b Me llamo Cristóbal, soy mexicano. Soy de San Diego, California. Hablo inglés y español.
c Me llamo Mario, soy chileno. Soy de Santiago. Hablo español.

Unit 2

Activity 5

– ¿Dónde vive usted, Silvia?
– En Barcelona. Vivo en el Barrio Gótico, en la Plaza del Rey.

– ¿Dónde vives, Francisco?
– Vivo en la ciudad de México, en el Paseo de la Reforma.

– Y tú Julio, ¿dónde vives?
– Vivo en la calle de la Libertad.

Activity 7

a – ¿Número?
 – Por favor, ¿el teléfono del hotel Sancho?
 – El hotel Sancho tiene el número 612 2018.
 – Muchas gracias.
 – De nada.
b – ¿Qué número desea?
 – El número de teléfono del señor Martín Ramos, por favor.
 – Martín Ramos. Un momento, por favor.
 – Es el 792 5436.
 – Gracias.

Unit 3

Activity 2

a – ¿La habitación del señor Luis García, por favor?
 – Es la número cuarenta y ocho.
b – Por favor, ¿la oficina de la señorita Sáez?
 – La treinta y seis.
c – Buenos días, ¿Cuál es la habitación de los señores Silva, por favor?
 – Un momentito, por favor. Los señores Silva tienen la habitación número cien.

Unit 4

Activity 5

Turista 1   ¿Dónde está la avenida del Mar?
Guía   Está a la izquierda, a dos cuadras del hotel.
Turista 2   ¿Y la playa?
Guía   La playa está al final de la avenida del Mar.
Turista 2   ¿Y correos, dónde está?
Guía   Está en la calle España, la tercera a la izquierda, al lado de un supermercado.
Turista 3   Y el museo, ¿dónde está?
Guía   El museo está en la calle Picasso, al lado de la catedral.

Unit 5

Activity 2

a Oiga, ¿nos trae otra botella de vino tinto, por favor?
b ¿Me pasas la sal?
c Por favor, ¿me traes dos aguas minerales sin gas del supermercado?
d ¿Me trae más azúcar, por favor?
e Por favor, ¿nos trae otros dos cafés y un té?
f ¿Me pasas una servilleta?

Activity 4

Camarero	Buenas noches. ¿Qué van a tomar?
Ramón	¿Qué tapas tiene?
Camarero	Hay champiñones, gambas, calamares y tortilla de patatas.
Ramón	¿Qué vas a tomar tú, Silvia?
Silvia	Para mí, una de calamares y una cerveza.
Ramón	¿Y para ti, Clara?
Clara	Yo quiero un bocadillo.
Camarero	Tenemos de jamón, queso, salchichón y chorizo.
Clara	De queso.
Camarero	¿Y para beber?
Clara	Un cortado.
Camarero	¿Y para usted?
Ramón	Yo, champiñones y un vino blanco.
Camarero	¿Algo más?
Ramón	No, nada más.

Unit 6

Activity 3

Buenos días. Soy Inés Suárez, de Iberiatur. Llamo para confirmar su vuelo a Lima, Perú, para el jueves dieciséis. El avión sale de Madrid a las veintitrés treinta y llega a Lima el viernes a las diez menos veinte de la mañana, hora local. La hora de presentación en el aeropuerto es a las veintiuna y treinta.

Unit 8

Activity 1

– Buenos días. Quisiera cambiar libras a euros. ¿A cuánto está el cambio? Tengo billetes.
– El cambio de la libra está a ... un euro con cincuenta y cinco céntimos. ¿Cuánto quería cambiar?
– Ciento setenta y cinco libras.

– ¿Dígame?
– Buenas tardes. Tengo unos cheques de viaje en francos suizos y quería cambiarlos a euros. ¿A cuánto está el cambio?
– Francos suizos ... un momento, por favor. Sí, mire, está a setenta céntimos.
– Quiero cambiar doscientos cincuenta.
– Bien, ¿me permite su pasaporte, por favor?

– Por favor, quisiera cambiar ciento veinte coronas suecas a euros. ¿Puede decirme a cuánto está el cambio?
– La corona sueca está a diez céntimos.

Unit 9

Activity 4

– ¿Su nombre, por favor?
– Antonio Bravo Miranda.
– ¿Qué edad tiene?
– Cincuenta y dos años.
– ¿Su estado civil?
– Casado.
– ¿Cómo se llama su esposa?
  Elena Castro García.
– ¿Qué edad tiene ella?
– Cuarenta y tres años.
– ¿Tienen hijos?
– No, no tenemos hijos.

Unit 10

Activity 3

– ¿A qué te dedicas?
– Soy profesora en una universidad.
– ¿Y cuánto tiempo hace que trabajas allí?
– Hace seis años.
– Ah, seis años. ¿Y qué horario de trabajo tienes?
– De 9.00 a 12.30 en la mañana. En la tarde, de 3.00 a 5.00–5.30. Ése es mi horario.
– Y vacaciones, ¿cuántas vacaciones tienes al año?
– Cinco días para Semana Santa, dos semanas en invierno y alrededor de dos meses en verano.

Activity 7

Hola, me llamo Ricardo García. Soy español, de Madrid. Soy intérprete y trabajo en una organización internacional desde hace cinco años. Trabajo desde las nueve de la mañana hasta las dos de la tarde, de lunes a viernes. Los sábados no trabajo. Tengo cuatro semanas de vacaciones al año.

Me llamo Mercedes Donoso. Soy española, de Salamanca. Hace dos años que estudio psicología en la universidad de Salamanca. También estudio inglés. Mis clases de inglés en la universidad son por la tarde, de seis a ocho, los lunes, miércoles y viernes.

Unit 11

Activity 3

– ¿Cómo es un día normal para ti? ¿Qué haces en un día normal?
– En un día de trabajo me levanto temprano, me levanto a las 7.00. Me ducho, tomo desayuno, me voy al trabajo para estar … para llegar a las 9.00. Almuerzo a la 1.00 y regreso a casa a las 6.00.

Unit 12

Activity 2

– ¿Qué te gusta hacer en tu tiempo libre?
– Bueno, me gusta viajar, salir de paseo los fines de semanas, me encanta trabajar en el jardín, y también me gusta leer y ver televisión.
– ¿Qué tipo de programas te gustan?
– Me encantan los programas cómicos y los documentales.
– ¿Y qué te gusta hacer en tus vacaciones?
– Me gusta viajar al interior y al exterior del país.

Activity 9

a   Me llamo Angélica y soy secretaria. Me gusta mucho mi trabajo y
     me encanta mi jefe. Es muy simpático. Pero lo que no me gusta es
     el sueldo. Gano muy poco dinero.

b   Me llamo Cristóbal y soy portero en una fábrica. Detesto mi
     trabajo y el horario tampoco me gusta. ¿Y mi jefe? Mi jefe es
     horrible. No me gusta nada.

Unit 13

Activity 2

Voy a salir para Bogotá el martes 5 a las cinco menos veinte de la tarde.
Allí voy a estar cuatro días en total. La reserva del hotel aún no está
confirmada, pero espero quedarme en el hotel Eldorado. El número de
teléfono es el 5 19 20 42. El sábado 9 al mediodía voy a continuar viaje
a Caracas. Allí voy a estar tres días, desde el sábado hasta el lunes
inclusive. En Caracas tengo una reserva en el hotel Plaza. El número de
teléfono es el 7 38 55 17. El vuelo de regreso a Madrid es el martes 12
y espero volver a la oficina el miércoles 13.

Unit 14

Activity 2

Voz   ¿Dígame?
Raquel   ¿Está Lorenzo, por favor?
Voz   Está duchándose en este momento. ¿De parte de quién?
Raquel   Soy Raquel.
Voz   ¿Quieres dejarle algún recado?
Raquel   Sí, dile que tengo las entradas para el concierto de esta
          noche.
Voz   Vale.

Activity 4

Voz   ¿Dígame?
Javier   Quería pedir hora con la doctora Gómez, para mañana.
Voz   Lo siento, pero no hay hora disponible hasta el jueves, a las
          once y cuarto o a las cuatro menos cuarto.
Javier   A las cuatro menos cuarto me va bien.
Voz   ¿Su nombre, por favor?
Javier   Javier Urrutia.

Unit 15

Activity 10

Nublado y precipitaciones débiles, aumentando a fines del día, con extremas probables de cinco y doce grados anunció para hoy en la región metropolitana la Dirección Meteorológica de Chile. Perspectivas para mañana miércoles 5 de julio, nublado y precipitaciones, declinando en la tarde. Extremas probables de mañana, siete y catorce grados.

Unit 16

Activity 6

Me llamo Nicolás Rivas y nací en Guadalajara, México, el 30 de diciembre de 1955. Empecé la carrera de diseño industrial en 1974 y terminé los estudios en 1978. Trabajé como diseñador industrial en Metromex desde enero de 1982 hasta finales de octubre de 1987. Fui nombrado gerente de diseño en Industrias Metalsa en noviembre de ese mismo año. Al año siguiente conocí a Margarita, mi primera mujer. Nos casamos en Mérida el 20 de marzo de 1990. Tuvimos un hijo en junio de 1991. Nos divorciamos dos años después.

Unit 17

Activity 7

José   ¿Qué tal tu jefe?

Carmen   Me encanta. Es muy simpático. Es una persona muy agradable y bastante inteligente y tiene una personalidad muy interesante. Además, es guapo. Es muy diferente al jefe que tenía antes. Ése era horrible, no me gustaba nada. Era muy antipático y bastante temperamental, y perezoso, también. Tenía un carácter muy agresivo y poco sentido del humor. Y además, era muy feo.

Unit 18

Activity 6

Begoña   ¿A qué te dedicabas antes, Esteban?

Esteban   Trabajaba en un restaurante. Era camarero.

Begoña   ¿Y ahora qué haces?

Esteban   Soy programador. Trabajo en una compañía especializada en programación.

Begoña	Y tú, Víctor, ¿qué hacías antes de llegar a España?
Víctor	Era estudiante. Estudiaba idiomas. Ahora soy intérprete y trabajo por mi cuenta.
Begoña	Pues yo trabajaba en una línea aérea. Era azafata. Y ahora estoy sin trabajo.

Unit 19

Activity 1

Buenos días. Soy María Bravo de Málaga. Ha sido imposible encontrar billete para el 28 de marzo. Todos los vuelos están completos. He tenido que aplazar el viaje para el 2 de abril. Viajo en el vuelo 732 de Iberia que llega allí a las once y media de la mañana. He reservado una habitación en el hotel Intercontinental. Adiós, gracias.

Activity 3

Laura	Buenas tardes.
Recepcionista	Buenas tardes.
Laura	Mire, mi marido y yo hemos pedido una habitación con vistas al mar, y usted nos ha dado una con vistas al aparcamiento. ¡Esto no puede ser! Además, la habitación no tiene ni baño completo ni terraza. Y el hotel no está a cien metros de la playa como ponía en el anuncio. Y no tiene piscina ni solarium. ¡Es el colmo! Hemos venido aquí varias veces y ésta es la primera vez que nos pasa algo así.
Recepcionista	Perdone usted, señora, pero ha sido una equivocación de su agencia de viajes. No es culpa nuestra. Yo no puedo hacer nada.
Laura	¡Esto es increíble!

Unit 20

Activity 2

- Esta tarde se inaugurará en el Centro de Arte Reina Sofía una exposición de pinturas y esculturas del artista colombiano Fernando Botero. La exposición estará abierta hasta el 25 de abril.
- Mañana lunes llegará a Madrid en visita oficial el presidente de la República Argentina, quien será recibido en el aeropuerto de Barajas por el presidente del gobierno español.

- El consorcio europeo Airbus anunció que construirá un nuevo avión que podrá transportar 555 personas. Éste tendrá dos pisos, una sala de conferencias, un gimnasio y varios dormitorios.
- Un tren de alta velocidad unirá muy pronto las ciudades de París y Bruselas. A una velocidad de 300 kilómetros por hora, el viaje entre las dos capitales se hará en sólo una hora y 26 minutos.
- El tiempo: Nuboso y con posibles precipitaciones se presentará mañana el tiempo en Madrid. Se estima una temperatura mínima probable de ocho grados y una máxima de quince.

Unit 21

Activity 4

a – Oye, Lucía, ¿quieres venir a tomar una copa conmigo después del trabajo?
– Imposible, he quedado con María para ir de compras. Otro día, ¿qué te parece?
– Vale. Otro día.

b – Buenas tardes, señor Flores. Esta tarde hay un cóctel para darle la bienvenida al nuevo director. ¿Quiere usted venir?
– Lo siento, pero no puedo. Tengo hora con el dentista.

c – Hola Mario. ¿Tienes algún plan para el martes por la noche?
– No, ninguno.
– ¿Por qué no vienes a mi fiesta de cumpleaños? Voy a celebrarlo en casa.
– Encantado.

Unit 23

Activity 2

Al salir del hotel tome la calle Palacio que está aquí enfrente y gire a la derecha en la calle Triunfo. Siga de frente por la calle Triunfo hasta la Plaza de Armas, cruce la plaza y después tome la calle Garcilaso. El hostal está una calle más arriba a la izquierda, en la esquina.

Unit 24

Activity 2

a

Doctor	¿Qué le pasa?
Señora	Me siento muy cansada, doctor, y no duermo bien por la noche. Estoy constantemente nerviosa, intranquila. No sé qué hacer, doctor.
Doctor	Usted está estresada evidentemente. Tiene que descansar. Debería tomarse unas vacaciones.

b

Señor	Doctora, no sé qué me pasa. Desde hace dos días tengo un dolor de estómago horrible. No puedo comer nada. Me siento muy mal, doctora.
Doctora	¿Le duele aquí?
Señor	Ay, sí, doctora, me duele muchísimo.
Doctora	¿Tiene diarrea?
Señor	Sí, tengo diarrea.
Doctora	Bueno, probablemente se trata de una infección estomacal. Le voy a recetar unas pastillas. Tiene que tomar dos cada seis horas. Con esto se le pasará.

Unit 25

Activity 7

Alfonso	Creo que ya es hora de buscar una nueva persona para el departamento de relaciones públicas, ¿no crees tú?
Isabel	Sí, creo que sí.
Alfonso	Tendrá que ser alguien que sepa relacionarse bien con la gente. Ese requisito es fundamental. Y que tenga dos o tres años de experiencia como mínimo.
Isabel	Por supuesto. Necesitamos una persona que hable inglés y preferiblemente también algo de francés.
Alfonso	Sí, sí, claro. Y que tenga conocimientos de informática y que sepa conducir.
Isabel	Para relaciones públicas queremos una persona que sea dinámica, creativa y que esté dispuesta a trabajar en equipo. Espero que encontremos a alguien.
Alfonso	No creo que sea difícil.

key to the activities

Introductory unit

A.3 a Hola. **b** Buenos días. **c** Buenas tardes. **d** Buenas noches.
e Hola, buenas noches.
B.3 a ¿Cómo te llamas? **b** Me llamo ...; ¿Cómo se llama Vd.?
C.2 a ¿Que significa *dinero*? **b** Más despacio, por favor.
c ¿Cómo dice?/¿Puede repetir, por favor? **d** ¿Habla Vd.
inglés?
D.1 1 a 2 c 3 d 4 b
D.2 a Adiós. **b** Hasta luego. **c** Adiós. **Check what you have
learnt:** llama/llamo/usted/entiendo/puede/habla.

Unit 1

Dialogues

1.2 ¿De dónde eres?
2.1 a F **b** F **c** F **d** V
2.2 a Usted es español, ¿verdad? **b** Y usted, ¿de dónde es?
3.1 a No. **b** Spanish.
3.2 a ¿Habla Vd. ...? **b** Hablo ...
 4 Catalan, Spanish and some English

Practice

 1 a-6-E, b-4-D, c-5-F, d-7-G, e-1-C, f-3-B, g-2-A
 2 a Española. Barcelona. Español y catalán. **b** Mexicano.
San Diego, California. Inglés y español. **c** Chileno.
Santiago. Español.
 3 a Me llamo Boris. Soy de Moscú. Hablo ruso. **b** ... Paco.
... de Granada. ... español. **c** ... Ingrid. ... de Berlín. ...

alemán. **d** … Marguerite. … de París. … francés. **e** … Mark. … de Nueva York. … inglés. **f** … Mª Ángeles. … de Monterrey, México. … español.
4 Me llamo … soy … Soy …, hablo.
5 Follow Activity 4.
6 **a** Palma. **b** Guillermo. **c** Córdoba, España.
7 ¿Cómo se llama Vd.?/Me llamo …, ¿de dónde es Vd.?/Soy de … ¿Habla Vd. inglés?/Sí, hablo un poco de español.

Unit 2

Dialogues

1.1 a Are you señora Rivas? **b** Yes, I am.
1.2 Mucho gusto. Encantado.
2.1 a Muy bien, ¿y tú? **b** Bien, gracias.
2.2 a Te presento a … **b** Éste es Felipe.
3.1 a He lives in La Coruña. **b** She lives in Madrid.
3.2 a ¿Dónde vives? **b** Vivo en …
4.1 a 712 6973/603 5823. **b** –/520 1417.
4.2 ¿Qué número de teléfono tienes?

Practice

1 **a** eres/soy/soy/estás. **b** es/es/está/está/es.
2 **a** – **b** la **c** la **d** el **e** – **f** una **g** un
3 ¿Vd. es el señor Barrios?/Yo soy …/ Encantado/a, señor Barrios./Le presento a John, un compañero de trabajo.
4 **a** Te presento a mi marido/mujer. **b** … mi novio/a. **c** … mi padre/madre. **d** … mi hermano/a. **e** Ésta es … **f** Éste es … **g** Éste es … **h** Ésta es …
5 **a** la ciudad de México, en el Paseo de la Reforma **b** … la calle de la Libertad. **c** … Barcelona, en el Barrio Gótico, en la Plaza del Rey.
7 **a** 612 2018 **b** 792 5436
8 **a** Vivo en (*city*). **b** Vivo en (*area*). **c** Vivo en la calle (*name of street*). **d** (*Your telephone Nº*). **e** Sí/No tengo teléfono. **f** (*Telephone Nº at work*). **g** Sí/No tengo. **h** (*Extension Nº*).
9 *Horizontales*: 1 tiene 2 tienes 3 usted 4 vivo 5 eres
Verticales: 1 vive 2 mi 3 tengo 4 su 5 tu

Unit 3

Dialogues

1.1 Para una persona. Para seis noches. Sin desayuno. Con baño.

1.2 a ¿Para cuántas noches? **b** Hasta el veintiocho. **c** Todas las habitaciones tienen baño. **d** Su carnet de identidad, por favor.

2.1 Doble/treinta y cinco.

2.2 a Tenemos una habitación reservada. **b** ¿Cómo se escribe su apellido, por favor? **c** ¿Dónde se puede cambiar dinero, por favor?

Practice

1 Treinta y seis, cuarenta y cinco, cincuenta y nueve, sesenta y cuatro, setenta y seis, ochenta y ocho, noventa y tres.

2 **a** Hab. cuarenta y ocho. **b** Of. treinta y seis. **c** Hab. cien.

3 **a**-5 **b**-1 **c**-6 **d**-3 **e**-4 **f**-2

4 Rooms with a balcony and private bathroom, air conditioning, colour cable TV, telephone, beach club, swimming pool, jacuzzi, restaurant, piano bar, night club, complete programme of activities from scuba diving to cycling, horse-riding, tennis, windsurfing, etc., direct access to golf course.

5 **a** queremos **b** quieren **c** podemos **d** puede **e** puede

6 **a** F **b** V **c** V **d** V

7 **a** Air conditioning in lounge, dining-room and bar, telephone, bar, fire exit. **b** Air conditioning in room, individual safe-deposit box. **c** In four- and five-star hotels/In all hotels.

9 Check Activity 8.

10 Check Activity 8.

Unit 4

Dialogues

1.1 a Perdone. **b** Una oficina de cambio, un hotel. **c** ¿Hay una oficina de cambio …? ¿ … hay un hotel …? **d** A la izquierda, a la derecha.

1.2 Nº 1, Nº 7, Nº 9.

2.1 a The tourist office. **b** I don't know. **c** Nº 11.

2.2 a (Está) al final de esta calle. **b** A cinco minutos de aquí.
3 **a** ¿Dónde están los servicios? **b** They are on the first floor, at the end of the corridor.

Practice

1 **a** hay **b** está **c** hay **d** está **e** están **f** hay
2 **a** ¿Hay un restaurante por aquí cerca? **b** ¿ ... una librería ...?
  c ¿ ... una tienda de ropa ...? **d** ¿ ... una tienda de
  comestibles ...? **e** ¿Dónde está la estación de autobuses?
  f ¿ ... la iglesia? **g** ¿ ... la biblioteca? **h** ¿ ... la plaza Mayor?
3 sabes; sé; conozco; conozco; conoces; conozco.
4 *Possible answers*: **a** Hay dos, uno detrás de la plaza de la
  Luz y otro detrás del cine. **b** Hay uno en la esquina, al
  lado de un restaurante. **c** Está entre el museo y la estación
  de metro. **d** Hay dos, uno delante de la gasolinera y otro
  delante de la estación de metro. **e** Está en la primera calle,
  a la derecha, al final de la calle. **f** Hay una al lado de la
  parada de autobuses, a la izquierda. **g** Hay una en la
  primera calle, a la derecha, al lado de un restaurante.
  h Está detrás de la iglesia/Correos.
5 **a** It's on the left, two blocks from the hotel. **b** At the end
  of *Avenida del Mar*. **c** On *calle España*, the third turning
  on the left, next to a supermarket. **d** It's on *calle Picasso*,
  next to the cathedral.
6 *Possible answers*: **a** Está en (*name of street/area*). **b** Hay
  una parada de autobús a cinco minutos de mi casa. **c** Hay
  un supermercado, tiendas de ropa, una panadería, etc.
  d Hay un museo, una biblioteca, un parque.

Unit 5

Dialogues

1.1 a Gazpacho and grilled hake and a salad. **b** Peas and ham
  and chicken and chips. **c** Still mineral water. **d** Red wine.
1.2 a Queremos el menú del día. **b** Para mí **c** De primero/
  segundo. **d** Yo prefiero.
2.1 Antonio orders more bread and Marisol another mineral
  water. M. wants a chocolate ice cream and A. creme
  caramel.
2.2 a ¿Nos trae ...? **b** ¿Me trae ...?

Practice

1 para mí/de primero/de segundo/con arroz/para usted/a la
plancha/con puré/para beber/ ¿con o sin gas?/con gas/sin gas.

2 **a** Vd. **b** tú **c** tú **d** Vd. **e** Vd. **f** tú

3 *Possible answers*: De primero ..., De segundo quiero ...,
Prefiero ..., ¿Qué tiene de postre?, Quiero/prefiero ...,
¿Me trae un café y la cuenta, por favor?

4 Silvia: squid/a beer, Clara: cheese sandwich/white coffee,
Ramón: mushrooms/white wine.

5 **a Montealpino**: central European, inc. Swiss, German,
French and Italian food; **Salvaje**: international cuisine.
b Mont.: 24.000 for two people; **Sal.**: 9.000 for two
people. **c Mont.**: sports or formal; **Sal.**: informal. **d**
Salvaje; **e** Salvaje.

6 *Pescado*: atún, merluza. *Carne*: pollo, cordero, cerdo.
Verdura: lechugas, ajo, cebollas. *Fruta*: piñas, uvas,
manzanas. *Utensilios*: cuchillo, cuchara, tenedor, plato.

7 **a** F **b** F **c** V **d** F

Unit 6

Dialogues

2.1 a To Barcelona. **b** Return. **c** Second class. **d** Non-smoker.

2.2 a veinte cuarenta y cinco. **b** dieciséis quince.

3.1 a F **b** F **c** V

3.2 a ¿Qué línea tengo que tomar? **b** Tienes que tomar... **c** Te
bajas en ... **d** Está allí mismo.

Practice

1 ¿Qué hora es en (*name of city*)? **a** Son las seis de la tarde.
b Son las cinco de la tarde. **c** Es la una de la mañana.
d Son las nueve de la mañana. **e** Es la una de la tarde.
f Son las doce/Es mediodía.

2 **a** A las ocho menos diez, a las doce y veinte, a las siete
menos veinte de la tarde. **b** A las once menos dos, a las
cuatro y diecisiete minutos de la tarde, a las diez y tres
minutos de la noche.

3 *Destination*: Lima, Perú *Departure*: Thursday 17th, 11.30
p.m. *Arrival*: Friday, 9.40 a.m., local time. 21.30 at
airport.

4   100, 299, 500, 900, 3500, 100,000, 2,000,000
5   *Examples*: Trescientos dieciocho euros/novecientos treinta y tres euros/mil cuatrocientos dieciocho euros.
6   Buenos días. ¿Cuánto cuesta un billete de ida y vuelta en avión a Cartagena? Quisiera/quiero reservar un billete para el viernes por la mañana. ¿A qué hora hay vuelos? Prefiero el vuelo de las ocho y cuarto. ¿A qué hora llega a Cartagena? Está bien.
7   a ¿Qué línea tengo que tomar para ir de Sol a Lista? b …, cambias en Goya y tomas un tren en dirección a Diego de León. Lista está una estación antes de Diego de León.

Unit 7

Dialogues

1.2   One and a half kg oranges, one kg bananas, two kg tomatoes, one lettuce, two kg potatoes.
1.3   a Me da … b ¿Cuánto valen? c ¿Algo más?
2.1   a-4 b-6 c-1 d-3 e-5 f-2
2.2   Black trousers, a white shirt
2.3   a ¿Puedo probármelos? b ¿Cómo le quedan? c Me quedan muy bien. d Me los llevo.

Practice

1   1-d 2-e 3-a 4-f 5-b 6-c
2   Quería un kilo y medio de tomates. ¿Cuánto cuestan/valen las fresas? Me da/Deme un kilo. ¿Tiene pimientos verdes? Quiero cuatro. Sí, quiero perejil también. Nada más, gracias.
3   a harina b aguacate c galleta
4   …esos zapatos marrones – ¿Éstos? – Sí, ésos – ¿… probármelos? – ¿… quedan? – … quedan grandes; … esa camiseta amarilla – ¿Ésta? – Sí, ésa – ¿ … probármela? – ¿ … queda? … – … queda estrecha; …ese abrigo gris – ¿Éste? – Sí, ése – ¿ … probármelo? – ¿ … queda? – … queda estrecho.
5   a Quisiera ver (*item*). b ¿Cuánto cuesta(n)/vale(n)? c Lo/a(s) quiero en la talla (*size*). d Lo/a(s) prefiero en (*colour*). e ¿Puedo probármelo/la(s)? f Me queda/n bien. g Me queda/n demasiado corto/a(s). h Me lo/a(s) llevo.

Unit 8

Dialogues

1.1 a F b V c F
1.2 a Quisiera cambiar … b ¿A cuánto está el cambio? c ¿Qué dirección tiene?
2.1 a F b V c V d F
2.2 42.
2.3 a ¿Qué nos recomienda? b ¿Podemos pagar con tarjeta de crédito?

Practice

1 libras, 1.55 euros, 175; francos suizos, 0.70 céntimos, 250; coronas suecas, 0.10 euros, 120.
2 Quisiera cambiar … ¿A cuánto está el cambio? – …de viaje. – … seiscientos setenta./ ¿ … cambiar? – Doscientos … – ¿a cuánto está? – … novecientos setenta y seis. ¿Cuántas … cambiar? – Ciento ochenta … – (*Address*).
3 ¿Cuál es tu dirección?/(*Your address*)/(*business address*).
4 me, le, lo, lo, lo.
5 a ¿Cuánto cuesta/vale el alquiler del Ford Escort? b ¿Está incluido el seguro obligatorio? c ¿Están incluidos los impuestos? d Y la gasolina, ¿está incluida? e ¿Podemos pagar con tarjeta de crédito? f ¿Podemos llevarlo ahora mismo?
6 *Horizontales*: 1 efectivo 2 alquilar 3 quisiera 4 tarjeta 5 incluidos 6 gasolina 7 recomiendo *Verticales*: 1 alquiler 2 cuánto 3 firmar 4 cambiar 5 billetes 6 viaje 7 casa (L.Am.)

Unit 9

Dialogues

1.1 a F b V c V d F
1.2 a Estás casada, ¿verdad? b ¿Tú estás soltero? c Tengo veintidós años. d El mayor, la menor.
2.1 a It is not bad. It has four bedrooms, a large sitting-room, a fitted kitchen, two bathrooms, and it is very bright. b It is very good and quieter than the city centre. c It is not as big as María's flat, but it is very comfortable. It has three bedrooms, the sitting-room, kitchen, bathroom, and independent heating.

2.2 **a** Gracia. **b** Génova.

Practice

1. **a** llamo **b** tengo **c** estoy **d** vivo **e** padres **f** mayor **g** llama
    h tiene **i** que **j** menor
2. **a** se llama **b** tiene **c** está **d** Vive con su madre, sus tres
    hermanos y su abuela. **e** Sus padres ... **f** Él es el menor.
    g llama **h** tiene **i** que **j** menor es su hermana ...
3. *Possible answer*: Me llamo Luisa, tengo cuarenta y cinco
    años, estoy casada. Mi marido se llama Pedro y tiene
    cuarenta y siete años. Tengo tres hijos. La mayor se llama
    Teresa y tiene veintitrés años, después viene Raquel, que
    tiene veinte, y el menor es mi hijo Felipe, que tiene
    diecisiete años.
4. **Antonio Bravo Miranda:** – 52 años – casado. **Elena Castro
    García:** 43 años – no tienen hijos.
5. *Possible answer*: Me llamo ..., estoy casado/a. Mi
    marido/mujer se llama ... y tiene ... Tengo ... hijos. El/La
    mayor se llama ... y tiene ... años, después viene ..., que
    tiene ... años, y el/la menor se llama ..., y tiene ... años.
6. **a** Tiene dos. **b** Es estupendo, mucho mejor que el anterior
    y más barato. **c** Es muy tranquilo. **d** Tiene calefacción y
    aparcamiento.
7. **a** 1, 4, 5, 6, 7, 9 **b** 1, 3, 8 **c** 2, 4, 5, 6, 7, 8 **d** El piso
    más grande es el **a** y tiene cuatro habitaciones.
8. **a** *See example*. **b** El piso de la calle Lorca es más grande
    que el piso de la avenida Salvador. **c** ... Salvador es más
    céntrico que ... Lorca. **d** ... Lorca es tan cómodo como ...
    Salvador. **e** ... Lorca es más seguro que ... Salvador.
    f ... Lorca es tan tranquilo como ... Salvador.
9. Use Elena's letter in Activity 6 as a model.

Unit 10

Dialogues

1.1 **a** V **b** F **c** V **d** F
1.2 ¿Cuánto tiempo hace que trabajas allí? Desde hace un año
solamente.
2.1 **a** siete **b** ocho/mañana, tres/tarde **c** viernes **d** tres/año

Practice

1 a-4 b-9 c-6 d-1 e-8 f-7 g-3 h-10 i-5 j-2
2 a-2 b-4 c-1 d-3
3 Profesora/una universidad/seis años/9.00 a 12.30/3.00 a
   5.00–5.30; vacaciones: Semana Santa: 5 días; invierno:
   2 semanas; verano: alrededor de 2 meses
4 a Mónica, (93) 209 36 48 b Victoria c Mª Ángeles d (94)
   637 96 35 e Eugenia f Mónica, (93) 787 61 70
5 *Model*: Tengo ... años y busco trabajo como (*occupation*),
   preferentemente por las mañanas/tardes. Tengo
   experiencia. Llamar a partir de las (*time*) horas. (*Your
   name, telephone N° and city*).
6 a ¿Cuánto tiempo hace que estás aquí? Estoy aquí desde
   hace dos meses y medio *or* Hace dos meses y medio que
   estoy aquí. b ¿ ... que estudias inglés? Estudio inglés ...
   dos meses. c ¿... que vives en este barrio? Vivo en este
   barrio ... tres semanas. d ¿... conoces a Paul? Conozco a
   Paul ... un año y medio.
7 *Possible answers*: a Soy (*occupation*), trabajo en (*place of
   work*) desde hace (*number of months/ years*). Trabajo ...
   horas al día, de (*time*) a (*time*). No trabajo los fines de
   semana. Tengo ... semanas de vacaciones al año. b Estudio
   español desde hace (*number of months/years*). Estudio por
   mi cuenta/en una universidad. Tengo clases de (*time*) a
   (*time*), de (*day*) a (*day*).

Unit 11

Dialogues

1.1 a 6.45 b 9.00 c autobús d casi una hora e un restaurante
    f 7.00 g 8.00
1.2 me levanto, empiezas, tardo, voy, comes, salgo
2.1 b, d, g, h, i, k, l, n
2.2 a sobre las 9.00 b después de cenar c a veces veo la
    televisión d nunca me acuesto antes de las once y media

Practice

1 a 2, 6, 8, 9. b 3, 4, 7 c 1, 5
2 a Me levanto a las seis. b Me ducho. c Me afeito. d Me
   lavo los dientes. e Me peino. f Me visto/pongo la ropa.
   g Desayuno. h Leo el periódico.
3.1 a-2 b-3 c-4 d-1

3.2 regresa, almuerza.

4 **a** ¿A qué hora te levantas? **b** ¿Cómo vas al colegio?
c ¿Cuánto tiempo tardas en llegar allí? **d** ¿A qué hora
empiezas las clases? **e** ¿Dónde almuerzas? **f** ¿A qué hora
sales? **g** ¿A qué hora vuelves a casa? **h** ¿Qué haces por la
noche? **i** ¿Qué haces los fines de semana?

5 Use Activities 1–4 and the introductory dialogues as a
model.

6 **a** He tries not to accept any engagement and tries to do
absolutely nothing. He stays at home, he rehearses,
studies, reads and tries not to speak. **b** He eats a very light
meal, perhaps some grilled chicken or some veal and soup.
c Eight hours on a normal day, but when he has a
performance he tries to sleep up to eleven hours.
d Most of the time by the seaside.

Unit 12

Dialogues

1.1 **a** She likes playing the guitar and singing. She loves
literature and going to the cinema. **b** Soap operas.
c Documentaries or sports programmes. **d** Football.

1.2 **a** tocar la guitarra y cantar – la literatura – el cine. **b** el
cine – ver la televisión – las telenovelas. **c** el cine –
películas españolas – telenovelas. **d** el fútbol.

2.1 1-c 2-e 3-a 4-f 5-b 6-d

2.2 **a** Because the salary is not bad, the working hours are
good, and the atmosphere is excellent. **b** Swimming, sun-
bathing and sleeping until late. **c** To go camping, riding a
bicycle and travelling abroad.

2.3 **a** ¿Qué tal tu trabajo? **b** No está mal.

Practice

1 *Examples*: Me encanta escuchar música; me gusta ir al
cine; no me gusta (nada) realizar tareas domésticas;
detesto asistir a cursos.

2.1 b, d, e, f, h

2.2 She likes comedies and documentaries.

3.1 **a** David **b** Gabriela **c** Yadira **d** Yadira **e** David **f** Víctor

3.2 Follow the models.

4 Follow the examples.

5 me gusta – me encanta – detesto – me interesa – me gusta
– prefiero – preferimos – nos encanta – nos gusta

6 Follow Activity 5 as a model.
7 ¿Qué tipo de comida le gusta? – A mí también me gusta. ¿A Vd. le gusta el teatro? – A mí también. Me encanta el teatro inglés. ¿Y a Vd. también? – ¿Le interesa la pintura? Hay una galería de arte excelente en la ciudad. – A mí tampoco me gusta.
8 *Examples*: Me encanta mi trabajo. Me gustan mis compañeros de trabajo. Detesto escribir informes.
9 A Angélica le gusta mucho su trabajo y le encanta su jefe, pero no le gusta el sueldo. Cristóbal detesta su trabajo, y el horario tampoco le gusta. Su jefe no le gusta nada.

Unit 13

Dialogues

1.1 a Nieves, 3. Miguel, 2. Eduardo, 1. b Flamenco. c No. d Because he is very tired.
1.2 a ¿Qué vas a hacer? b ¿Qué piensas hacer? c Voy a ir al cine. d Voy a cenar.
2.1 a N … b M … c N… d M …

Practice

1 a Voy a ir al teatro. b Madame Raquin. c En el teatro Apolo. d A las seis de la tarde.
2 *Destino 1*: martes 5 a las 4.40 de la tarde – 4 – Eldorado, 519 20 42. *Destino 2*: sábado 9, al mediodía – 3 – Plaza, 738 55 17.
3 vamos – pensamos – quieres – vamos.
4 a Pensamos ir a Cuba. b Vamos a visitar La Habana y Varadero. c Vamos a estar ocho días. d En Varadero vamos a quedarnos en el hotel Sol Palmeras y en La Habana en el Copacabana. e No, vamos a tomar media pensión. f Vamos a viajar en Cubana.
5 Use Activities 2 and 4 and Dialogue 1 as a model.
6 a ¿Qué vas a hacer este verano? b ¿Dónde vas a ir? c ¿Cuánto tiempo vas a quedarte? d ¿Dónde vas a quedarte? e ¿Cuándo piensas viajar/salir? f ¿Cuándo vas a volver?
7 *Fernando*: conseguir – seguir – mudarme. *Tina y Paco*: ahorrar – casarnos – viajar.
8 a *Fernando*: Espera conseguir … – Quiere seguir … – Piensa mudarse … b *Tina y Paco*: Van a ahorrar … –

Esperan casarse … – Piensan viajar …

9 **a** algún/ninguno. **b** algunos/ algún **c** alguna/ninguna
10 *Possible answers*: Tengo muchos planes: voy a continuar con el español, pienso buscar otro trabajo, espero ir a la universidad, pienso comprar un coche, voy a viajar a (Turquía), quiero ahorrar dinero para comprar un piso, quiero casarme, espero tener muchos hijos.

Unit 14

Dialogues

1.1 a 2 **b** She offers to take a message. **c** To tell him that she is going to phone later.
1.2 a ¿De parte de quién? **b** No puede ponerse en este momento. **c** Por favor, dígale que …
2.1 a Quisiera hablar con … **b** … no es ésta. **c** Es la … **d** Sí, ahora mismo …
2.2 a Se ha equivocado. **b** En seguida le pongo. **c** Está comunicando. **d** ¿Me puede poner con …?
3.1 a Llamo por el anuncio **b** Monday at 9.30.
3.2 a I'm calling about the advertisement. **b** I wanted an interview. **c** May I have your name, please?

Practice

1 ¿Está Leonor? – ¿De parte de quién? – ¿Quiere dejarle algún recado?
2 **a** 3 **b** She says she's got the tickets for tonight's concert.
3 ¿Dígame? – La señora Smith está hablando con un cliente en este momento. ¿De parte de quién? – ¿Quiere dejarle algún recado? – Muy bien, le daré su recado.
4 For Thursday at 3.45.
5 **a** Llamo por el anuncio para el puesto de … **b** Quería hablar con el/la encargado/a. **c** Quería solicitar una entrevista. **d** (El miércoles a las cuatro y media) me va bien.

Unit 15

Dialogues

1.1 a She loved Mexico. **b** 10 days/ 5 days/a weekend. **c** A week ago.

1.2 a ¿Estuviste en ciudad de México? b Conocí mucha gente y salí muchísimo. c Fui a Guanajuato.

2.1 a It's very pleasant, it's not very warm, although at this time of the year it rains a lot. b Because it rained only once. c It was very hot.

2.2 ¿Qué tal el tiempo? Es muy agradable, (no) hace mucho calor, llueve bastante, llovió, hizo muchísimo calor.

Practice

1 salió/fue/hice/cené/me acosté/tuve/fui/gustó/pasé/salí.

2 1-c, nadó 2-f, tomó el sol 3-a, salió a bailar 4-d, conoció … 5-b, fue a … 6-e, hizo vela

3 a ¿Adónde fuiste en tus vacaciones? b ¿Con quién fuiste? c ¿Dónde estuviste? d ¿Cuánto tiempo estuviste (en cada ciudad)? e ¿Te gustó San Francisco? f ¿Cuándo volviste?

4 a Salimos a las 9.00 de la mañana. b Almorzamos en Córdoba. c Visitamos la mezquita, la sinagoga y el barrio judío. d Cenamos en Sevilla. e No, tomamos la media pensión. f Visitamos la ciudad. g Fuimos a Jerez. h Duró tres días.

5 Follow Activities 1 and 3 and Dialogue 1 as a model.

6 a See example. b ¿… viajaste …?/Viajé … hace … c ¿… hiciste …?/ Hice … d ¿… comenzaste …?/Comencé … e ¿…te mudaste …?/Me mudé … f ¿ conociste …?/Conocí …

7 Empecé a trabajar/estudiar hace (*months/years*). Empecé a estudiar … hace (*months/years*).

8.1 1-c 2-f 3-a 4-h 5-b 6-e 7-g 8-d

8.2 a Hace sol y viento. b Hace sol. c Está nublado. d Está cubierto. e Está lloviendo. f Está nublado y hace viento.

9 a Hizo dieciocho grados. b Hizo siete grados. c En La Habana y Panamá hizo más calor. d En La Paz hizo más frío. e En San Juan hizo más calor.

10 a V b F c F d V

Unit 16

Dialogues

1.1 a He was born in San Clemente, on 23 April 1968. b He went to secondary school in Cuenca, and in Valencia he worked as an office clerk in a company. c ten years

1.2 me fui – terminé – me fui – trabajé – llegué – entré – dejé – me dediqué

Practice

1 1-c 2-e 3-b 4-d 5-f 6-a

2 terminé – trabajé – me fui – ingresé – desempeñé – ocupé – perdí

3.1 **a** Trabajé cuatro años. **b** Ingresé en 1989. **c** Ascendí a … en 1990.

3.2 **a** Ocupo el cargo de directora … **b** Estudié empresariales. **c** Luego de terminar. **d** Dos años más tarde.

4 **a** ¿Dónde nació? **b** ¿Cuándo nació? **c** ¿Dónde hizo sus estudios universitarios? **d** ¿Qué estudió? **e** ¿Cuándo terminó sus estudios? **f** ¿Dónde trabaja actualmente? *or* ¿A qué se dedica actualmente?

5.1 Antonio Banderas.

5.2 nació – nacer; filmó – filmar; hicieron – hacer; adoptó – adoptar; asignó – asignar; tuvo – tener; hubo – haber; se casó – casarse; tuvieron – tener; seleccionó – seleccionar; estrenó – estrenar.

6 **a** 30 de diciembre de 1955 **b** 1974 **c** 1978 **d** enero de 1982/finales de octubre de 1987 **e** noviembre **f** al año siguiente **g** 20 de marzo de 1990 **h** junio de 1991 **i** dos años después

7 1-c ¿Cuánto tiempo llevas haciendo atletismo? Llevo tres años …; 2-d ¿… trabajando como enfermera? Llevo un año …; 3-b ¿… estudiando inglés? Llevo un año y medio …; 4-a ¿… viviendo en Londres? Llevo dos años …

8 *Possible answers*: **a** Me llamo … **b** Nací en (*place*). **c** Nací el (*date*). **d** Hice mis estudios … en … **e** Los empecé/terminé en … **f** Además, estudié … **g** Actualmente trabajo en … **h** Llevo (*months/years*) estudiando/ trabajando allí. **i** Anteriormente estudié/trabajé en … **j** Estuve (*months/years*) allí.

Unit 17

Dialogues

1.1 **a** Because the company where he worked was very small, there weren't many opportunities for promotion, and the salary wasn't very good. **b** They were very nice. **c** He had a very difficult character.

1.2 **a** La empresa era muy pequeña. **b** No había muchas posibilidades de ascenso. **c** El sueldo no era muy bueno. **d** No me sentía a gusto.

2.1 Hotel Bellavista.
2.2 See dialogue.

Practice

1 **a** ¿Por qué ...? – 3 Porque ... **b**-5 **c**-6 **d**-1 **e**-4 **f**-2
2 **a** Tenía dos plantas. **b** Tenía dos. **c** Había sólo un baño.
d El comedor estaba en la planta baja, y el baño estaba en el primer piso. **e** La cocina estaba en la planta baja, y los dormitorios estaban en el primer piso.
3 *Possible answers:* **a** Estaba en (*place*). **b** Era muy pequeño/a, pero cómodo/a. **c** Tenía sólo un dormitorio.
d Tenía un pequeño jardín. **e** El barrio era tranquilo, pero mis vecinos eran muy ruidosos. **f** (No) Me gustaba vivir allí porque estaba muy lejos/cerca de mi trabajo.
4 **a** se llamaba **b** estaba **c** tenía **d** era **e** había. Answers require the same verbs.
5 **a** Se llamaba (*name*). **b** Estaba en (*place*). **c** Era muy grande, moderno, y muy tranquilo y agradable. **d** (No) Me sentía a gusto/bien.
6.1 **a** aburrido **b** alegre **c** tímido **d** inteligente **e** arrogante
f descortés **g** pesimista **h** antipático **i** débil **j** agradable
k perezoso **l** responsable **m** maduro **n** seguro
6.2 Completed word square at the end of Unit 17.
7 **a** simpático, muy agradable y bastante inteligente/una personalidad muy interesante. **b** horrible, muy antipático y bastante temperamental, y perezoso también/un carácter muy agresivo y poco sentido del humor.
8 **a** Mi jefe(a)/profesor(a) era (*name*). Era una persona muy inteligente/amable/seria/estricta. **b** Mis compañeros(as) eran divertidos(as)/simpáticos(as)/ antipáticos(as).
9 **a** 26,188,000 inhabitants. **b** Population decreased. **c** There will be fewer children and more old people.

Unit 18

Dialogue

1.1 **a** She lived in Almería. **b** She had a good job and knew a lot of people. **c** They used to meet in a café in the evenings, sometimes they went out for dinner, and the weekends they used to go to the cinema or dancing.
d She was a teacher in a school.

1.2 vivías/vivía: **vivir**; gustaba: **gustar**; encantaba: **encantar**;
tenía: **tener**; conocía: **conocer**; veía: **ver**; reuníamos: **reunir**;
salíamos: **salir**; pasábamos: **pasar**; hacías: **hacer**; trabajaba:
trabajar.

Practice

1 1-e, se levantaba 2-c, iba 3-f, comía 4-a, dormía 5-d, hacía
   6-b, jugaba
2 vivía – trabajaba – iba – empezaba – salía – ganaba –
   estaba – tenía – se llamaba – nos veíamos – dábamos –
   hablábamos
3 **a** He used to visit his grandmother. **b** His cousins. **c** At the
   Hotel Royal. **d** It was a bit like his own home and it had a
   special charm.
4.1 **a** F **b** V **c** F 4.2 **a** conservadores **b** infancia **c** paseábamos
   d se equivocaban
5 *Possible answer*: Cuando era pequeño/a vivía en (*place*).
   Mi padre era (*occupation*) y trabajaba en (*place*) y mi
   madre era (*occupation*). Mi (*person*) me llevaba a la
   escuela. Me encantaba/No me gustaba ir a la escuela.
   Pasaba mis vacaciones en (*place*). Allí nadaba, salía con
   mis amigos/as …, etc.
6 **Esteban**: c. trabajaba/era; f. soy/trabajo. **Víctor**: e.
   era/estudiaba, a. soy/trabajo; **Begoña**: b. era/trabajaba, d.
   estoy
7 **a** Contestaban … **b** Leían … **c** Mandaban … **d** Trabajaban
   … **e** Atendían … **f** Servían …
8 **a** Contestábamos … **b** Leíamos … **c** Mandábamos …
   d Trabajábamos … **e** Atendíamos … **f** Servíamos …
9 **a** ¿Qué hacía Vd. antes?/¿A qué se dedicaba? **b** ¿Dónde
   trabajaba? **c** ¿Cuánto ganaba? **d** ¿Cuántas semanas de
   vacaciones tenía al año?
10 *Possible answers*: **a** Antes era (*occupation*). **b** Estudiaba/
   trabajaba en (*place*). **c** Ahora soy (*occupation*). **d** Estudio/
   trabajo en (*place*).

Unit 19

Dialogues

1.1 **a** … confirmar el vuelo a México. **b** … el sábado 2 de
   septiembre. **c** … el día 3.

1.2 a me ha dicho **b** ha recibido un fax
2.1 a F **b** F **c** V
2.2 a pedido **b** dado **c** sido
2.3 The person complaining claims that the hotel administration does not accept responsibility for the damage caused to her car while it was in the hotel car park.
3.1 It's a blue, checked umbrella.
3.2 a He comido aquí. **b** He olvidado mi paraguas.

Practice

1 María Bravo, from Málaga, has phoned. She says it has been impossible to find a ticket for the 28th of March. All the flights are full. She has had to postpone her trip until April 2nd. She is travelling on Iberia flight 732 which arrives at 11.30 a.m. She has booked a room at the Intercontinental hotel.
2 ha aparecido – he escrito – he llamado – he tenido – he recibido – ha causado.
3.1 Hotel Condes
3.2 a V **b** F **c** F
4 a The heating, the air conditioning, the television, the hot/cold tap … isn't working. **b** The toilet, the wash basin, the bath … is blocked. **c** There isn't any soap, shampoo, toilet paper. **d** There aren't enough towels.
5 a La calefacción no funciona. **b** El lavabo está atascado. **c** Falta/No hay jabón en el baño. **d** Necesito más mantas en mi cama.
6 Although she is well qualified and young, she claims she has been unable to find work because she is a woman.
7 She left a briefcase with some documents. She says it is a black leather briefcase.
8 *Possible answers*: Perdone, he estado aquí al mediodía y he olvidado/dejado un libro de español/un jersey gris de manga larga/un bolso negro.
9 a See example. **b** See example. **c** ¿Ha pedido hora con …? Sí, ya la he pedido. **d** ¿Ha escrito a …? Sí, ya les he escrito. **e** ¿Ha hecho el pedido de …? No, todavía no lo he hecho. **f** ¿Ha visto a …? Sí, ya la he visto. **g** ¿Ha abierto la …? No, todavía no la he abierto.
10 a ¿Ha estado aquí antes? **b** ¿Qué lugares ha visto ya? **c** ¿Qué ha hecho hoy? **d** ¿Ha almorzado ya?

Unit 20

Dialogues

1.1 a Viaja a Barcelona. **b** Sale mañana por la noche. **c** Llega el viernes a las siete y media de la mañana.
1.2 She is not taking her car because it is too small, so she is borrowing Rafael's car.
1.3 a salgo **b** vendrás **c** supongo **d** traerás **e** pediré **f** tengas
2.1 a There was a lot of turbulence and he couldn't sleep all night. **b** She will take him home so that he can sleep for a while. **c** She suggests going out for dinner.
2.2 a ... estás bien ... **b** ... hace bueno ...
2.3 a No he dormido en toda la noche. **b** Estarás muy cansado, ¿no? **c** Me imagino que querrás ... **d** Seguro que mañana ...

Practice

1 saldré – llegaré – me quedaré – llamaré – llevaré
2 a F **b** F **c** V **d** V **e** V
3 a-4, b-5, c-1, d-2, e-3
4 a See example. **b** ... te entrevistarán. **c** ... te lo ofrecerán. **d** ... será muy bueno. **e** ... te lo darán.
5 a See example. **b** ... vendrá solo. **c** ... tendrá nuestra dirección. **d** ... sabrá cómo llegar aquí. **e** ... entenderá algo de español.
6 a su – mío – el mío. **b** sus – mías – las mías.
7.1 a F **b** V **c** V **d** F **e** V
7.2 a dos tercios **b** en un plazo de **c** las ciudades **d** habitantes **e** incremento **f** países en desarrollo

Unit 21

Dialogues

1.1 a Quiere ir al cine. **b** Quiere ver *La flor de mi secreto*. **c** Porque es muy difícil aparcar. **d** Empieza a las 9.00.
1.2 a ¿Qué te parece si ...? **b** ¿Qué te apetece ver? **c** Me gustaría verla.
2.1 a Los invita a cenar con él el próximo viernes **b** Ha invitado a Julio también. **c** Porque tiene un compromiso.
2.2 a Yo encantada. **b** A mí me encantaría, pero no puedo. **c** ¿Otro día quizás?

Practice

1 **a** haría **b** lavaría **c** escribiría **d** llamaría **e** saldríamos
 f veríamos **g** tendríamos **h** podríamos

2 Soy (*your name*). ¿Tienes algún plan para esta noche?
 ¿Qué te parece si vamos al cine o al teatro? Me gustaría
 ver (*film or play*). ¿La has visto? La ponen en el Olimpia y
 empieza a las 7.00. Podríamos quedar en el café enfrente
 del cine/teatro a las 6.30. ¿Qué te parece?

3.1 Racismo. **3.2** b.

4 *Lucía* is being invited to have a drink with someone after
 work. She doesn't accept because she is going shopping
 with María.
 Sr. Flores is being invited to a cocktail party to receive the
 new Director, but he can't accept because he has an
 appointment with the dentist.
 Mario is being invited to a birthday party, and he accepts
 the invitation.

5 He is inviting me to see Joaquín Cortés and he suggests we
 meet in the bar which is next to the theatre at 7.30.

6 *Example*: ¿Qué te parece si vamos al concierto de …
 mañana por la noche? Es en el teatro (*name of theatre*) a
 las (*time*). Podríamos quedar delante del teatro a las
 (*time*). ¿Qué te parece? Llámame.

7 The Chamber of Commerce of Santa Cruz has pleasure in
 inviting you to the inauguration ceremony for our new
 offices. The opening ceremony, which will be attended by
 the local authorities, will take place on Avenida del
 Libertador, 52, on Tuesday 25th May, at 19.30.

Unit 22

Dialogues

1.1 **a** She had never been to Guanajuato. **b** She thinks it is a
 very beautiful city.

1.2 **a** ¿Había estado aquí antes? **b** Nunca había venido a
 Guanajuato. **c** ¿Qué le parece la ciudad?

2.1 **a** Lleva pescado. **b** ¿Quiere un poco más? **c** Are you sure?
 – Sure, thank you.

2.2 **a** Está buenísimo. **b** Está delicioso. **c** Es una especialidad
 mexicana.

3 1-c,d 2-a,b

Practice

1 1-d: había aprendido 2-c: había viajado 3-e: había hecho
   4-f: había estudiado 5-a: había escrito 6-b: había
   terminado.
2 a ¿Había estado aquí antes? b ¿No había visitado nunca
   esta compañía/empresa? c Usted se había quedado/había
   estado en este hotel antes, ¿verdad? d Usted no había
   comido esto antes, ¿verdad?
3 No había estado nunca aquí antes. Es un país muy
   bonito./ Los mariscos están buenísimos./Están
   deliciosos./Sí, pero sólo un poco./No, gracias./¿De
   verdad?/Sí, de verdad, gracias. No puedo beber más
   porque tengo que conducir.
4 *Possible answers*: a ¿Le sirvo otra taza de café? b ¿Le sirvo
   un poco más de tarta? c ¿Quiere un poco más de coñac?
   d ¿Quiere más agua mineral?
5 a *por* tu regalo b *ha* sido c mucho *de* d conocer*la*
6 agradecer – mujer – estancia – placer – poder – visita

Unit 23

Dialogues

1.1 a the post office b turn right c a la izquierda/a la derecha
1.2 a ¿Podría decirme dónde está correos? b ¿Hay que tomar
     la avenida de Mijas?
2.1 a F b V c F
2.2 por/hasta/dc
3.1 a de 9.00 a 11.30 de la mañana y por la tarde de 4.00 a
     6.00 b al 642 2109 c el 759 5532
3.2 a marque b llame c indique d haga

Practice

1 1-d 2-g 3-a 4-f 5-h 6-c 7-e 8-b
2 He/she is staying at Hotel Monasterio and is looking for
   the Hostal Los Marqueses.
3 siga – gire – tome – siga – suba – pregunte
4 Sí, siga todo recto/de frente y tome/coja la tercera (calle) a
   la izquierda, luego tome/coja la primera a la derecha y siga
   todo recto/de frente hasta el final de la calle. El banco está
   enfrente de la estación.
5 *Possible answer*: Al salir del hotel, tome/coja la calle San
   Antonio que está a la izquierda, después gire a la izquierda

en la esquina y luego tome/coja la primera a la derecha.
Ésa es la avenida de Bailén. La estación está al final de la
avenida dc Bailén, a la izquierda.
6 a envíelo b llámela c hágalo d tráigalas e mándelas
   f enséñemelo

Unit 24

Dialogues

1.1 a por favor/de agua b tengo c un momento
1.2 a ¿Qué te pasa? b Vuelvo en seguida.
2.1 a She is not feeling well. b Because she is too hot. c To rest
     for a while and to try to sleep.
2.2 a No me encuentro bien. b Me duele la cabeza. c Por
     favor, abre la ventana. d ¿Por qué no descansas?

Practice

1 Germany, the Netherlands (Low Countries) and Spain.
2 a Fatiga, ansiedad/insomnio/problemas digestivos. b To
   rest and take a holiday/Some tablets, two every six hours.
3 a me encuentro/siento b me duele c tengo dolor d tengo
   e me duele f me siento
4 No me encuentro/siento bien. – Tengo un dolor de cabeza
   horrible y tengo fiebre. – Por favor, tráeme un vaso de agua
   mineral. Tengo mucha sed. – ¿ Podrías abrir la puerta?
   Tengo mucho calor. – No, gracias, no tengo hambre.
5.1 Rosa: She constantly puts on and loses weight. Nelson: At
     the end of the day he suffers from terrible headaches
     which prevent him doing anything. He also has nausea
     which usually ends up in vomiting.
5.2 a constantemente b sucede c hacer dieta d en realidad
5.3 a diarias b devastador c por lo general d concluyen
6 Rosa: b, c, f. Nelson: a, d, e.

Unit 25

Dialogues

1.1 a cerca del centro b tres o cuatro c no más de seiscientos
     euros d lo quiere amueblado

1.2 the one which costs 580 euros *or* the one which costs 520 euros.

2.1 a V b F c V d F

2.2 a Espero que encuentres a alguien. **b** No creo que sea fácil.

Practice

1.1 a *Tel.* 330 16 87 **b** *Tel.* 894 69 05 **c** *Tel.* 426 55 42 **d** *Tel.* 357 26 71 **e** *Tel.* 418 50 05/Begoña **f** *Tel.* 443 05 65/ Carlota

1.2 *Tel.* 907 44 04 57

 2 viva – alquile – haya – puedan – esté

 3 Follow Activities 1 and 2 as a model.

 4 a sea **b** esté **c** sepa **d** tenga **e** le gusten **f** se lleve

5.1 a to know languages **b** ... how to drive **c** ... how to relate to people **d** to be creative **e** ... dynamic **f** to have experience **g** to be presentable **h** to have a degree **i** to be familiar with computers **j** to have own car **k** to be willing to travel **l** to be available immediately

6.1 a, i, g, h, l

6.2 ability to carry out minor tasks and experience (in similar job)

7.1 c, a, i, b, e, d

7.2 sepa relacionarse – tenga – de experiencia – hable inglés – francés – tenga – informática – sepa

 8 a La carrera de empresariales y un máster de una universidad británica. **b** Sabe inglés y francés. **c** Es extrovertido y simpático. **d** No tiene. **e** Experiencia. **f** Está muy desesperado.

 9 *Possible answers*: a Es (un poco – bastante – muy) difícil – fácil **b** Los jóvenes y las mujeres tienen más dificultad **c** Buscan personas que tengan experiencia, que sepan idiomas, que sean dinámicas y creativas, que estén disponibles de inmediato, etc.

key to 'testing yourself'

Units 1–5

1 **a** ¿Cómo? **b** ¿Cómo? **c** ¿dónde? **d** ¿Qué? **e** ¿Cuál?
f ¿Dónde? **g** ¿Qué?

2 estás; estoy; es; eres; soy; soy; está; Está

3 **a** Buenas tardes, me llamo (*your name*), soy (*nationality*).
b See alphabet in Unit 3. **c** Hablo (*languages*). **d** Mucho
gusto/Encantado/a. **e** Le presento a Sarah Johnson, una
compañera de trabajo/colega. **f** Vivo en (*place*) y mi
(número de) teléfono es el (Nº).

4 Buenas tardes. Quiero una habitación individual, con
baño, para tres noches./¿Dónde está el restaurante?/
¿Puedo/Se puede cenar ahora?/¿Hay un banco por aquí
(cerca)? Quiero cambiar dinero./Más despacio, por favor.

5 **a** un banco **b** la iglesia **c** el museo **d** el Hotel Nacional
e correos **f** Estados Unidos **g** Avenida Independencia

6 **a** queremos **b** quiero **c** quieres **d** prefiero **e** tiene
f tenemos **g** trae

Units 6–10

1 **a** Es la una y cuarto. **b** Son las tres menos veinte. **c** A las
seis menos cuarto. **d** A las seis y media. **e** Son las cuatro y
diez. **f** A la una.

2 **a** ¿Cuánto cuestan esas gafas? – ¿Éstas? – Sí, ésas. **b** ¿...
cuesta ese perfume? – ¿Éste? – Sí, ése. **c** ¿... cuesta esa
crema ...? – ¿Ésta? – Sí, ésa. **d** ¿... cuestan esos zapatos? –
¿Éstos? – Sí, ésos.

3 **a** las **b** probármela **c** le **d** me/me los **e** deme **f** nos **g** les
4 **a** El hotel P.B. está más cerca de la playa que el hotel C.A.
  b ... P.B. tiene mejor vista que el hotel C.A. **c** ... C.A. es
  tan tranquilo como el hotel P.B. **d** ... C.A. es más barato
  que el hotel P.B. **e** Las habitaciones del hotel C.A. son tan
  grandes como las habitaciones del hotel P.B. **f** C.A. es más
  cómodo que el hotel P.B.
5 tengo; estoy; tengo; soy; trabajo; tiene; es; trabaja;
  estamos; vivimos.
6 **a** ¿Cuánto tiempo hace que estás aquí? **b** ¿Estás aquí con
  tu familia? **c** ¿A qué te dedicas? **d** ¿Cuánto tiempo hace
  que trabajas allí? **e** ¿Cuántas semanas de vacaciones tienes
  al año?

Units 11–15

1 te levantas – se levanta; salgo – sale – salimos; voy – vas –
  vamos; empiezo – empiezas – empieza; vuelvo – vuelve –
  volvemos; como – comes – comemos; me acuesto – te
  acuestas – se acuesta
2 me levanto – me ducho – desayuno – salgo – llego –
  almuerzo – trabajo – vuelvo – leo – veo.
3 me encantan – me gusta – le gustan – prefiere – les fascina
  – nos encanta – te gusta.
4 **a** ¿Qué vas a hacer? Voy a escribir ... **b** ¿Qué vais a hacer?
  Vamos a contestar ... **c** ¿Qué va a hacer Vd.? Voy a recibir
  ... **d** ¿Qué van a hacer Vds.? Vamos a realizar ...
5 **a** ¿Dígame? **b** Se ha equivocado de número. **c** ¿De parte de
  quién? **d** En seguida le pongo. **e** En seguida se pone.
  f ¿Quiere dejar algún recado? **g** Quisiera hablar con el ...
  h ¿Me puede poner con la ...? **i** Quisiera/ Quería
  solicitar/concertar una entrevista con el/la gerente. **j** Por
  favor, dígale que he llamado.
6 regresé – pasé – Estuve – encantó – fui – me quedé –
  visitamos – volvimos – tomé – Llegué – empecé
7 Estuvo – encantó – fue – se quedó – visitaron – volvieron
  – tomó – Llegó – empezó.

Units 16–20

1 nació – fue – abdicó – se educó – ingresó – realizó – se casó – fue – empezó.

2 conocí – tenía – estaba – era – tenía – vivía – trabajaba – vi – iba – volvía – saludé – respondió – vi – hablé – fue

3 a *See example*. b he hecho c he enviado d he hablado e he asistido f *See example*. g hemos escrito – enviado h entrevistado i hemos ido j hemos vuelto

4 *Examples*: Julio ha llegado, ha hecho, etc. Rafael y Silvia han despachado, han escrito, etc.

5 a iré b saldré c viajaré d hará e llegaré f me quedaré g volveré

6 a irá b saldrá c viajará d hará e llegará f se quedará g volverá

Units 21–5

1 a trabajaría b haría c compraría d pondría/viviría e podríamos f enviaríamos g ayudaríamos h nos iríamos

2 a ¿Había estado en (*place*) antes? b ¿Qué le parece la ciudad? c ¿Le sirvo (un poco) más? d ¿Quiere (un poco) más (de) vino? e Lo/la llevaré a su hotel en mi coche. f Me alegro de haberlo/la conocido.

3 … gire a la izquierda … está a la derecha … entre Antonio Varas y Manuel Montt

4 a Siga todo recto/de frente y luego tome la tercera (calle) a la izquierda. El banco está al final de esa calle. b Suba por esas escaleras hasta el primer piso. Los servicios están a la derecha pasados los teléfonos.

5 a-3 b-6 c-5 d-1 e-4 f-2

6 a … sea – tenga – fume – quiera b … sea – sepa – se lleve – esté

a *to*
abierto/a *open*
abogado/a *lawyer*
abrigo (m) *coat*
abrir *to open*
abuelo/a *grandfather/grandmother*
aburrido/a *boring*
acabar de *to have just*
aceite (m) *oil*
acerca de *about*
acostarse (o > ue) *to go to bed*
actriz (f) *actress*
actual *present*
actualmente *presently, at present*
acuerdo: de – *fine, O.K., that's all
right*
adelantar *to overtake*
además *besides*
administrativo/a *clerk*
afección (f) *complaint, illness*
afeitarse *to shave*
afueras (f pl) *outskirts*
agencia de viajes (f) *travel agency*
agradable *pleasant*
agradecimiento (m) *thanks*
agua (f) *water*
agua caliente/fría: el – *hot/cold water*
aguacate (m) *avocado*
ahora *now*; – mismo *right now*
aire acondicionado (m) *air
conditioning*
ajo (m) *garlic*
albaricoque (m) *apricot*
albergue juvenil (m) *youth hostel*
aldea (f) *village*
alegrarse *to be glad*

alegre *cheerful*
alemán/alemana *German*
Alemania *Germany*
algo *something, anything*; ¿ – más?
anything else?
algodón (m) *cotton*
alguien *somebody, someone*
algunos/as *some, any*
alimento (m) *food*
almacenes (m pl) *department store*
almíbar (m) *syrup*
almorzar (o > ue) *to have lunch*
almuerzo (m) *lunch, mid-morning
snack*
alojamiento (m) *accommodation*
alquilar *to hire, to rent, to let*
alquiler (m) *rent*
alrededor *around*
allí *there*; – mismo *right there*
ama de casa (f) *housewife*
amarillo/a *yellow*
ambiente (m) *atmosphere*
amigo/a *friend*
amistad (f) *friendship*
amplio/a *large, wide*
ancho/a *wide*
andar *to walk, to go for a walk*
ansiedad (f) *anxiety*
anteayer *the day before yesterday*
antecedentes (m pl) *professional
record*
anterior *previous*
antes *before*; – de ayer *the day
before yesterday*
antipático/a *unpleasant*
anular *to cancel*

anuncio (m) *advertisement*
año (m) *year*
aparcamiento (m) *car park, parking*
aparcar *to park*
aparecer *to appear*
apasionar *to love*
apellidarse: ¿cómo se/te apellida/s?
  what's your surname?
apellido (m) *surname*
apetecer *to like, to fancy*
aplazar *to postpone*
apreciar *to notice*
aprender *to learn*
aptitud (f) *flair*
apuntarse *to register*
aquel/aquella *that*; aquél/aquélla *that
  one*
aquellos/as *those*; aquéllos/as *those ones*
aquí *here*; – mismo *right –*; – tiene –
  you are por – *nearby, this way*
arreglar *to tidy up*
arreglarse *to get ready*
arroz (m) *rice*
artículo (m) *article*
asado *roast*
ascender (e > ie) *to come up to, to be
  promoted*
ascenso (m) *promotion*
ascensor (m) *lift*
asiento (m) *seat*
asimismo *likewise, also*
asistir *to attend*
atún (m) *tuna fish*
audaz *bold*
aumentar *to increase*
aún *even*
aunque *although, even though,
  though*
autocar (m) *coach*
auxiliar administrativo/a
  administrative assistant
avería (f) *fault*
avión (m) *aeroplane*
ayer *yesterday*
ayudar *to help*
azafata (f) *air stewardess*
azúcar (m or f) *sugar*
azul *blue*

bachillerato (m) *secondary education*
bailar *to dance*

bajar *to go down*
bajarse *to get off*
bajo/a *low*
baloncesto (m) *basketball*
banco (m) *bank*
bañarse *to have a bath*
bañera (f) *bathtub*
baño (m) *bathroom, toilet*
barra (f) *loaf*
barrio (m) *neighbourhood, area*
bastante *quite, rather, fairly*
beber *to drink*
bello *beautiful*
beso (m) *kiss*
biblioteca (f) *library*
bibliotecario/a *librarian*
bien *fine, well*
bienestar (m) *welfare*
billete (m) *ticket, banknote*
blanco/a *white*
bocadillo (m) *sandwich*
boletín informativo (m) *news
  broadcast*
bolsa (f) *bag*
bonito/a *beautiful, pretty*
botas (f pl) *boots*
bote (m) *jar*
botella (f) *bottle*
brevedad: a la mayor – *as soon as
  possible*
británico/a *British*
bruto/a: *gross (salary)*
buceo (m) *skin-diving*
buenas tardes *good afternoon/evening*
bueno *well*
bueno/a *good*
buscar *to look for*

cabeza (f) *head*
cada *each, every*
cadena (f) *chain*
café (m) *café, coffee*; – con leche (m)
  white coffee; – cortado (m) *coffee
  with a dash of milk*
caída (f) *fall*
caja (f) *box*; – fuerte *safe deposit box*
calamar (m) *squid*
calcetines (m pl) *socks*
calcomanía (f) *transfer*
calefacción (f) *heating*
calidad (f) *quality*

calor (m) *heat;* hace – *it is warm*
calle (f) *street;* a la – *facing the street*
cama (f) *bed*
camarero/a *waiter, waitress*
cambiar *to change*
cambio (m) *change*
camión (m) *lorry*
camisa (f) *shirt*
camiseta (f) *vest, T-shirt*
campo (m) *country*
canción (f) *song*
cansado/a *tired*
cargo (m) *post*
carne (f) *meat*
carnet de identidad (m) *identity card*
caro/a *expensive*
carpeta (f) *file*
carpintero/a *carpenter*
carrera (f) *career, studies*
carta (f) *menu, letter*
cartera (f) *briefcase*
cartero/a *postman/woman*
casa de huéspedes (f) *boarding/guest
  house*
casa (f) *house, home;* – de cambio (f)
 bureau de change (L.Am.)
casado/a *married*
casarse *to get married*
casi *almost*
catapultar *to shoot to fame*
categoría (f) *class*
cebolla (f) *onion*
ceder el paso *to give way*
cena (f) *dinner*
cenar *to have dinner*
céntrico/a *central*
centro comercial (m) *shopping centre*
cerca *near;* por aquí – *nearby*
cerdo (m) *pork*
cerrar (e > ie) *to close, to shut*
cerveza (f) *beer*
champiñon (m) *mushroom*
chaqueta (f) *jacket*
cheque de viaje (m) *traveller's cheque*
chorizo (m) *hard pork sausage*
cita (f) *appointment*
ciudad (f) *town, city*
ciudadano/a *citizen*
cobrar *to claim*
cocina (f) *kitchen*
cocinar *to cook*

coche (m) *car*
coger *to take, to catch*
colegio (m) *school*
colgar (o > ue) *to hang*
coliflor (f) *cauliflower*
comedor (m) *dining room*
comer *to eat, to have lunch*
comerciante (m f) *merchant*
comestibles (m pl) *groceries*
comida (f) *lunch, meal, food*
como *as, like*
cómo *how, what*
comodidad (f) *comfort*
cómodo/a *comfortable*
compañero/a *colleague*
compartir *to share*
compra (f) *purchase, shopping;* hacer
 la – *to do the shopping*
comprar *to buy*
compromiso (m) *engagement*
computador/a *computer* (L.Am.)
con *with*
concierto (m) *concert*
concurso (m) *contest*
conducir *to drive*
conductor/a *driver*
conmigo *with me*
conocer *to know, to meet*
conocimiento (m) *knowledge*
conseguir *to get*
consejo (m) *advice*
conservador/a *conservative*
constar: hacer – *to state, to make
  known*
consulta (f) *surgery*
consumir *to consume*
contable (m f) *accountant*
contar (o > ue) *to tell*
contar con *to have*
contrato fijo (m) *permanent contract*
convenir *to agree*
copa (f) *drink*
corazón (m) *heart*
corbata (f) *tie*
cordero (m) *lamb*
correos: la oficina de – (f) *post office*
cortés *polite*
corto/a *short*
cosa (f) *thing*
costar *to cost*
costumbre (f) *custom*

criatura (f) *child*
cruce (m) *crossing*; – de peatones (m)
 zebra –
cuadros: de – *check*
cuál *what, which*
cualquier/a *any*
cuándo *when*
cuánto/a *how much*
cuántos/as *how many*
cuarto/a *fourth*
cuarto (m) *quarter*
cubierto *overcast*
cuchara (f) *spoon*
cuchillo (m) *knife*
cuenta (f) *bill*; por mi – *on my own*
cuento (m) *short story*
cuerpo (m) *body*
cuidado: con – *carefully*
cuidar *to look after*
culpa (f) *fault*
cumpleaños (m sing) *birthday*
cumplir *to meet (requirements)*
cumplir ... años *to become/turn ...*
 years old
curso (m) *course*

damasco (m) *apricot* (L.Am.)
dar *to give*; – a *to face*
datos (m pl) *data, information*
de *from, of*
deber *to have to, must*
deberes (m pl) *homework*
débil *weak*
decidir *to decide*
declinar *to come down, decrease*
dedicación exclusiva (f) *full-time*
 commitment
dedicarse *to devote oneself to, to go*
 in for
dedicas: ¿a qué te – ? *what do you do*
 for a living?
dejar *to leave*
del (de + el) *of the*
delante de *in front of*
demasiado/a *too, too much*
deme *give me*
dentro *inside*
departamento (m) *flat* (L.Am.)
dependiente/a *shop assistant*
deporte (m) *sport*
deportivo/a (adj.) *sports*

derecha (f) *right*; a la – *on the –*
derecho (m) *law*
desagradable *unpleasant*
desayunar *to have breakfast*
desayuno (m) *breakfast*
descansar *to rest*
descapotable *convertible*
descortés *impolite*
descubrir *to discover*
descuento (m) *discount*
desde ... hasta *from ... to*
desear *to want, to wish*; ¿qué desea?
 what would you like? can I help you?
desempeñar *to hold* (a job)
desempleo (m) *unemployment*
desesperado/a *desperate*
despacho (m) *office*
despierto/a *bright*
después *then, later, afterwards*
destino (m) *destination*
detrás de *behind*
día (m) *day*; al – *per day, daily*
diario/a *daily*
dibujar *to draw*
difícil *difficult*
dígame *can I help you? hello?*
 (telephone)
digestivo *digestive*
dinero (m) *money*
diplomado/a *qualified person*
dirección (f) *address*
director/a gerente *general manager*
dirigirse *to address*
diseñador/a *designer*
disminuir *to slow down*
disponer de *to have*
disponibilidad (f) *availability*
disponible *available*
dispuesto/a a *willing to*
distinto/a *different*
divertido/a *amusing*
divorciado/a *divorced*
divorciarse *to get divorced*
docena (f) *dozen*
documental (m) *documentary*
dolor (m) *pain*; – de cabeza *headache*
domingo *Sunday*
dominio (m) *command*
dónde *where*
dormir (o > ue) *to sleep*
dormitorio (m) *bedroom*

ducha (f) *shower*
ducharse *to take a shower*
durar *to last*
durazno (m) *peach* (L.Am.)

e *and* (before i, hi)
echar de menos *to miss*
echarse una siesta *to have a siesta*
edad (f) *age*
edificación (f) *building*
edificio (m) *building*
efectivo: en – *cash*
ejemplar (m) *copy*
ejemplo (m) *example*
el *the* (masculine)
él *he*
elegir (e > i) *to choose*
ella *she*
ellos/as *they*
empezar (e > ie) *to start, to begin*
empleado/a *clerk, employee*
empresa (f) *company, firm*
empresariales (f): ciencias – *business
  studies*
empresario/a *businessman/woman*
en *in, on, at*
en seguida *right away*
encantado/a *pleased to meet you*
encantar *to love, to like a lot*
encanto (m) *charm*
encargado/a *person in charge,
  manager*
encontrar (o > ue) *to find*
encontrarse (o > ue) *to meet; –
  bien/mal to feel well/badly*
encuentro (m) *encounter*
enfermero/a *nurse*
enfrente de *opposite, in front of*
enmarcación (f) *framing*
ensalada (f) *salad*
ensayo (m) *essay*
enseñar *to show, to teach*
entender (e > ie) *to understand*
entonces *then*
entrada (f) *ticket*
entrar *to start, to begin* (school,
  work)
entre *between*
entretenimiento (m) *entertainment*
entrevista (f) *interview*
entrevistar *to interview*

envejecer *to get old*
enviar *to send*
envío (m) *dispatch, sending*
equipado/a *fitted*
equipaje (m) *luggage*
equipo (m) *team*
equivocación (f) *mistake*
equivocado/a *wrong*
equivocarse *to be wrong, to have the
  wrong number*
escalera (f) *stairs*
escaparate (m) *shop window*
escasos/as *few*
escribir *to write*
escuchar *to listen*
escuela (f) *school*
escultura (f) *sculpture*
ese/a *that*; ése/a *that one*
eso (neuter) *that*
esos/as *those*; ésos/as *those ones*
español/a *Spanish*
esperanza de vida (f) *life expectancy*
esperar *to hope, to expect, to wait*
esposo/a *husband/wife*
esquiar *to ski*
esquina (f) *corner*
estación (f) *station*
estacionamiento (m) *car park* (L.Am.)
estado civil (m) *marital status*
estancia (f) *stay*
estar *to be*
este/a *this*; éste/a *this one*
estimado/a *dear*
esto (neuter) *this*
estómago (m) *stomach*
estos/as *these*; éstos/as *these ones*
estrecho/a *tight*
estrella (f) *star*
estrenar *to show for the first time*
estudiar *to study*
estudios superiores (m pl) *higher
  education*
estupendo *great*
evento (m) *event* (L.Am.)
evitar *to avoid*
exigir *to demand*
éxito (m) *success*; tener – *to succeed*
exposición (f) *exhibition*
exterior *facing the street*
extranjero (m) *abroad, overseas*
extraño/a *stranger*

fábrica (f) *factory*
falda (f) *skirt*
fatal *terrible*
fatiga (f) *fatigue*
fecha (f) *date*
feliz *happy*
feo/a *ugly*
ferroviario *railway* (adj.)
festivo (m) *holiday*
ficha (f) *card*
fiebre (f) *fever*
filmar *to film*
fin (m) *end*; poner – a *to put an – to*
fin (m) de semana *weekend*
final (m) *end*; al – de *at the – of*
firmar *to sign*
flan (m) *creme caramel*
flor (f) *flower*
floristería (f) *florist's*
fondo: al – (de) *at the end (of)*
formación (f) *education, training*
fracaso (m) *failure*
francés/francesa *French*
fregar (e > ie) *to wash up*
frente: de – *straight on*
fresa (f) *strawberry*
frío/a *cold*; hace frío *it is cold*
frito/a *fried*
fruta (f) *fruit*
frutería (f) *fruit shop*
fuera *out*
fuerte *strong*
fumador/a *smoker*
fumar *to smoke*
función (f) *performance, show*
funcionar *to work*

galleta (f) *biscuit*
gamba (f) *prawn*
gasto (m) *expense*
gato (m) *cat*
generalmente *generally, usually*
gente (f) *people*
gerente (m f) *manager*
girar *to turn*
gobierno (m) *government*
gracias *thank you*
gran *big, large*
grande *big, large*
grasa (f) *fat*
grifo (m) *tap*

gris *grey*
guapo/a *good-looking*
guerra (f) *war*
guisante (m) *pea*
guisar *to cook*
gustar *to like*

habitación (f) *room*
habitante (m f) *inhabitant*
habla (m): de – española *Spanish-speaking*
hablante (m f) *speaker*
hablar *to speak*
hacer la compra *to do the shopping*
hacer dieta *to go on a diet*
harina (f) *flour*
harto/a *fed up*
hasta *until, as far as*
hay *there is/are*
hecho (m) *fact*
helado (m) *ice cream*
hermano/a *brother, sister*
hijo/a *son, daughter*
hilo musical (m) *piped music*
hogar (m) *home*
hola *hello, hi*
holandés/holandesa *Dutch*
hombre (m) *man*
hora (f) *hour, time*
horario (m) *timetable, working hours*
hostal (m) *small, cheap hotel*
hoy *today*
huevo (m) *egg*

ida: de – *single (ticket)*
ida y vuelta *return (ticket)*
idioma (m) *language*
igual *same*
imaginarse *to imagine*
implicar *to mean, to imply*
imprescindible *essential*
impuesto (m) *tax*
incendio (m) *fire*
incluso *even*
incorporación (f) *joining*
incremento (m) *increase*
individual *single*
informática (f) *computing*
informe (m) *report*
ingeniería (f) *engineering*
Inglaterra *England*

inglés/inglesa *English*
ingresar *to join*
inmaduro/a *immature*
inseguro/a *insecure*
insomnio (m) *insomnia*
instituto (m) *secondary school*
interesar *to interest*
interior *facing onto a central patio*
interpretación (f) *interpreting*
intranquilo *anxious, worried*
inútilmente *in vain*
invierno (m) *winter*
invitar *to invite*
ir *to go*
irse *to leave, to go*
izquierda (f) *left*; a la – *on the* –

jabón (m) *soap*
jamón (m) *ham*
jardín (m) *garden*
jardinera (f) *window box*
jefe/a *boss*
jersey (m) *sweater*
jitomate (m) *tomato* (Mexico)
jornada intensiva (f) *working day
 with a short break*
joven *young*
jóvenes (m pl) *the young*
joyas (f pl) *jewellery*
jubilado/a *retired*
judías verdes (f pl) *green beans*
judío/a *Jewish*
jueves *Thursday*
jugar (u > ue) *to play*
junto/a a *next to*

la (f) *the; it, her, you* (formal)
lado: al – de *next to*; al otro – de *on
 the other side of*
lago (m) *lake*
lamentar *to regret*
lana (f) *wool*
lapso (m) *period*
largo/a *long*
lata (f) *tin*
lavado (m) *washbasin*
lavandería (f) *launderette*
lavar *to wash*
lavarse *to wash*; – los dientes *to
 brush one's teeth*
lectura (f) *reading*

leche (f) *milk*
lechuga (f) *lettuce*
leer *to read*
legumbre (f) *pulse*
lejos *far*
lengua (f) *language*
levantarse *to get up*
libra (f) *pound*
libre *free*
librería (f) *bookshop*
libro (m) *book*
licenciado/a *graduate*
ligero/a *light*
limón (m) *lemon*
limpiar *to clean*
línea (f) *line*
línea aérea (f) *airline*
lino (m) *linen*
lo (m) *it, him, you* (formal)
localizarse *to be located*
loco/a *crazy, mad*
Londres *London*
lugar (m) *place*
lujo (m) *luxury*
lujoso/a *luxurious*
luminoso *bright*
luz (f) *light*

llamada (f) *call*
llamar *to call*
llamarse *to be called*
llave (f) *key*
llegada (f) *arrival*
llegar *to arrive*
llevar *to take, to carry*
llevarse bien con *to get on well with*
llover (o > ue) *to rain*

madre *mother*
maduro/a *mature*
maleta (f) *suitcase*
malo/a *bad*
malva *mauve*
mandar *to send*
manejo (m) *command*
manera (f) *way*; de – que *so that*
manta (f) *blanket* (Spain)
manzana (f) *apple*
mañana *tomorrow*; (f) *morning*
maquillarse *to put on make-up*
maquinaria (f) *machinery*

mar (m f) *sea*
maravilloso/a *wonderful*
marcar *to dial*
marido (m) *husband*
marrón *brown*
martes *Tuesday*
más *else, more*; el/la – *the most*; ¿qué
– ? *what else?*
mayor *older, larger, greater*; el – *the oldest*
me *me, myself*
mecanógrafo/a *typist*
media (f) *average*
media pensión (f) *half board*
mediana edad: de – *middle-aged*
mediano/a *medium (sized)*
medio/a *half*
mediodía (m) *noon, midday*
mejor *better*; el – *the best*
melocotón (m) *peach*
menor *younger, smaller, lesser, minor*
menos *less, minus*
mensual *monthly*
menudo: a – *often*
mercado (m) *market*
mercancía (f) *merchandise*
merecer *to deserve*
merluza (f) *hake*
metro (m) *undergound railway, metre*
mi *my*
mí *me*
miércoles *Wednesday*
minuto (m) *minute*
mío/a *mine*
mirada (f) *look*
mirar *to look*
mitad *half*
mixta *mixed*
mobiliario (m) *furniture*
molestar *to bother*
moneda (f) *currency*
montar *to ride*
mucho gusto *pleased to meet you*
mudarse *to move house*
mueble (m) *piece of furniture*
muerto/a *dead*
mujer (f) *wife, woman*
mundo (m) *world*
museo (m) *museum*
muy *very*

nacer *to be born*
nacionalidad (f) *nationality*
nada *nothing, not at all*; de – *you are welcome*
nadar *to swim*
naranja (f) *orange*
nata (f) *cream*
natación (f) *swimming*
necesitar *to need*
nene/a *baby* (L.Am.)
nevar *to snow*
niebla (f) *fog*
ninguno/a *no, one, not any*
niño/a *child*
niños (m pl) *children*
nivel (m) *level*
nocturno *night, evening* (adj.)
noche (f) *night*
nombrar *to appoint*
nombre (m) *name*
nos *us*
nosotros/as *we*
noticia (f) *news*
novio/a *boyfriend/girlfriend*
nublado/a *cloudy*
nuboso *cloudy*
nuestro/a *our, ours*
nuevamente *again*
nuevo/a *new*
número (m) *number*
nunca *never*

o *or*
obra (f) *play, work*: – de teatro (f) *play*
ocio (m) *leisure*
ocultar *to hide*
oeste (m) *west*
oficina (f) *office*; – de turismo (f) *tourist* –; – de cambio *bureau de change*
ofrecer *to offer*
olvidar *to leave behind, to forget*
optar *to choose*
ordenador (m) *computer* (Spain)
orgulloso/a *proud*
oriente (m) *east*
orilla (f) *shore*
os *you* (informal, plural)
oscuro/a *dark*
otro/a *another*

otros/as *others*

padecer *to suffer*
padre *father*
padres (m pl) *parents*
pagar *to pay*
país (m) *country*
palabra (f) *word*
pan (m) *bread*
pana (f) *corduroy*
panadería (f) *baker's*
pantalones (m pl) *trousers*
papa (f) *potato* (L.Am.)
papel (m) *role, paper;* – higiénico (m)
toilet –
papelería (f) *stationery*
par (m) *pair*
para *for, in order to*
parada de autobuses (f) *bus stop*
parador (m) *state-run hotel* (Spain)
paraguas (m) *umbrella*
parar *to stop*
parecer *to seem*
paro (m) *unemployment*
parque (m) *park*
parrilla (f) *grill*
parte (f) *part;* ¿de – de quién? *who's
calling?*
partir: a – de *starting*
pasado/a *past, last*
pasaje (m) *ticket* (L.Am.)
pasajero/a *passenger*
pasar *to pass, to happen, to spend
(time), to come in*
pasarlo bien *to have a good time*
pasear en bicicleta *to ride a bicycle*
paseo: dar un – *to go for a walk*
pasillo (m) *corridor*
pastilla (f) *tablet*
patata (f) *potato;* patatas fritas (f pl)
chips
pedido (m) *order*
pedir (e > i) *to ask for;* – hora *to ask
for an appointment* (with a
doctor/dentist)
peinarse *to comb*
película (f) *film*
pelota (f) *ball*
pensar (e > ie) *to think*
pensión (f) *boarding/guest house;* –
completa *full board*

pepino (m) *cucumber*
pequeño/a *small*
perder (e > ie) *to lose*
perdone/a (formal/informal) *sorry,
excuse me*
perejil (m) *parsley*
perezoso/a *lazy*
periódico (m) *newspaper*
periodista (m f) *journalist*
permitir *to let, to allow*
pero *but*
perro/a *dog*
pescado (m) *fish*
pescar *to fish*
peso (m) *weight;* currency (L. Am.)
piel (f) *leather* (Spain), *fur*
pimiento verde/rojo (m) *green/red
pepper*
pintura (f) *painting*
piña (f) *pineapple*
piscina (f) *swimming pool*
piso (m) *floor, flat* (Spain)
placer (m) *pleasure*
plancha: a la – *grilled*
planchar *to iron*
planta (f) *floor;* – baja (f) *ground* –
plantilla (f) *staff*
plátano (m) *banana*
plato (m) *dish*
playa (f) *beach*
plaza (f) *square*
población (f) *population*
poblado/a *populated*
poco/a *little;* un poco de *some*
poder (o > ue) *to be able to, can*
poesía (f) *poetry*
pollo (m) *chicken*
pone: ¿me –? *will you give me* –? (in a
market, bar)
poner *to put, to put through, to show
(film), to say* (in writing)
pongo: ¿qué le –? *what would you
like?*
ponerse *to put on;* – al teléfono *to
come to the phone*
por, *for, by, in, per;* – aquí *nearby,
this way*
por favor *please*
por qué *why*
porque *because*
portero/a *doorman/woman*

postal (f) *postcard*
postre (m) *dessert*
precio (m) *price*
precisar *to need, to require*
preferentemente *especially*
preferir (e > ie) *to prefer*
presentación (f) *introduction*
presentar *to introduce*
pretensión (f) *expectation*
primero/a first; de primero *first course*
primo/a *cousin*
principios: a – (de) *at the beginning (of)*
probador (m) *fitting room*
probarse *to try on*
problema (f) *problem*
profesor/a *teacher*
programador/a *programmer*
pronunciar *to pronounce*
propio/a *own*
protagonizar *to star in*
próximo/a *next*
publicidad (f) *advertising*
pueblo (m) *small town*
puerto (m) *port*
pues *well*
puesto (m) *post, job;* – directivo *executive post*
punto: en – *sharp*

que *that, which, who*
qué *what, which*
quedar *to fit, to agree to meet*
quedarse *to stay*
queja (f) *complaint*
quejarse *to complain*
querer (e > ie) *to want*
querido/a *dear*
queso (m) *cheese*
quién *who*
quinto/a *fifth*
quisiera *I'd like* (from querer)
quizás *perhaps*

rato (m) *while*
realizar *to carry out, to make*
recado (m) *message*
recetar *to prescribe*
recibir *to receive*
reclamo (m) *complaint*

recordar (o > ue) *to remember*
recto: todo – *straight on*
regalo (m) *present*
régimen (m) *diet*
regresar *to come back*
regreso (m) *return*
reina (f) *queen*
relajarse *to relax*
remuneración (f) *salary*
repartir *to deliver*
repasar *to rehearse*
representante (m f) *representative*
requisito (m) *requirement*
reserva (f) *reservation, booking*
resfriado (m) *cold*
respuesta (f) *answer*
retraso (m) *delay*
reumatismo (m) *rheumatism*
reunirse *to meet*
revista (f) *magazine;* – del corazón *true-romance magazine*
rey (m) *king*
río (m) *river*
rodeado/a *surrounded*
rojo/a *red*
ropa (f) *clothes*
rosa *pink*
ruidoso/a *noisy*

sábado *Saturday*
saber *to know;* – de memoria *to know by heart*
sal (f) *salt*
sala (de estar) (f) *sitting-room*
salchichón (m) *salami-type sausage*
salida (f) *departure, exit;* – de incendio (f) *fire exit*
salir *to leave, to go out*
salón (m) *sitting-room*
salvar *to save*
sed (f) *thirst*
seda (f) *silk*
seguida: en – *right away*
seguido por *followed by*
seguir (e > i) *to continue*
segundo/a second; de segundo *second course*
seguramente *surely*
seguridad (f) *security*
seguro/a *confident, safe*
seguro *sure*

seguro (m) *insurance*
semana (f) *week*
semanal *weekly, per week*
sentir (e > ie) *to be sorry*
sentirse (e > ie) a gusto *to feel at ease*
señal (f) *signal*
señor (m) *gentleman, sir*
señora (f) *lady, madam*
señorita (f) *young lady*
se *himself, herself, yourself, (formal),
  itself, yourselves, themselves; one,
  you* (impersonal)
ser *to be*
servicio (m) *service*
servicios (m pl) *toilets, facilities*
servilleta (f) *napkin*
servir *to serve*
si *if*
sí *yes*
siempre *always*
siento: lo – *I am sorry*
siguiente *following*
simpático/a *nice*
sin *without*
sin embargo *however*
sino *but*
sitio (m) *place*
situación (f) *location*
sobre *about* (with the time)
socio/a *member*
sol (m) *sun*
solamente *only*
soleado/a *sunny*
soler (o > ue) *to usually* (do, etc.)
solicitar *to request, to arrange*
  (interview/ appointment)
solo/a *alone*
sólo *only*
soltero/a *single*
soñar *to dream*
sopa (f) *soup*
su *your* (formal), *his, her, its, their*
subir *to go up*
sueldo (m) *salary;* – líquido (m) *net* –
suerte (f) *luck;* tener – *to be lucky;*
  ¡qué –! *how lucky!*
suéter (m) *sweater* (L.Am.)
superficie (f) *area*
supermercado (m) *supermarket*
suponer *to suppose*
supuesto: por – *of course*

suyo/a *yours* (formal), *his, hers, its,
  theirs*

tal: ¿qué –? *how are you?, hi,* ¿qué –
  es? *what is it like?;* – vez *perhaps*
talla (f) *size*
tamaño (m) *size*
también *also, too*
tampoco *neither, not ... either*
tan ... como *as ... as*
tapa (f) *snack* (Spain)
tardar *to take* (time)
tarde (f) *afternoon; late*
tareas domésticas (f pl) *household
  chores*
tarjeta (f) *card;* – de crédito *credit
  card*
tasa de natalidad (f) *birth rate*
taza (f) *cup*
te *you, yourself* (informal)
té (m) *tea*
teatro (m) *theatre*
telenovela (f) *soap opera*
teleserie (f) *TV serial*
tendero/a *shop keeper*
tenedor (m) *fork*
tener *to have, to be* (age)
tener éxito *to succeed*
tener que *to have to*
tercero/a *third*
ternera (f) *veal*
terraza (f) *balcony*
ti *you* (informal)
tiempo (m) *weather, time;* – libre
  spare time; hace – *a long time ago*
tienda (f) *shop*
tímido/a *shy*
típico *typical*
tipo (m) *kind*
título (m) *degree*
tocar la bocina *to sound one's horn*
todavía *still, yet*
todo/a *whole, all, every, everything*
tomar *to drink, to take, to have;* – el
  sol *to sunbathe*
tonto/a *fool, silly*
tormenta (f) *storm*
tortilla (f) *omelette*
tostadas (f pl) *toast*
trabajador/a *worker, hardworking*
trabajar *to work*

trabajo (m) *work*
traducción (f) *translation*
traductor/a *translator*
traer *to bring*
traje (m) *suit*
tranquilidad (f) *quietness*
tranquilo/a *quiet*
trastorno (m) *disorder, illness*
tratar de *to try to*
través: a – de *through*
tren (m) *train*
tribunal (m) *court*
triste *sad*
trozo (m) *piece, slice*
tú *you* (informal)
tu *your* (informal)
turco/a *Turk, Turkish*
tuyo/a *yours* (informal)

u *or* (before 'o')
ubicación (f) *location*
último/a *last*
un/a *a*
unos/as *some, about*
único/a *only*
unos *some, around*
urgir *to be urgent*
urna (f) *box*
usted *you* (formal, singular)
ustedes *you* (formal, plural)
utilizar *to use*
uva (f) *grapes*

vacaciones (f pl) *holiday(s)*
vagón (m) *carriage*
vale *O.K., all right*
valer *to cost*
valorar *to be an advantage*
vaqueros (m pl) *jeans*
variedad (f) *variety*
varios/as *several, various*
vaso (m) *glass*
váter (m) *W.C.*
veces: a – *sometimes*
vecino/a *neighbour*
vela (f) *sail*; hacer – *to sail*
velocidad: alta – *high speed*
vender *to sell*
venir (e > ie) *to come*
venta (f) *sale*; en – *for sale*
ventana (f) *window*

ver *to see, to watch*
veranear *to go on a summer holiday*
verano (m) *summer*
verdad (f) *true*; ¿verdad? *isn't it?, do you?, etc.*; ¿de –? *sure?*
verde *green*
verduras (f pl) *vegetables*
verificar *to certify*
verse *to see each other*
vestido (m) *dress*
vestirse (e > i) *to get dressed*
vez (f) *time*; de – en cuando *from – to –*; una – *once*
viajar *to travel*
viaje (m) *trip, journey*; – de negocios (m) *business trip*; cheque de – *traveller's cheque*
vida (f) *life*
viejo/a *old*
viento (m) *wind*; hacer – *to be windy*
viernes *Friday*
vino blanco/tinto (m) *white/red wine*
visitante (m f) *visitor*
víspera (f) *eve*
vistas: con – a *with a view to*
vivienda (f) *housing*
vivir *to live*
volver (o > ue) *to come back*
vosotros/as *you* (informal, plural)
vuelo (m) *flight*
vuestro/a *your, yours* (informal, plural)

y *and*
ya *yet, already*
yo *I*

zanahoria (f) *carrot*
zapatos (m pl) *shoes*
zumo (m) *juice*

about (3.00 p.m.) *sobre (las 3.00 de la tarde)*
about *acerca de, sobre*
abroad *en el extranjero*
accommodation *alojamiento* (m)
accountant contable (m/f), *contador/a* (L.Am.)
actress *actriz*
address *dirección* (f)
advertisement *anuncio* (m)
advertising *publicidad* (f)
advice *consejo* (m)
aeroplane *avión* (m)
after *después*
afternoon *tarde* (f)
afterwards *después*
again *otra vez, de nuevo, nuevamente*
age *edad* (f)
air conditioning *aire acondicionado* (m)
air *aire* (m)
airline *línea aérea* (f)
airport *aeropuerto* (m)
allow: to – *permitir*
almonds *almendras* (f pl)
almost *casi*
alone *solo/a*
already *ya*
also *también, asimismo*
although *aunque*
always *siempre*
amusing *divertido/a*
anchovies *anchoas* (f, pl)
and *y, e* (before *i, hi*)
ankle *tobillo* (m)

another *otro/a*
answer *respuesta* (f)
anxiety *ansiedad*
anxious *intranquilo/a*
appear: to – *aparecer*
apple *manzana* (f)
appoint: to – *nombrar, designar*
appointment *cita* (f)
apricot *albaricoque, damasco* (L.Am.)
April *abril*
area *superficie* (f)
arm *brazo* (m)
around *alrededor*
arrival *llegada* (f)
arrive: to – *llegar*
art gallery *galería* (f) *de arte*
article *artículo* (m)
as *como*
as ... as *tan ... como*
as far as *hasta*
ask: to – *preguntar*
ask: to – for *pedir* (a > i)
asparagus *espárragos* (m pl)
aspirin *aspirina* (f)
at *en*
athletics *atletismo* (m)
atmosphere *ambiente* (m)
attend: to – *asistir*
August *agosto*
aunt *tía*
availability *disponibilidad* (f)
available *disponible*
average *media* (f)
avocado *aguacate* (m), *palta* (f) (Southern Cone, L.Am..)
avoid: to – *evitar*

back *espalda* (f)
bad *malo/a*
bag *bolsa* (f)
baker´s *panadería* (f)
balcony *balcón* (m)
ball *pelota* (f)
banana *plátano* (m)
bank *banco* (m)
banknote *billete* (m)
basketball *baloncesto* (m), *basquetbol* (m)
bath: to have a – *bañarse*
bath *baño* (m)
bathe: to – *bañarse*
bathroom *baño* (m)
be: to – *ser, estar*
beach *playa* (f)
beautiful *bonito/a, bello/a, lindo/a, hermoso/a*
because *porque*
bed *cama* (f)
bedroom *dormitorio* (m)
beer *cerveza* (f)
before *antes, delante*
beginning: at the – of ... *a principios de ...*
behind *detrás*
besides *además*
better *mejor*
between *entre*
bicycle *bicicleta* (f)
big *grande, gran* (before a noun)
bill *cuenta* (f)
birth rate *tasa de natalidad* (f)
birthday *cumpleaños* (m, sing)
biscuit *galleta* (f)
black coffee *café solo* (m)
black *negro/a*
blanket *manta* (f, Spain), *cobija* (f, México), *frazada* (f, Southern Cone, L.Am.)
blood *sangre* (f)
blouse *blusa* (f)
blue *azul*
boarding house *casa* (f) *de huéspedes*
boat *barco* (m)
body *cuerpo* (m)
boiled *hervido/a*
bold *audaz*
book *libro* (m)
bookshop *librería* (f)

boots *botas* (f, pl)
boring *aburrido/a*
born: to be – *nacer*
boss *jefe/jefa*
bother: to – *molestar*
bottle *botella* (f)
box *caja* (f)
boyfriend *novio*
bread *pan* (m)
breakfast *desayuno* (m)
breakfast:: to have – *desayunar, tomar desayuno*
briefcase *cartera* (f), *portadocumentos* (m sing)
bright *luminoso/a*
bring: to – *traer*
British *británico/a*
broken *roto/a*
brother *hermano*
brother-in-law *cuñado*
brown *marrón*, (colour) *café* (L.Am.)
building *edificio* (m), *edificación* (f)
bureau de change *oficina* (f) *de cambio, casa* (f) *de cambio* (L.Am.)
burned *quemado/a*
bus stop *parada* (f) *de autobuses*
bus *autobús* (m)
businessman/woman *empresario/a*
but *pero*
butter *mantequilla* (f)
buy: to – *comprar*
by *por*

cake shop *pastelería* (f)
call *llamada* (f)
call: to – *llamar*
campsite *camping* (m)
can *poder*
cancel: to – *anular*
car *coche* (m), *carro* (L.Am.)
car park *aparcamiento* (m), *estacionamiento* (L.Am.)
card *tarjeta* (f), *ficha* (f)
career *carrera* (f)
carefully *cuidadosamente, con cuidado*
carriage *vagón* (m)
carrot *zanahoria* (f)
carry: to – *llevar*
cash *efectivo* (m)
cat *gato/a*

cauliflower *coliflor* (f)
celery *apio* (m)
cerdo *pork* (m)
chain *cadena* (f)
chair *silla* (f)
change: to – *cambiar*
change *cambio* (m)
charm *encanto* (m)
cheerful *alegre*
cheese *queso* (m)
chemist´s *farmacia* (f)
cherries *cerezas* (f, pl)
chess *ajedrez* (m)
chest *pecho* (m)
chicken *pollo* (m)
child *niño/a*
children *niños*
chips *patatas/papas* (f pl, L.Am.)
  fritas
choose: to – *elegir* (e > i)
chop *chuleta* (f)
cigarrette *cigarrillo* (m)
cinema *cine* (m)
citizen *ciudadano/a*
city *ciudad* (f)
clean: to – *limpiar*
clean *limpio/a*
clerk *administrativo/a*
close: to – *cerrar*
clothes shop *tienda* (f) *de ropa*
clothes *ropa* (f)
cloudy *nublado, nuboso*
coach *autocar* (m), *autobús* (m)
coat *abrigo* (m)
cod *bacalao* (m)
coffee *café* (m)
cold: it is – *hace frío* (weather)
cold *frío*
colleague *colega* (m/f), *compañero/a*
comb: to – *peinarse*
come: to – *venir*
come back: to – *regresar, volver* (o >
  ue)
comfort *comodidad* (f)
comfortable *cómodo/a*
complain: to – *quejarse*
complaint *queja* (f), *reclamo* (m)
computer programmer *programador/a*
computer *ordenador* (m),
  computador/a (m/f) (L.Am.)
computing *informática* (f)

concert *concierto* (m)
confident *seguro/a*
continue: to – *continuar, seguir*
  (e > i)
cook: to – *cocinar, guisar*
cooked meats *fiambres* (m pl)
cookery *cocina* (f)
copy *ejemplar* (m)
corner *esquina* (f)
corridor *pasillo* (m)
cost: to – *costar* (o > ue), *valer*
cotton *algodón* (m)
country *país* (m), *campo* (m)
course *curso* (m)
court *tribunal* (m)
cousin *primo/a*
crab *cangrejo* (m)
crazy *loco/a*
credit card *tarjeta de crédito* (f)
creme caramel *flan* (m)
crisps *patatas/papas* (f pl, L.Am.)
  fritas
cucumber *pepino* (m)
cup *taza* (f)
currency *moneda* (f)
custom *costumbre* (f)
customs *aduana* (f)

daily *diario*
dance: to – *bailar*
dark *oscuro*
date *fecha* (f)
daughter *hija*
day before yesterday: the – *anteayer,
  antier* (México)
day *día* (m)
dead *muerto/a*
dear (in letters) *querido/a, estimado/a*
December *diciembre*
degree *título* (m)
delay *retraso* (m)
deliver: to – *repartir*
demand: to – *exigir*
dentist *dentista* (m/f)
department store *grandes almacenes*
  (m pl)
departure *salida* (f), *partida* (f)
designer *diseñador/a*
dessert *postre* (m)
dial: to – *marcar*
diet *dieta* (f), *régimen* (m)

different *diferente, distinto/a*
difficult *difícil*
dining room *comedor* (m)
dinner: to have – *cenar*
dinner *cena* (f)
dirty *sucio/a*
discount *descuento* (m)
dish *plato* (m)
dispatch *envío* (m)
divorced *divorciado/a*
doctor *médico/a, doctor/a*
dog *perro/a*
door *puerta* (f)
doorman/woman *portero/a*
double room *habitación* (f) *doble*
dozen *docena* (f)
dream: to – *soñar* (o > ue)
dress *vestido* (m)
drink: to – *beber*
drink *copa* (f)
drive: to – *conducir*
driver *conductor/ora*
driving licence *permiso* (m) *de conducir*
Dutch *holandés/holandesa*

each *cada*
ear *oreja* (f) (outer), *oído* (m) (inner)
east *este* (m), *oriente* (m)
eat: to – *comer*
education: higher – *estudios* (m pl) *superiores*
education *educación* (f), *formación* (f)
egg *huevo* (m)
else *más*
employee *empleado/a*
encounter *encuentro* (m)
end: at the – *al final, al fondo*
end *fin* (m)
engagement *compromiso* (m)
engineer *ingeniero/a*
engineering *ingeniería* (f)
England *Inglaterra*
English *inglés* (m) (language); *inglés/inglesa*
entertainment *entretenimiento* (m)
especially *especialmente, preferentemente*
essay *ensayo* (m)
essential *imprescindible, fundamental, esencial*
eve *víspera* (f)

even though *aunque*
even *incluso, aun*
every *todos/as, cada*
example *ejemplo* (m)
excuse me (sorry) *perdone* (formal)/*perdona* (informal)
executive *ejecutivo/a*
exhibition (f) *exposición*
exit *salida* (f)
expect: to – *esperar*
expense *gasto* (m)
expensive *caro/a*
eye *ojo* (m)

face *cara* (f)
fact *hecho* (m)
factory *fábrica* (f)
failure *fracaso* (m)
fall *caída* (f)
family *familia* (f)
far *lejos*
fat *grasa* (f); *gordo/a*
father *padre*
fault *culpa* (f)
fault *avería* (f)
February *febrero*
fed up *harto*
feel: to – well/badly *encontrarse* (o > ue) *bien/mal*
fever *fiebre* (f)
few *pocos, escasos*
fifth *quinto/a*
file *carpeta* (f)
film: in cinema *película* (f)
film: roll of – *rollo* (m) *de película*
film: to – *filmar*
find: to – *encontrar* (o > ue)
fine *de acuerdo, bien*
finger *dedo* (m)
fire *incendio* (m)
first *primero*
fish: to – *pescar*
fish *pescado* (m)
fitted *equipado/a*
fitting room *probador* (m)
fizzy (mineral water) *con gas*
flat *apartamento*, piso (m), *departamento* (m) (L.Am.)
flight *vuelo* (m)
floor (1st/2nd, etc.) *planta* (f), *piso* (m)
florist's *floristería* (f), *florería* (L.Am.)